Ziauddin

D1606820

SCIENCE
DEMONSTRATIONS
FOR THE
ELEMENTARY CLASSROOM

SCIENCE
DEMONSTRATIONS
FOR THE
ELEMENTARY CLASSROOM

Dorothea Allen

PARKER PUBLISHING COMPANY
West Nyack, New York 10995

©1988 *by*

PARKER PUBLISHING COMPANY, INC.

West Nyack, NY

All rights reserved.
No part of this book may be reproduced
in any form or by any means,
without permission in writing from the publisher.

10 9 8 7 6 5 4 3 2 1

Printed in the United States of America

Library of Congress Cataloging-in-Publication Data

Allen, Dorothea.
   Science demonstrations for the elementary classroom / Dorothea
Allen.
      p.   cm.
   Bibliography: p.
   ISBN 0-13-794652-X
   1. Science—Study and teaching (Elementary) 2. Science—
—Experiments. I. Title.
LB1585.A46 1988
372.3′5044—dc19   88-4137
                                         CIP

ISBN 0-13-794652-X

PARKER PUBLISHING COMPANY
BUSINESS & PROFESSIONAL DIVISION
A division of Simon & Schuster
West Nyack, New York 10995

To Allen and Sissy

Introduction

Science Demonstrations for the Elementary Classroom is a compendium of demonstration lessons, organized and presented in a form that is ready to use. It is divided into three broad areas—Physical Science, Environmental Science, and Life Science—which comprise the major concerns of elementary science today, with further subdivisions within these areas to help the teacher locate an appropriate lesson for pointing up a specific aspect of a topic being developed. A wide selection of demonstrations is included within each area, allowing for a spiral development of each major topic at successive grade levels.

Each demonstration lesson is complete and is developed logically, according to an easy-to-follow pattern. The format includes:

- **DEMONSTRATION TITLE:** The topic of the demonstration lesson is stated in direct terms, immediately establishing its main thrust, which may be the presentation of a scientific law or principle, the illustration of a scientific phenomenon or event, the application of an investigation-oriented discovery to a new situation, or the employment of a technique or method that is useful in scientific endeavors.

- **INTRODUCTION:** Guidelines are provided for helping to prepare young students for viewing the demonstration. Some pertinent introductory remarks attach an importance to the demonstration topic by suggesting the main area of focus and some associated key points to which students can relate in a meaningful way.

- **LEARNING OBJECTIVES:** A list of the expected outcomes of each lesson is provided to give purpose and direction to the demonstration. These specify the basic scientific concepts, laws, and principles to be understood, as well as the attitudes and approaches to be developed. Special emphasis is placed on the development of an awareness of how the science involved in the demonstration applies to situations in everyday life.

- **MATERIALS REQUIRED:** A list of all materials needed in the performance of the demonstration is included. Where applicable, alternative materials that can serve as satisfactory substitutes are suggested.

- **PRESENTATION:** Step-by-step instructions, an accompanying line drawing, and, where applicable, recommendations for precautionary measures to be taken are included for use in both practice run-throughs and the actual performance of a safe and successful demonstration. This simplicity and clarity of design makes most demonstrations suitable for some degree of student involvement in the presentation. Except in specific cases, indicated as "Suitable for teacher-only presentation," teacher discretion is encouraged for the involvement of students—in the role of assistants, manipulators, or presenters—with the necessary supervision of the teacher.

- **RATIONALE:** Attention is drawn to a valid scientific explanation that accounts for *how* and *why* the demonstration works as it does. It establishes the demonstration within the realm of true science and serves as a handy resource and reference guide for teachers.
- **DISCUSSION AND FOLLOW-UP:** Suggestions and guidelines are offered for ways to channel student interest and enthusiasm into discussion and activities related to the demonstration being performed, thus giving broad meaning to the demonstration lesson. Both group interaction and individual activities may be included to provide opportunities for each student to become actively involved and to develop an understanding of the demonstration. A particular focus on practical applications is emphasized to help students gain some insight into the science that is involved in a wide variety of everyday life experiences.

Most of the demonstrations included require only the simplest of materials that are easy to obtain and inexpensive to implement. The procedures are simple to follow and, in most cases, a single advance run-through will prepare the demonstrator sufficiently to deliver an effective presentation. While suggested grade levels are indicated for each demonstration lesson, it is recommended that teachers use discretion and apply these lessons flexibly so as to accommodate properly the interest, maturity, and experience levels of their students. It is also suggested that students maintain written records that indicate an understanding of the demonstration performed, with each student preparing some prescribed form of an account of each lesson in a personal Science Demonstrations notebook, designated specifically and exclusively for this purpose.

Students, generally, are enthusiastic about teacher and/or student-performed demonstrations and rate them high on their list of favorite and most useful science class experiences. Direct, well-defined, purposeful, and live activities, they represent the essence of real science and may be used as a source of reference in the further development of a major topic or to reinforce learning and heighten motivation and interest levels.

Effective demonstrations make important contributions to Elementary Science education. They lend a balance to the overall program, complementing the action-based hands-on approach that is central to the design of a good science program; they serve to enrich students' experiences in science as well as in matters of developing desirable attitudes and approaches to the study; and, when presented as a follow-up of investigative activities, they help to refine and clarify concepts that originated in the hands-on endeavors.

The influence that demonstrations have on individual students is also considerable: techniques employed during teacher demonstrations serve as models for students to emulate during their own demonstrations and hands-on investigations; individuals build self-confidence and understanding as they share findings of their discovery-oriented activities and apply them to new situations that are real and meaningful; and, of course, students find demonstrations to be exciting and enjoyable—a fun type of learning experience.

To make demonstrations an effective and integral part of the elementary school science program requires careful planning, judicious selection, and a well-orchestrated presentation of course-related topics at appropriate maturity and experience levels for the students.

Science Demonstrations for the Elementary Classroom is offered as a practical resource book for helping elementary teachers to use demonstration lessons effectively and with confidence—thereby enriching the science education of their students and, in the attainment of that goal, making their own task a little bit easier and their efforts a lot more productive.

Dorothea Allen

Contents

Part I

Physical Science • 1

Part II

Environmental Science • 111

Chapter 5   **Demonstrations Pertaining to
Earth Science** **113**

Chapter 6   **Demonstrations Pertaining to
Ecology** **146**

Part III
Life Science • 169

Chapter 7   **Demonstrations Pertaining to Plants** **171**

Chapter 8   **Demonstrations Pertaining to Animals** **197**

PART I

PHYSICAL SCIENCE

Simple, direct, and uncomplicated demonstrations relating to topics in Physical Science help students to develop an awareness of the scientific world around them and to understand some of the methods that are used to discover new knowledge about it. Demonstrations that focus on **matter, energy, physical forces,** and **physical and chemical changes** afford opportunities for students to speculate on the outcome of a structured presentation and provide strong motivation for them to sharpen their skills of observation and to analyze the happenings as they check out the predictions made or questions raised.

Physical Science-based demonstration lessons are both enjoyable and satisfying experiences. Students respond well when materials that are familiar are used in a setting to which they can relate. As a result, many of the scientific laws and principles upon which our high-tech society depend take on new meaning.

1

CHAPTER 1

Demonstrations Pertaining to Matter

* Suitable for teacher-only presentation.

1–1: THE BUOYANCY OF SALT WATER
(elementary level)

INTRODUCTION

Those who have bathed in ocean water at a seaside resort report the great buoyant force of the water, which allows them to float with greater ease than is possible in a freshwater lake. Ships also are known to ride higher in salt water than in fresh water. The buoyant force of salt water can be demonstrated in the classroom using tap water to which table salt has been added.

LEARNING OBJECTIVES

As a result of the demonstration lesson, students should

- understand the concept of density.
- develop an awareness of relative density as it relates to an object and a liquid in which it is placed.
- relate the demonstration to other situations that illustrate relative density.
- explain the floating and/or sinking of an object in water in terms of *key words:* **density**, **buoyancy**, and **relative density**.

MATERIALS REQUIRED

2 drinking glasses; tap water; table salt; 2 fresh eggs

PRESENTATION

1. Obtain two identical drinking glasses and distinguish them by markings: "S" (for salt water) and "F" (for fresh water).
2. Pour tap water into the glasses until each is two-thirds full.
3. Add two tablespoons of table salt to the water in "S" and allow it to dissolve completely.
4. Gently lower a fresh egg into each of the glasses.
5. Observe what happens to the egg placed in each environment.

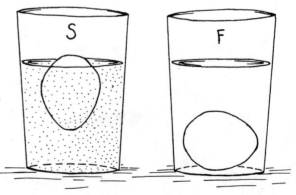

RATIONALE

The buoyant force of water is determined by the relative density of the water and the object placed in it. An object that is less dense than water will float; one that is more dense will sink. Only by changing the density of the water will the same object be caused to float or sink when placed in water. Adding salt to water makes it more dense and increases its buoyancy.

DISCUSSION AND FOLLOW-UP

- Students will immediately observe that the egg placed in salt water floats, while the one placed in fresh water sinks to the bottom of the glass.
- They should relate the buoyant force of the salt water to the salt that was added, making the water "thicker," or more dense, with the ability to hold up objects more easily than in the "thinner," less dense fresh water.
- They should also be encouraged to report their experiences in swimming in bodies of fresh water and salt water, and to predict what might reasonably happen if they went swimming in the Great Salt Lake, where the salt concentration is about six times as great as that in the ocean.
- At the end of the discussion period, students should be asked to indicate their understanding of the demonstration by writing answers to questions:
  - How is the density of water affected by the addition of salt?
  - What causes an object to float in water? What causes an object to sink in water?
  - Will a ship ride higher or lower in the water as it passes from New York harbor into the Atlantic Ocean?
  - How did the demonstration illustrate "density" and "buoyancy"?

1–2: POURING A GLASS OF AIR
(elementary level)

INTRODUCTION

After drinking the milk in a milk carton or the soda in a bottle or can, we refer to the container as "empty." Actually, air occupies the space in these "empty" containers, just as it does in an enclosed space within a bicycle tire, a football, or an inflated balloon. The basic scientific fact that "All matter occupies space" can be reinforced by way of a demonstration in the classroom, using air as a representative form of matter.

LEARNING OBJECTIVES

After the demonstration lesson has been completed, students should be able to

- show evidence of an understanding of three related aspects of a basic scientific principle:
    — All matter occupies space.
    — Air is a form of matter.
    — Two things cannot occupy the same space at the same time.
- prepare a list of five situations in which air is actually present in places we refer to as "empty" or of which we say that "there is nothing there."
- describe how the demonstration worked, using *key words*: **matter** and **displacement**.

MATERIALS REQUIRED

aquarium or large transparent bowl; 2 small drinking glasses or baby food jars; water; food coloring

PRESENTATION

1. Fill an aquarium tank until it is about three-fourths full of water. Then add a few drops of food coloring and mix so that the water becomes uniformly colored throughout the container.

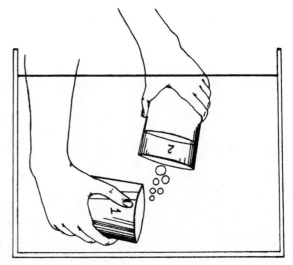

2. Lower drinking glass #1 into the water until it is completely submerged, tilting the open end upward slightly to allow it to fill with water.

6

3. Submerge glass #2 also, keeping the open end directed downward, but do not allow water to enter it.

4. Hold glass #2 (containing air) mouth downward, just above the rim of glass #1 (filled with water).

5. Carefully and slowly tilt glass #2 slightly to allow air to escape into glass #1.

RATIONALE

All substance in the universe is referred to as matter, and matter is defined as anything that has mass and occupies space. The fact that air is a form of matter is often overlooked when a substance is removed from a container, leaving "nothing" behind. Actually, under normal conditions a substance cannot be removed from a container until it is displaced by another substance, usually air, which replaces it in the container.

In the demonstration, water could not enter glass #1 until the air was removed by transferring it to glass #2. One form of matter was exchanged for another so that the glasses contained either air or water, but in every case the space was occupied by some form of matter.

DISCUSSION AND FOLLOW-UP

- As the demonstration progresses, students should respond to pertinent questions:
    — What was the evidence that neither glass was empty when initially submerged, mouth downward, in the aquarium?
    — Why did water enter glass #1 but not glass #2 when placed under water?
    — How was it possible to fill glass #1 with air while it was underwater?
    — How could you explain to your friends that it is possible to pour a glass of air?
- Students should be encouraged to name other examples of matter that cannot be seen and to identify some examples of displacement of one form of matter by another.
- They should be asked to suggest ways to verify that something is really present in a so-called empty container and to make predictions as to what would happen to the container if it were really empty.
- After the demonstration lesson has been reviewed and discussed, students should be asked to prepare a diagram and a short report about the demonstration in their Science Demonstrations notebooks.

1–3: EFFECT OF TEMPERATURE ON VOLUME OF AIR
(elementary level)

INTRODUCTION

Bicycle and automobile tires appear to become firmer during periods of warm weather or after having been ridden on for a while. The accompanying increase in pressure, however, is only temporary because the process may be reversed. During cold weather, or when the car or bike has remained idle for a time, the pressure returns to its lower level. For this reason it is recommended that air pressure in tires should be measured when the tires are "cold."

With provisions for heating and cooling the air in the classroom, the effect of temperature on volume and pressure exerted by air can be demonstrated.

LEARNING OBJECTIVES

Upon the completion of this demonstration lesson, students should be able to

- understand how a change in temperature affects the volume of air in a container.
- relate the concept of the demonstration to at least one experience in everyday life.
- describe the demonstration, using *key words:* **temperature**, **volume**, and **pressure**.

MATERIALS REQUIRED

large toy balloon; string; electric fan or air-conditioning unit

PRESENTATION

1. Select a fairly large toy balloon and inflate it until it is near its capacity volume.

2. Tie the stem of the balloon with string and check to be sure that there are no leaks.

3. Tie a string around the middle of the balloon, outlining its circumference.

4. Hold the balloon or hang it near an electric fan or air-conditioner.

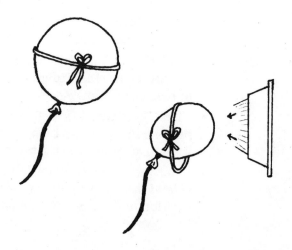

5. Turn off the fan and, after a time, observe what happens.

6. Return the balloon to a warmer section of the room and observe again.

RATIONALE

The volume of a gas (air) depends upon the conditions under which it is measured. Although there is no change in the number of air particles present in an inflated balloon, when the air is cooled, the air particles are slowed in their motion and have less force. The pressure they exert on the inside surface of the balloon then decreases, causing the balloon to contract. The system also works in reverse; when air in the balloon is heated, the air particles gain energy and move more rapidly. As a result, the pressure on the inside surface of the balloon increases and the balloon may be seen to expand.

DISCUSSION AND FOLLOW-UP

- When the balloon has been placed near the electric fan, students should be asked to make predictions about what they think will happen.
- They should then watch closely as the balloon is being cooled and report any changes observed.
- When all have observed that the string around the middle of the balloon becomes very loose, they should offer suggestions for the reasons and compare the observations with their predictions made earlier.
- If the string should become so loose that it falls off the balloon, it can be gently replaced and held in position as the balloon is moved to a warmer location.
- Discussion should center upon the change in size of the balloon and the change in volume of the air within it. Since no air escaped, students should relate the effects to the heating of all substances in which molecules gain energy, allowing them to move farther apart and take up more space. The opposite effect, brought about by lowering the temperature, should also be applied.
- Attention should be given to the effect of temperature on the air in bicycle and automobile tires. Students should be encouraged to observe and then describe the appearance of a relatively soft bicycle tire after the bike has been ridden for a while, during which time the air in it has been warmed.
- After the discussion has been completed, students should express their understanding of the demonstration by explaining why it would not be advisable to add air to automobile tires after the car has been driven for over an hour. This should be recorded in their Science Demonstrations notebooks.

1–4: MAKING AN OBJECT FLOAT AND/OR SINK
(elementary level)

INTRODUCTION

The engineering design of a submarine enables it to make adjustments in its average density in order to submerge or surface at appropriate times.

How objects can be made to rise or sink in water can be demonstrated with the use of a one-liter plastic soda bottle and a medicine dropper.

LEARNING OBJECTIVES

After having participated actively in this demonstration lesson, students should be able to

- recognize that a gas, such as air, is more easily compressed than a liquid, such as water.
- relate the demonstration to a practical application in the design and operation of a submarine.
- construct and manipulate a "personal" model, patterned after the demonstration model.
- explain the phenomenon of sinking and of floating, using *key words:* **density, average density, buoyancy,** and **compression.**

MATERIALS REQUIRED

one-liter plastic soda bottle; medicine dropper; water

PRESENTATION

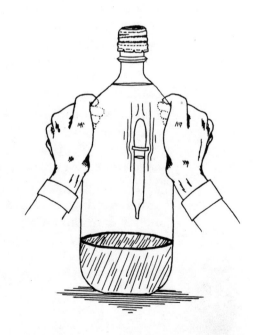

1. Pour water into a one-liter soda bottle until it is nearly full.
2. Draw water into a medicine dropper until it is about half full of water.
3. Lower the dropper, bulb side up, into the water in the bottle and, if necessary, adjust the amount of water in the dropper until it barely floats, with the bulb bobbing at the surface.
4. Place the cap on the bottle.
5. Using the palms of both hands, press hard on the sides of the bottle.

10

6. Observe the dropper.

7. Release the pressure on the sides of the bottle and observe the effect on the dropper.

8. Repeat, if necessary, so that all students may observe the changes produced in the content of the dropper as well as the overall effect.

RATIONALE

The medicine dropper floats when the correct proportion of air and water in it makes the average density of the dropper just barely less than the density of the water. When the sides of the bottle are pressed, the increased pressure causes the air to compress, forcing more water into the dropper. With additional water, which increases the average density of the dropper so that it is now greater than that of water, the dropper sinks. Releasing the pressure on the sides of the bottle reverses the chain of events, and the dropper is allowed to float once more.

DISCUSSION AND FOLLOW-UP

- Interaction between students should be kept at a lively pace as they respond to discussion questions:
  - Under what conditions does the medicine dropper float?
  - What happens to the air in the dropper when pressure is applied to the sides of the bottle?
  - What causes the dropper to sink?
  - What causes it to rise again?
  - How does the motion of the medicine dropper resemble that of a submarine?
- After the discussion has been completed, students should be asked to bring in a soda bottle for the next science class. At that time, in a follow-up class, they can construct personal models and reinforce their understanding of the manner in which they work—both in class and at home, where they may demonstrate and explain the mechanism to a friend or a family member.

1–5: THE WHOLE IS NOT ALWAYS EQUAL TO THE SUM OF ITS PARTS
(intermediate level)

INTRODUCTION

It seems reasonable to expect that the addition of an equal volume of one substance to a different one already in a container will result in the doubling of the total volume. However, this is not always true. Using seeds of different sizes, the phenomenon can be demonstrated and related to the molecular composition of matter.

LEARNING OBJECTIVES

After having completed the demonstration lesson, students should

- have an awareness that materials are made up of individual particles, with some spaces between them.
- understand how the particles of one substance can occupy some of the space between particles of another.
- relate the demonstration to the molecular composition of matter.
- name two examples of situations in which the concept of the demonstration is illustrated.
- exhibit an understanding of the meaning and proper usage of *key words:* **particle**, **molecule**, **volume**, and **mixture**.

MATERIALS REQUIRED

2 identical measuring cups, marked for ½-cup measure; radish seeds; pea seeds

PRESENTATION

1. Place a sufficient quantity of pea seeds in a measuring cup to fill it to the halfway mark.

2. Using a second measuring cup, measure out one-half cup of radish seeds.

3. Carefully transfer the radish seeds to the cup containing the pea seeds, applying gentle agitation to encourage the seeds to intermingle.

4. Allow students to take a volume reading of the mixture of seeds and to observe closely their distribution in the cup.

5. Interpret the results in terms of the observations made.

RATIONALE

When radish seeds and pea seeds are mixed together, the radish seeds tend to take up some of the space between the pea seeds, with the result that less than a full cup of mixed seeds is formed when one-half cup of each are mixed together. This applies also at the molecular level; spaces between the individual molecules of one substance may provide spaces in which molecules of another can fit, allowing the two kinds of molecules to intermingle when they form a mixture.

DISCUSSION AND FOLLOW-UP

- Before the two kinds of seeds are combined, students should be asked to predict the final volume resulting from the mixture.
- Special attention should be drawn to close and careful observations of the mixture in order to detect how the radish seeds found and occupied spaces between the pea seeds.
- Examples of other situations illustrating this same effect should be called for, with students relating the demonstration to experiences in which they have added sand to a bucketful of seashells or have witnessed the making of mixtures of sand and gravel.
- They should also relate the demonstration to molecules making up all substances and identify mixtures of salt and water and/or sugar and water as examples of the intermingling of particles where the molecules of one substance fit in the spaces between molecules of the other.
- When there are indications that all students understand the concept of the demonstration, each should be asked to prepare a diagram using different symbols or colors to indicate the intermingling of molecules that results when the molecules of one fit between the spaces of another, and making use of the *key words* to label the diagram appropriately.

1–6: AIR-FILLED COLUMNS PROVIDE GREAT STRUCTURAL SUPPORT

(intermediate level)

INTRODUCTION

Finding ways to avoid excess weight is a prime consideration for engineers who design airplanes. By studying the design of nature's flying machines, they gain important insights into possible solutions to this problem. The bones of a bird, for example, are mostly hollow and filled with air. This makes the skeleton exceptionally light and amazingly strong—a combination of features that is desirable in many structural designs.

LEARNING OBJECTIVES

After this demonstration lesson has been completed, students should be able to

- identify nature as a model for some "inventions."
- understand the benefits of strength and light weight, which accompany the use of hollow supports in both living and nonliving situations.
- name three practical applications of the scientific principle demonstrated.
- add another dimension to their previous learning of the basic topic and thereby reinforce their understanding of it.

MATERIALS REQUIRED

several Styrofoam coffee cups; white casein glue; several books

PRESENTATION

1. Using white glue, bind together two Styrofoam coffee cups, rim-to-rim, to form a hollow column.
2. Set the air-filled column aside and allow the glue to dry thoroughly.
3. Place two Styrofoam cups side-by-side on a table top where all students can view them so that one cup is resting on its side, the other on its base.
4. Place a heavy book on each of the cups and compare the manner in which they are able to support the book.

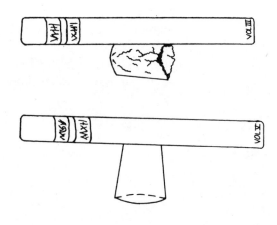

5. Place the two-cup column upright on the table top. Carefully place a book on the top of the column. Then add additional books, to the capacity of the column to support them.

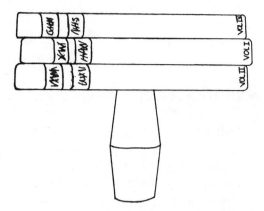

6. Observe and compare the results with those noted when the cups were used singly.

RATIONALE

A book that crushes an "empty" cup that is set on its side is easily supported by one that is standing upright. Air in the cup, which may be forced out when the end is left open, is trapped when there is no escape route and remains in the "column." The same effect can be observed in the greater support offered by the walls of a rolled paper tube when placed on end rather than on its side. This knowledge is useful to engineers who design hollow or air-filled columns to be used as lightweight supporting structures.

DISCUSSION AND FOLLOW-UP

- Students will observe differences in the manner in which the cups function as supporting structures for the books.
- Attention should be given to the reasons for these differences.
- Discussion should focus on the different conditions demonstrated as they relate to the design of lightweight columns that are capable of supporting weight in both natural and person-made situations.
- Investigations of hollow bones of birds, architectural designs of public buildings of today as well as those of ancient Greece and Rome, and some modern designs that make use of hollow tubes can be assigned for reporting.
- As a follow-up, motivated students can determine the maximum number of books that can be supported by a single Styrofoam cup in an upright position and of a four-cup column constructed by gluing two two-cup columns base to base.
- After all discussion has been completed, students should prepare a written report in their Science Demonstrations notebooks in which they explain their understanding of the demonstration and its applications.

1–7: SIZE VERSUS SHARP DETAILS IN A PHOTOGRAPH ENLARGEMENT
(intermediate level)

INTRODUCTION

Although small photographs and pictures are often enlarged to produce prints of more suitable size, the quality of the photograph is often diminished as the picture, spread over a larger surface, appears somewhat fuzzy. It is a case of "bigger is not necessarily better." This can be demonstrated in the classroom with the use of halftone photographs taken from a newspaper and pieces of equipment generally found in most classrooms.

LEARNING OBJECTIVES

After having participated in this demonstration lesson, students should be able to

- understand the means by which light rays are used to magnify an image.
- recognize that enlarging a picture involves sacrificing some of the sharpness of details.
- describe the appearance of a photograph enlargement and explain how these results were obtained, using *key words:* **magnification** and **resolution**.

MATERIALS REQUIRED

opaque projector; hand lens magnifiers; projection screen or wall area; halftone newspaper photographs or pictures

PRESENTATION

1. Position an opaque projector close to the viewing screen or wall in a darkened classroom.
2. Turn on the projector light and observe the size of the lighted area on the screen.
3. Place a newspaper halftone photograph on the projector and focus its image on the screen.
4. Observe the size and sharpness of the details of the picture being projected.
5. Move the projector to the back of the room and again turn on the

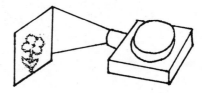

16

light, noting the change in size and brightness of the lighted area on the screen.

6. Adjust the focus, as needed, and compare the size, brightness, and sharpness of the details of the projected image with the same features of the image produced when the projector was close to the screen.

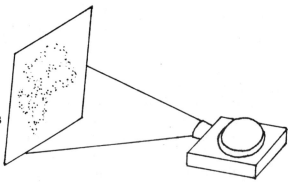

RATIONALE

Distributing the same amount of light over a larger surface results in both an enlargement of the projected image and a reduction in the sharpness of visible details. In an enlargement of a newspaper photograph, for example, the individual dots making up a halftone photograph are spread farther apart to cover the larger area. Consequently, details, such as the outer edges, are less well-defined and appear to be indistinct and fuzzy.

DISCUSSION AND FOLLOW-UP

- During the demonstration, after students have viewed the halftone picture projected on the screen at close range, they should be asked to suggest ways to produce a larger picture on the screen.

- Their suggestions can be checked out, including, eventually, the main thrust of the demonstration; the projector should be moved a greater distance from the viewing screen until the lighted area fills the entire screen.

- Attention should focus on the quality of the projected image as well as its size. The relationship between the amount of magnification and sharpness of details (resolution) should be determined for this and other examples, such as enlargements of small snapshots and comparisons of large screen/ small screen TV viewing.

- As a follow-up, student groups should use hand lens magnifiers for individual viewing of halftone newspaper photographs.

- They should note the spreading out of the individual dots making up the picture and relate this to the decrease in number of light rays reaching the eye from any given area of the enlarged picture. How this leads to an image that is less bright and that shows details less clearly should then be discussed.

- To check for student understanding of the demonstration, each should be asked to explain why a picture of Donnie Smith, which appears very clear in postage-stamp size as a part of his sixth-grade class picture, loses its clear detail and appears to be fuzzy when enlarged to an 8 x 10 portrait of Donnie alone.

1–8: SURFACE AREA AND REACTION RATE
(elementary level)

INTRODUCTION

When a substance dissolves in water, all of its particles do not necessarily distribute themselves immediately throughout the solution. Heat or some form of agitation, such as shaking or stirring, is commonly used to shorten the time it takes for the particles to intermingle. The effect of surface area on the rate at which a substance dissolves in water can be demonstrated in the classroom.

LEARNING OBJECTIVES

After the students have completed the demonstration lesson they should be able to

- explain how stirring and shaking shorten the time required for the making of a solution.
- relate the speed with which a substance goes into solution with the amount of exposed surface of the substance.
- apply the concept of the demonstration to three everyday life situations.
- describe the demonstration and how it works, using *key words:* **solvent**, **solute**, **dissolve**, and **surface area**.

MATERIALS REQUIRED

2 baby bottles (glass or clear plastic); 2 sugar cubes; spoon; very hot water

PRESENTATION

1. Select two identical heat-proof baby bottles and distinguish them with markings I and II.
2. Place a sugar cube in bottle I.
3. With the bowl end of a spoon, crush another sugar cube and place the crushed crystals in bottle II.
4. Pour hot water into the bottles until each is two-thirds full of water.
5. Place both bottles in a place where students can observe the reaction.

RATIONALE

Surface area refers to the amount of a solid substance that is available to take part in a reaction. When crushed, individual particles of sugar are widely separated,

18

with much surface available to mingle with the molecules of water. This enables them to engage in a greater number of successful collisions than is possible when the sugar particles are tightly packed in the form of a cube. As the surface area of the sugar is increased, the rate at which it dissolves in water increases also.

DISCUSSION AND FOLLOW-UP

- While the demonstration is in progress, a discussion of the events that are unfolding should include student responses to pointed questions:
  - Why was hot water used in the demonstration?
  - Is there more sugar in bottle I than in bottle II?
  - What evidence is there that the sugar is dissolving?
  - Would it be safe to make a "taste" test?
  - What could be done to speed the rate of reaction in bottle I?
  - Which material in the bottles is the solute? Which is the solvent?

- At the end of the demonstration, students should summarize their observations by discussing fully how the surface area of a solute affects the speed of its reaction in a solvent. Specific information from the demonstration and from personal experiences cited can be combined to formulate a generalization.

- As a test of their understanding of the concept of the demonstration, students should write a short report in which they tell the rate at which, under identical conditions, samples of coal representing large, medium, and small pieces will burn.

1–9:   A "LIGHTER THAN AIR" BALLOON
(intermediate level)

INTRODUCTION

The uses to which man puts hot air and/or gas balloons are many and varied. He uses them to send instruments aloft for gathering data that meteorologists find helpful in forecasting the weather; he uses them to relay radio and television programs to remote areas; and he uses them as a means for engaging in recreational sport, such as hot air balloon races. Although of various designs, the mechanics involved in all are based on simple scientific principles. A simple working model can be devised and operated in a cool room or outside on a cool day.

LEARNING OBJECTIVES

At the end of the demonstration lesson, students should be able to

- recognize that hot air is less dense than cold air.
- relate the demonstration to other examples of warm air rising above a mass of cooler air.
- apply information from the demonstration to explain how a hot air balloon works.
- show evidence of an understanding of the meaning and proper usage of *key words:* **density**, **weight**, and **volume**.

MATERIALS REQUIRED

plastic garment bag from a dry cleaner; tape; string; rubber band; vacuum cleaner with hose

PRESENTATION

1. Obtain a plastic garment bag from a dry cleaner and close the top opening with tape to make it airtight.
2. Place a piece of string around the bag, about four inches from its lower edge. Then, turn the lower edge up, encasing the string.
3. Tape the turned-up edge of the bag to hold it and the encased string in position.
4. Carefully pull on the two ends of the string, gathering the lower edge of the bag until the opening is only about three inches in diameter.

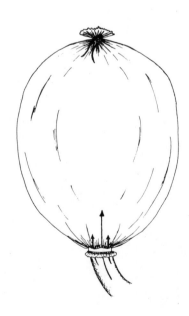

5. Turn on a vacuum cleaner and allow it to run for a few minutes until it warms up.
6. Fit the exhaust end of the vacuum cleaner hose into the bag opening, and draw the string tightly around it.
7. Turn on the warmed-up vacuum cleaner and fill the plastic bag with heated air.
8. Remove the hose from the bag and draw the string as tight as possible before tying the ends together to keep the bag closed. Use a rubber band for reinforcement, if necessary.
9. Release the inflated bag and observe.

RATIONALE

When air is warmed, the heat energy causes the motion of its molecules to speed up and move farther apart. These movements cause an overall expansion of the air and a lowering of its density. Consequently, a plastic bag containing warm air weighs less than the weight of the cooler air it displaces, and the displaced air provides an upward force, causing the bag to rise. For this reason, balloons are filled with "light" gases or with hot air, and provisions are made for adjusting the "lighter-than-air" craft to enable it to lift off, ascend to a higher altitude, descend, or to land.

DISCUSSION AND FOLLOW-UP

- The basic demonstration can be expanded through a discussion of factors that build on previous experiences and extend the learning.
- There are key points to be included in the discussion:
    - Why choose a cool room or a cool day for the demonstration?
    - Why does a balloon rise when warm air is used to fill it?
    - What other gases could be used for inflating balloons?
    - How would you rate the suitability of hydrogen, helium, and carbon dioxide for use in inflating a balloon?
    - How can the height be regulated in a hot air balloon?
    - What would be the maximum height that could be reached by a hot air balloon?
    - How are hot air and gas balloons used by people?
- As a follow-up, students should summarize the demonstration by writing a report on "lighter-than-air" craft in their Science Demonstrations notebooks.

1–10: LIGHTING A MATCH THAT HAS BEEN UNDERWATER
(elementary level)

INTRODUCTION

A glass, jar, bottle, or other container is generally said to be "empty" unless we can observe the specific taste, color, odor, weight, or texture of the substance that may be in it. It is more difficult to detect a substance that has no odor and that cannot be seen. The presence of such a substance can, however, be demonstrated in interesting ways and with simple materials.

LEARNING OBJECTIVES

At the end of this demonstration lesson, students should be able to

- recognize that not all substances have properties that can be detected by our senses.
- understand that all materials—even those we cannot see—occupy space.
- apply the scientific law that states that "Two substances cannot occupy the same space at the same time."
- name at least one example of an instance in which this scientific law is demonstrated.
- show evidence of an understanding of the meaning and proper usage of the *key word:* **matter**.

MATERIALS REQUIRED

soup can (cleaned out and with one end removed); drinking glass or jar; book of matches; bowl or basin; tape; towel

PRESENTATION

1. Using a small strip of tape, attach an unlighted match to the inside of a clean, dry soup can so that it lays flat on the bottom of the can and can easily be removed without harm to the match head.
2. Partially fill a bowl or basin with water and place it on a table where all students can view it clearly.
3. Holding the can by the bottom, lower it directly into the water, taking care to prevent its tipping or tilting in any direction.

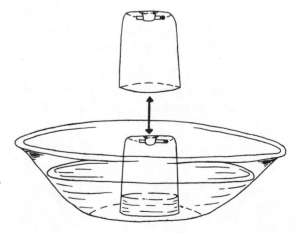

22

4. Completely submerge the can in water, holding it firmly in an upright position for one minute.

5. Carefully lift the can out of the water and wipe the lower edge of the can with toweling to remove any traces of water that may have adhered to it.

6. Turn the can over and remove the match. Then strike the match head against the emery strip of the matchbook to confirm that the match is still dry and workable.

7. When students' comments and questions indicate that there is some uncertainty as to *why* the match did not get wet, repeat the demonstration, this time replacing the can with a transparent glass or jar of about the same size.

8. Call attention to this "second look" for students to verify that the submerged match was never touched by water.

RATIONALE

When an open container is inverted and forced straight down into a body of water, water will not enter the container because air already occupies that space. Since water does not rise in the container, it is prevented from coming in contact with the match attached to the inside surface. The match therefore remains dry, allowing it to be ignited after having been "submerged" in water.

DISCUSSION AND FOLLOW-UP

- Discussion started during the demonstration should be continued, with students volunteering information about other experiences with "empty" containers placed underwater. The inability of water to enter a bottle until the air bubbles out of it is familiar to all, just as air-filled balloons, automobile and bicycle tires, footballs, and beachballs provide evidence that air occupies space.

- Attention should focus on this basic property of all matter and on the recognition of air as matter that is invisible.

- A short account of the demonstration and some applications from personal experience should then be written by the students in their personal Science Demonstrations notebooks.

1-11: EXPANSION OF SOLIDS WHEN HEATED*
(elementary level)

INTRODUCTION

Heat has an important effect on all forms of matter. For example, when liquids such as water are heated in a container, the heat causes the particles of the liquid to move more rapidly and to take up more space. Although it is more difficult to observe the expansion of solids when heated, it can be demonstrated in the classroom.

LEARNING OBJECTIVES

Upon the completion of this demonstration lesson, students should be able to

- understand the effect of heat on solids.
- relate the expansion of solids to the greater energy level of their molecules that, by becoming more active, move farther apart from each other.
- name at least three examples of situations in everyday life that illustrate the expansion of solids due to heat.
- explain the demonstration, using *key words:* **heat**, **energy**, **molecule**, **expansion**, and **contraction**.

MATERIALS REQUIRED

thin, bare copper wire; string; 2 chairs or other supporting structures; small candle; small weighted bell

PRESENTATION

1. Place two chairs at opposite ends of a table top or well separated on a cleared floor area where the demonstration will be clearly visible to all students.

2. Attach a length of bare copper wire to the backs of the chairs so that it stretches from one chair to the other.

3. At the center of the wire, tie one end of a piece of string that has a small weighted bell attached at the other end.

4. Make adjustments, as necessary, so that the bell is very close to the table top but still able to swing free and ring when the string is pulled.

5. Maintain these positions while holding a small candle below the wire on one side of the string.

6. Heat the wire by moving the candle flame back and forth over the length of the wire.

---

* Suitable for teacher-only presentation.

CAUTION: Do not bring the candle flame in contact with the string or allow any student to touch the heated wire.

7. Allow students to observe what happens to the distance between the bell and the table top and to the ability of the bell to swing free and ring.

8. Discontinue applying the flame to the wire and allow the wire to cool.

9. Again, call attention to the distance between the bell and the table top as you gently pull on the string and cause the bell to ring.

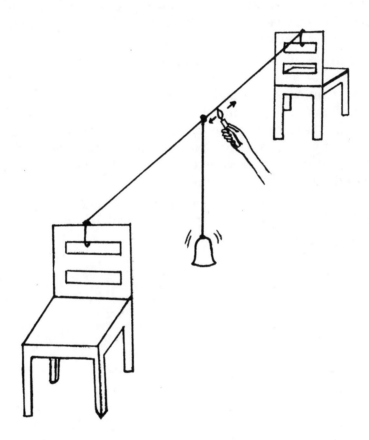

RATIONALE

Heat transferred from the candle flame increases the motion of molecules in the wire so that they move farther apart and take up more space. Consequently, the wire expands and sags a bit between the two supporting chairs. This allows the string attached to the wire to be lowered so the bell is brought closer to the table top. When the bell comes to rest on the surface, it is no longer able to swing free and ring. When the heat source is removed, the entire process is reversed. Molecules in the wire are slowed down, decreasing their distance from each other so that they take up less space, and causing the wire to contract, or shorten. The tightened wire lifts the string and the attached bell. Then, with enough clearance between the bell and the table top, the string is able to swing freely and the bell will ring.

DISCUSSION AND FOLLOW-UP

- As students observe the lowering of the bell until it is no longer able to move freely and ring, they should be encouraged to consider how this happens. Attention should be drawn to observations they report and to questions they raise.

- Discussion should center upon the slight sag in the wire, which is observable when the wire expands due to heating, and its association with the greater energy that causes the molecules to move more rapidly and spread farther apart. If a change in the length of the string is questioned, it can be measured before and after heat is applied to the wire.

- Students should be encouraged to give examples of other instances in which heat may be observed to cause the expansion of solids. They may relate the demonstration to personal matters, such as experiences they have had concerning how a ring, a bracelet, or a watchband fit when hands were hot as compared with times when hands were cold, or they may relate the demonstration to the expansion of pavements and the practice of providing narrow spaces between paved sections, without which buckling and cracking would occur due to expansion during hot weather.

- After the discussion has been completed, students should be asked to prepare a diagram and short report to explain the demonstration in their Science Demonstrations notebooks.

1-12: THE VOLUME OF AN IRREGULARLY SHAPED SOLID
(intermediate level)

INTRODUCTION

There are many times when it is necessary to find the volume, or the amount of space that is occupied by some form of matter. The measurement can be taken directly for substances whose particles allow them to be fitted into a precisely calibrated space, or calculated according to well-known formulas such as $V = l \times w \times h$ and $V = \pi r^3$ when applied to regularly shaped solids. The volume of an irregularly shaped solid, however, is generally determined by an indirect method, which can be demonstrated very easily.

LEARNING OBJECTIVES

At the end of this demonstration lesson, students should be able to

- infer that the volume of water displaced by a solid object is the volume of that object.
- name three objects whose volume can be determined by the displacement of water method.
- suggest ways to adjust this method to accommodate its use for objects less dense than water or the use of an immersing vessel that is uncalibrated.
- describe the demonstration and its applications, using *key words:* **displacement**, **volume**, and **meniscus**.

MATERIALS REQUIRED

graduated cylinder of suitable size; irregularly shaped rock or other dense object; water; string

PRESENTATION

1. Place water in the graduated cylinder to a convenient halfway mark.
2. Read the volume indicated, using the bottom of the meniscus.
3. Attach a rock or other heavy object to one end of a string, leaving several inches free at the other end.
4. Holding the string by the free end, carefully lower the rock into the water in the cylinder until the rock is completely submerged.

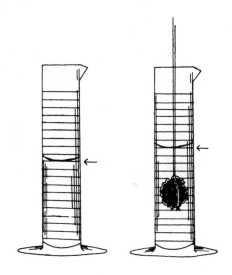

27

5. Observe the level of water in the cylinder and take another reading.

6. Using the string, raise the rock above the water level and confirm the volume of water only in the cylinder.

7. Determine the volume of water that was displaced by the rock.

RATIONALE

Volumes of irregularly shaped solids, which defy direct measurements, usually can be determined by indirect means. Based on the principle that "two things cannot occupy the same space at the same time," an insoluble solid can be completely submerged in a measured volume of water. The apparent change in volume of the water is equal to the volume of the solid that displaced it. With necessary adjustments, the basic method becomes versatile, accommodating special cases involving variations of objects and/or vessels employed; a sinker can be attached to the lower end of an object that is less dense than water, and water that overflows when an object is immersed in a completely filled but uncalibrated container can be collected and measured for a volume determination.

DISCUSSION AND FOLLOW-UP

- During the demonstration, students should be allowed to take volume readings, while developing skills involving the meniscus and appropriate units of volume.

- Throughout the discussion period, they should be encouraged to make comments, raise questions, and respond to pertinent questions:

  — What is meant by "displacement" of water?

  — Why is the volume of water displaced equal to the volume of the solid immersed?

  — What adjustments would be necessary to employ this method for finding the volume of an object that floats in water?

  — What variation can be suggested for using this method for objects that are too large to fit into a calibrated container?

- When the discussion has been completed, students should summarize the demonstration, explaining it through the use of *key words:* **meniscus**, **volume**, and **displacement**. They should then write a report of the demonstration and its applications in their Science Demonstrations notebooks.

CHAPTER 2

Demonstrations Pertaining to Energy

* Suitable for teacher-only presentation.

2–1: ENERGY TRANSFER DURING EVAPORATION*
(intermediate level)

INTRODUCTION

When water in a teapot is allowed to boil for a period of time, it disappears into the air as a vapor. Much of the activity involved in the process can be observed—the rapidity with which bubbles formed in the liquid are transferred to the surface increases, resulting in the production of steam which escapes through the spout and humidifies the surrounding air. Although usually associated with heat, evaporation is actually a cooling process. This feature can be demonstrated with water and a hot metal.

LEARNING OBJECTIVES

At the end of this demonstration lesson, students should be able to

- identify the process by which water changes its physical form from a liquid to a gas.
- relate the evaporation of a liquid to an increase in the energy level of its particles.
- infer that the energy needed for the evaporation of water is obtained from the immediate surroundings.
- give an explanation of the demonstration, using *key words:* **evaporation**, **heat energy**, **vaporization**, and **molecular energy**.

MATERIALS REQUIRED

iron skillet or other metal object with a flat surface; medicine dropper; oven, hot plate, or other heat source; water; hand protectors and/or tongs

PRESENTATION

1. Heat a cast iron skillet, large shortening can, or other flat-surfaced metal object in an oven or over an electric hot plate until it becomes very hot.
2. Using tongs, an oven mitt, or other hand protector, transfer the skillet in an upside-down position over a sink or catch basin of suitable size.

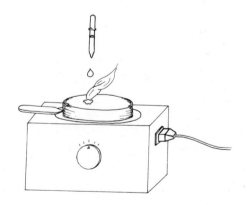

---

* Suitable for teacher-only presentation.

CAUTION: Keep students at a safe distance from the hot skillet. Do not touch or allow others to touch the hot metal with bare hands.

3. Fill a medicine dropper with cold water and, holding it several inches above the flat surface of the hot skillet, release one drop of water.

4. Observe the activity as the drop of water hits the hot surface.

5. Repeat the process, allowing a second drop of water to fall on the hot surface.

6. Continue to release water, one drop at a time, until the water begins to accumulate on the surface.

RATIONALE

Temperature has an effect on the way individual particles of a substance are joined together. At low temperatures water particles, having relatively little energy, move slowly and are packed closely together. As the temperature rises, the particles gain energy and are able to move more freely as they spread apart from each other. When the boiling point is reached, they have enough energy to move very rapidly and very far apart from each other, forming water vapor. The gain in energy is derived from an energy transfer from the immediate surroundings. Thus, having transferred some of its energy to the water, a hot object with which the water is in contact will be observed to lower its temperature as it is cooled.

DISCUSSION AND FOLLOW-UP

- Students should make auditory as well as visual observations of the activity as each drop of water hits the surface of the hot skillet. The sizzling, bouncing, and sputtering of the first drop that appears to fly off into the air should be related to the energy that is required for that activity and an inference should be made as to the source of that energy and what is happening to the skillet as each drop of water hits against its surface.

- As the activity subsides and water accumulates on the surface of the skillet, students can be asked to describe some of the practical uses of water as a cooling agent. The use of *key words*—**evaporation, heat energy, vaporization,** and **molecular energy**—should be used to explain the scientific concept involved in the demonstration and the effectiveness of evaporation as a cooling process.

2–2: CHANGING ENERGY FROM ONE FORM TO ANOTHER
(elementary level)

INTRODUCTION

When we turn on an electric switch, we may see evidence of electrical energy being changed (1) to light energy to illuminate a room; (2) to heat energy to cook foods; or (3) to mechanical energy to operate a rotary fan, a food blender, or an electric saw. In a similar manner, energy transformations occur when we use the chemical energy stored in a battery for a flashlight or any one of a multitude of other battery-operated appliances. The use of these devices illustrates a basic physical law, which states that "Energy cannot be created or destroyed but can be changed from one form to another."

LEARNING OBJECTIVES

After the demonstration lesson has been completed, students should be able to

- state the Law of Conservation of Energy.
- relate the demonstration and the physical law that is illustrated to personal experiences in everyday life.
- identify examples of different kinds of energy transformations.
- understand the meaning and proper usage of *key words:* **energy**, **forms of energy**, and **transformation of energy**.

MATERIALS REQUIRED

blocks of wood; sandpaper

PRESENTATION

1. Select two students to perform the demonstration: one to rub sandpaper briskly over a wood block for one minute and the other to put a hand on the surface that was "sanded" and make an observation.

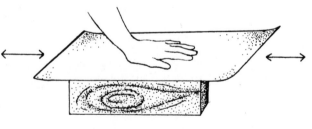

2. Select two additional students to repeat the demonstration.

3. Engage all students as participants in another demonstration:

- Rub the palms of both hands together, using brisk strokes.

- Observe the effect produced after one full minute of rubbing.

RATIONALE

Any one of six different forms of energy can be changed or converted to another form. Such changes in the form of energy are called energy transformations. In the demonstration, when the arm holding the sandpaper was moved back and forth, mechanical energy was "used." As the sandpaper was rubbed against the wood, friction was produced, resulting in the formation of heat energy. Hence, mechanical energy was converted to heat energy. The mechanical energy "used" to rub hands together also was not really lost. It too was converted to heat energy. The Law of Conservation of Energy, which states that "Energy cannot be created or destroyed but can be changed from one form to another," applies to the demonstration as well as to many other situations involving energy transformation.

DISCUSSION AND FOLLOW-UP

- Students should discuss the demonstration performed by the two student teams as well as that performed by all individuals. They should volunteer information and respond to direct questions:
  - In both demonstrations, what was the starting form of energy?
  - In both demonstrations, what was the resulting form of energy?
  - How do the demonstrations indicate that there was a change in the form of energy?
- Attention should also be directed to related situations, with students suggesting reasons that
  - there is a built-in fan on a film projector.
  - an electric appliance sometimes becomes overheated.
  - people rub their hands together or move briskly on a cold day.
- Examples of other energy transformations should be cited, drawing from experiences in school, at home, and at play.
- Some considerations should also be given to the long-range view of the Law of Conservation of Energy, with some thought given to whether all forms of energy are equally valuable and convenient for use by people.
- Each student should then prepare a list of six examples of energy transformation and a statement in which is expressed an understanding of the Law of Conservation of Energy.

2-3: CONVECTION CURRENTS IN WATER*
(elementary level)

INTRODUCTION

A pan of water being heated on a stove is a familiar sight. As the water at the bottom of the pan is heated, this water is forced upward by the cooler water that sinks around it. Heat is thus transferred from the bottom to the top of the pan by currents that are formed in the water. The direction of these currents can be traced by the pathway traveled by a material that is visible in the water.

LEARNING OBJECTIVES

At the end of this demonstration lesson, students should be able to

- identify heat as a form of energy.
- recognize that heat affects matter by causing its molecules to have more energy and engage in more rapid motion.
- understand that heat may be transferred when molecules move from one location to another.
- give an example of a situation in which the concept of the demonstration is illustrated.
- explain the demonstration, using *key words:* **heat energy**, **molecules**, and **convection**.

MATERIALS REQUIRED

beaker or heat-proof glass cooking utensil; water; heat source (hot plate, Bunsen burner, sterno heater, or other); coffee grounds

PRESENTATION

1. Fill a large beaker or heat-proof cooking vessel with water and place it over a heat source where students can view it clearly.
2. Place about one half a handful of coffee grounds in the water and allow them to sink to the bottom of the container.
3. Activate the heat source and apply gentle heat to the cooking vessel

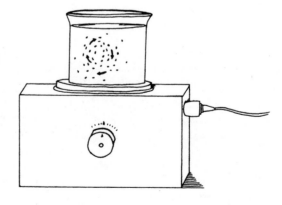

---

* Suitable for teacher-only presentation.

while students observe the activity of the water and coffee grounds.

NOTE: Safety precautions should be taken to prevent any mishap due to the heat source or the hot water.

4. Continue to observe as the water boils rapidly.

5. If the demonstration is repeated, a fresh supply of coffee grounds should be used.

RATIONALE

Transfer of heat by convection currents is limited to gases and liquids in which the molecules are held together very loosely by weak cohesive forces, enabling them to circulate freely. When the molecules are heated, they move farther apart, become less dense, and rise; when cooled, they are more closely packed and, being more dense, move to a lower level. In the demonstration, the currents created by this up-and-down movement of the water carry the coffee grounds, thus tracing the current's pathway.

DISCUSSION AND FOLLOW-UP

- As the demonstration proceeds, students should discuss what heat is and the methods by which it may be transferred.

- Building upon their comments, an awareness of the difference between heat and temperature can be developed.

- Observations of the demonstration should focus upon the movements of the coffee grounds from the area of heated water at the bottom of the vessel to the top, where they come in contact with relatively cool water, which carries them down again. These swirling up-and-down movements of water molecules trace the pathway of the convection currents as heat is transferred.

- Students should be encouraged to relate the demonstration to other situations encountered in which heat is transferred when a colder liquid or gaseous substance tends to move to a lower level while a warmer substance tends to rise, thus transferring the heat energy. Weather patterns, fireplaces, and cooking activities should be considered.

- Other methods of heat transfer should also be considered (if previously demonstrated) or planned as a study topic in a future demonstration lesson.

- After all discussion of the demonstration has been completed, students should be asked to write a report including the use of *key words*—**heat energy, molecules,** and **convection**—and a diagram of the demonstration in their Science Demonstrations notebooks.

2–4: HARNESSING ENERGY FROM THE WIND
(elementary level)

INTRODUCTION

The earth's dwindling supplies of fossil fuels and the many problems associated with nuclear energy have prompted a serious effort to find alternate energy sources that will meet our ever-increasing demands without bringing harm to our living and/or nonliving world. In addition to exploring new sources, researchers are taking a second look at some sources that have been used for many years. Windmills that have been used for centuries in the Netherlands for pumping water and grinding grain, for example, suggest that giant windmills, constructed in areas where the wind is strong enough, might be effective for the large-scale production of electric power. The force of moving air against a toy pinwheel can be used to demonstrate the force of wind against the blades of a windmill.

LEARNING OBJECTIVES

After the demonstration lesson has been completed, students should be able to

- identify the wind as a source of energy.
- understand the desire to put energy from a natural source to use in beneficial ways.
- recognize the windmill as a mechanism for harnessing energy from the wind.
- distinguish between harmful and beneficial aspects of wind and its energy.
- make appropriate use of *key words:* **kinetic energy**, **windmill**, and **wind storm**.

MATERIALS REQUIRED

toy pinwheels or materials to make them (paper, straight pins, scissors, and eraser-top pencils); air-conditioner, electric fan, or other source of moving air

PRESENTATION

1. Ask students to bring in a toy pin-wheel or provide them with materials and instructions for making one:
   - Make a pencil mark in the center of a four-inch square of colored paper.
   - Fold the square diagonally, twice, to make four triangular sections.

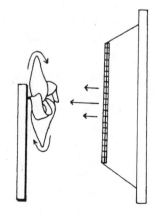

36

- With scissors, cut along folds in the paper from each corner to within one-half inch of the center mark.
- Fold back every other point to the center of the square and insert a straight pin through these corners, then through the center mark, and finally into the eraser at the top of a pencil.

2. Allow students to hold their pinwheels in front of a moving air source—electric fan, air-conditioner, fan on a filmstrip or opaque projector, or the student's mouth as breath is blown—so that air strikes against the blades.

3. Observe the activity.

RATIONALE

Wind, or air in motion, possesses kinetic energy that can do work. When directed toward a pinwheel, the moving air strikes against the nearest blade, forcing it away and bringing the next blade into the active area. As this is repeated with each blade in succession, the wheel is caused to turn and will rotate as long as the air continues to move and provide the necessary force. In windmills, the force that turns the wheel is then transmitted to a mechanism for pumping water or grinding grain. It is possible that it may also be used to generate electricity.

DISCUSSION AND FOLLOW-UP

- As students observe the activity of the pinwheel they should be encouraged to comment on the importance of a continuous supply of "wind" to keep the wheel rotating. Attention should also focus on the effects of the speed of the wind and the direction from which it strikes the blades. From this point they can discuss some of the weaknesses associated with the use of windmills for supplying a steady flow of power and suggest ways to overcome some of the problems.
- They should also be asked to report on examples of the destructive powers of uncontrolled wind, as in the case of tornadoes and cyclones, and to give meaning to the expression that something "looked as if a cyclone had hit it."
- When the discussion has been completed, students should prepare a report in their Science Demonstrations notebooks.
- A summary of the demonstration lesson should include:
  — The kind of energy possessed by moving air.
  — Ways in which this energy can be harmful to people.
  — Ways in which people can "harness" this energy to make it useful.

2–5: ACTION/REACTION
(elementary level)

INTRODUCTION

Only recently has Newton's Third Law of Motion, "For every action there is an equal and opposite reaction," become a popular phrase. This law, discovered by Sir Isaac Newton in the seventeenth century, has made possible some of our most important advances in space technology, and its impact has widened with the advent of jet airplanes and rockets. To develop a basic understanding of the law and its applications, a simple demonstration can be performed in the classroom.

LEARNING OBJECTIVES

At the end of this demonstration lesson, students should be able to

- state Newton's Third Law of Motion.
- explain how the law applies to a tennis racket hitting a ball, identifying the *action* and *reaction* involved.
- name three situations that illustrate Newton's Third Law of Motion.
- describe the demonstration, using correctly the *key words:* **action, reaction**, and **opposing force.**

MATERIALS REQUIRED

toy balloon; large pan; water

PRESENTATION

1. Blow up a toy balloon and twist the stem tightly by making several turns.
2. Hold the twisted stem securely between your fingers to prevent air from escaping.
3. Set the balloon on the surface of the water in a large pan and release your grip on the stem.
4. Observe the action of the balloon.

RATIONALE

When released, an inflated balloon resembles a rocket, as it is driven by internal air pressure in the direction opposite to that of its escaping jet stream.

In an actual rocket, the expanding fuel forces the exhaust gases downward from the bottom of the rocket (*action*) and the rocket itself is forced upward (*reaction*), resulting in a lifting of the rocket off its launch pad. Hot gases pushed out behind produce an unbalanced force on the rocket, accelerating its speed and possibly changing its direction. Both models operate because of unbalanced forces, and, in both, action and reaction are equal and opposite forces exerted on two different objects.

DISCUSSION AND FOLLOW-UP

- Students will no doubt request repeat performances of the demonstration.
- While the demonstration is being repeated, students may be invited to participate and to identify the action and reaction forces on the different objects.
- Other examples of action/reaction should be reported, with students encouraged to volunteer information about
  — experiences in which students have jumped from a boat, causing the boat to move away from the dock.
  — observations of television programs showing liftoff of spacecraft in which the spacecraft is propelled upward by rocket fuels, with exhaust at the rear.
  — observations of jet trails behind a jet plane that is flying at an enormous speed.
- After the discussion has been completed, students should be asked to write a report about the demonstration, using appropriate terms—**action, reaction, opposing forces**—to explain how it demonstrates Newton's Third Law of Motion. They may also be asked to name three examples of action/reaction situations and to design a more elaborate "rocket" or prepare another demonstration to be presented to the class.

2–6: LIGHT ORDINARILY TRAVELS IN STRAIGHT LINES
(intermediate level)

INTRODUCTION

Many everyday experiences tell us that light travels in straight lines. We cannot see around a corner unless we use a device to bend the light rays, we see narrow beams of light entering a dusty room or filtering through a cloud cover, and blocking the pathway of light shuts off our view of an object along that same pathway. Only through technological progress has this pathway been altered. These phenomena can be demonstrated to students.

LEARNING OBJECTIVES

When students have completed this demonstration lesson, they should

- understand that light waves ordinarily travel in straight lines.
- be aware of technological progress in making it possible for light to be guided around curves and corners.
- recognize some of the practical applications of our knowledge of how light travels.
- show evidence of an understanding of the meaning and proper usage of *key words:* **light energy**, **light waves**, **fiber optics**, and **technology**.

MATERIALS REQUIRED

flashlight; 4 pieces of blue construction paper; scissors; books; bookends; fiber optic light guide*

PRESENTATION

1. With scissors, cut a hole of equal size in the center of each of four pieces of blue construction paper.

2. Place four books between sturdy bookends on a table top. Then support each paper in a separate book so that the holes are all aligned at the same level.

3. Darken the room and hold a flashlight at the front end of the tunnel formed by the holes in the papers. Allow students to observe the light

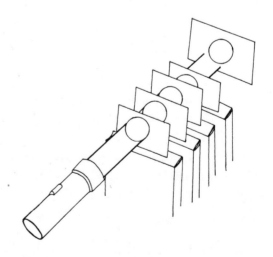

---

* A fiber optic light guide is available from Kurz-Kosch, Inc., Consumer Division, Dayton, Ohio 45401.

passing through the tunnel and forming a circle of light at the opposite end.

4. Raise the level of the third construction paper so that the hole in its center is no longer aligned with the holes in the other three papers.

5. Allow students to predict what will happen when the light is again directed into the tunnel.

6. Turn on the flashlight again and direct the light into the front end of the tunnel to allow students to check out their predictions.

RATIONALE

Light ordinarily travels in straight lines. Not only does this prevent us from seeing around corners, but it is responsible for the shadow cast by an opaque object through and around which light cannot travel. People have devised some unique ways for seeing around corners: the periscope has been used in submarines for many years, and recent developments in fiber optics, by which light can be guided through extremely thin strands of glass, now enable doctors to direct light to hard-to-see places in the bodies of their patients.

DISCUSSION AND FOLLOW-UP

- During the demonstration, students should be encouraged to give some additional examples of situations in which the straight-line path of light is blocked and unable to change its course to go around obstacles.

- Some students who may have observed a fiber optic light guide in use at home or in a doctor's office or who may have seen a television program featuring this technology may volunteer information about it. If not, its introduction as a follow-up demonstration will generate interest in technological progress.

- Several students should be allowed to use the SPECOLITE* to observe something in a difficult location, such as an inconveniently placed serial number on a projector. They should then report to the class how the bending of light around corners offered an advantage not available when light travels only in its normal straight-line pathway.

- A discussion of science and technology should point up the importance of inventiveness in furthering progress and in adjusting nature's methods to better advantage.

- After the discussion has been completed, students should be asked to incorporate *key words* —**light waves**, **light energy**, **fiber optics**, and **technology**—into a short written report of the demonstration illustrating natural and person-made pathways of light.

---

* A fiber optic light guide available from Kurz-Kosch, Inc., Consumer Division, Dayton, Ohio 45401.

2-7: TRANSFER OF ENERGY
(intermediate level)

INTRODUCTION

Students have an awareness of how they can forcibly move a classmate away by giving him a push or a shove. In the process, energy is transferred from the aggressor to the victim, whose body is caused to move involuntarily. A demonstration of how energy is transferred from one object to another can be developed for use in the classroom using a narrow trough and a few marbles.

LEARNING OBJECTIVES

After the demonstration lesson has been completed, students should be able to

- describe the demonstration to a friend and explain how it worked.
- prepare a list of three situations in which the scientific concept of energy transfer applies.
- tell how the demonstration helps to explain how light travels so rapidly through space.
- show evidence of an understanding of the meaning and proper usage of the *key word:* **electromagnetic energy**.

MATERIALS REQUIRED

pieces of wood or sturdy Styrofoam, 18–24 inches long; several marbles of equal size

PRESENTATION

1. Using pieces of wood or sturdy Styrofoam, prepare a long trough, with a channel that is slightly wider than the diameter of the marbles to be used.
2. Set the prepared trough on a table top where it will be clearly visible to all students.
3. Place three marbles, in a row and just touching each other, in the channel.
4. Have a student shoot a fourth marble into the row of three marbles in the channel.
5. Observe the shooter and the marbles in the row.
6. Repeat the demonstration, using other numbers of stationary marbles in the channel.
7. Observe the results, noting a common pattern in all cases.

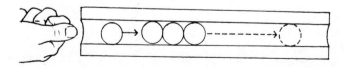

RATIONALE

When a rolling marble comes in contact with one that is stationary, the rolling marble is stopped and its energy is absorbed by the stationary one, causing it to move forward. When several stationary marbles are involved, energy from the moving one is passed on from one stationary marble to the next in line. Then, the end marble, being free to move, rolls forward. If two rolling marbles are directed into the lineup simultaneously, an energy transfer through the line will be set into motion, with the last two being moved forward.

It seems that the energy of a moving marble is not lost when the marble is stopped. Instead, it is transferred to the object it strikes, from which it may again be transferred, until it reaches an object that is free to move.

DISCUSSION AND FOLLOW-UP

- Students who express an interest in performing the demonstration on their own should be encouraged to do so, with further encouragement to vary the number of stationary marbles used, as well as the distance from which the stationary marbles are struck.

- Discussion should involve other situations in which a similar pattern of energy transfer has been observed, with some thought given to the importance of the conservation of energy. Electromagnetic energy should also be investigated and related to the demonstration.

- If a metal collision balls demonstrator is available from a high school physics class, this device will add a touch of added interest as students identify another demonstration of energy transfer with swinging balls.

- Students should be encouraged to relate the demonstration lesson to other forms of energy transfer, both from their science class and out-of-class experience. By way of review and summary, they should write a report about the energy transfer demonstration in their Science Demonstrations notebooks.

2–8: A CHAIN REACTION
(intermediate level)

INTRODUCTION

A chain reaction provides a vast amount of energy in a very short period of time. Basically, it occurs when the products of a reaction begin new reactions, and the reaction rate increases in what results in either a controlled or an uncontrolled manner. When the reaction proceeds slowly and in a controlled manner, the energy released can be used to perform useful work. It is only when the reaction cannot be slowed down that it becomes uncontrolled and leads to an explosion. The concept of a chain reaction can be demonstrated by setting up a group of dominoes in a well-designed pattern.

LEARNING OBJECTIVES

After completing this demonstration lesson, students should

- have an appreciation of the speed with which a chain reaction occurs.
- understand that, once set into motion, a chain reaction is difficult to stop.
- relate the domino demonstration to the concept of the release of nuclear energy by nuclear fission.
- suggest a scientific explanation for the mechanism involved in situations generally expressed by *key words:* **the domino effect** or **the domino theory**.

MATERIALS REQUIRED

dominoes; stopwatch (optional)

PRESENTATION

1. On a table top, set dominoes on end and according to a pattern such that starting with domino #1, each will fall against two others.

2. Gently push domino #1 toward the others in the pattern formation.

3. Watch the chain reaction.

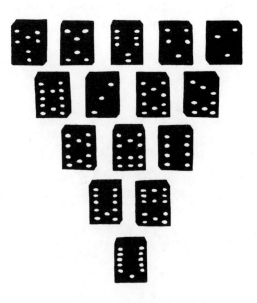

RATIONALE

In a chain reaction, some of the products of the initial reaction can be used to perpetuate the reaction. This brings about an increase in the reaction rate and releases an enormous amount of energy in a short period of time. For example, when an outside neutron hits an atom of Uranium 235, it causes the nucleus to split in two, releasing energy and setting free several inside neutrons. Each free neutron then causes the fission of another atom, and the chain reaction continues, with nuclear energy being released as a result of a chain reaction involving the nuclear fission of Uranium 235.

DISCUSSION AND FOLLOW-UP

- Students may wish to perform the demonstration many times, with different individuals supplying the initial push on domino #1. The demonstration can also be expanded to include a greater number of dominoes and variations of the pattern arrangement. If available, a stopwatch can be used to time the reaction from start to finish.

- Discussion should focus on the pattern by which an outcome of the toppling of domino #1 furthers the toppling of two or more dominoes and how the pattern continues until all dominoes have been toppled.

- Students should be encouraged to relate the demonstration to other activities, such as those involving bowling pins, billiard balls, and marbles. They should also be encouraged to engage in library research to find descriptions of a similar kind of chain reaction pattern that is involved in the release of nuclear energy by nuclear fission of Uranium 235.

- After the discussion has been completed, students should write a report in their Science Demonstrations notebooks in which they describe the demonstration and explain the **domino theory**.

2-9: PRODUCING A RAINBOW OF COLORS*
(intermediate level)

INTRODUCTION

The appearance of a rainbow after a rain shower is a beautiful sight. It is produced by sunlight shining through droplets of water, which causes the composite white light to be broken up into separate "colors of the rainbow." Flashes of color can also be seen from a sparkling diamond and from pieces of glass when light strikes against them. In the classroom, a color spectrum can be produced by directing a beam of strong sunlight through a glass prism or onto a mirror that has been placed underwater.

LEARNING OBJECTIVES

After having completed this demonstration lesson, students should be able to

- relate individual colors to rays of light with different wavelengths.
- identify the colors of the visible spectrum.
- account for the order of colors appearing in a color spectrum produced from white light.
- understand the meaning and proper usage of *key words:* **spectrum, wavelength, light energy,** and **refraction.**

MATERIALS REQUIRED

glass baking pan or clear plastic shoe box; water; square or rectangular pocket mirror; projection screen or wall surface

PRESENTATION

1. On a sunny day, place a glass baking dish or clear plastic shoe box on a table top near a window that receives direct sunlight.

2. Pour water into the container until it is nearly full of water.

3. Place a pocket mirror in the water so that it rests against one side of the container and receives rays of sunlight at an angle as they strike against its surface.

4. Adjust the angle of the mirror so that the light rays striking against

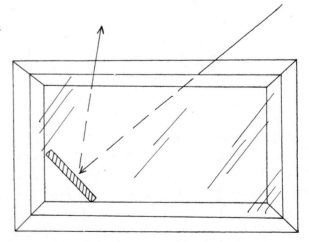

---

* Suitable for teacher-only presentation.

46

it are reflected on the wall or ceiling.

NOTE: Students should be cautioned not to look into the light that is being reflected.

5. Observe the color spectrum on the wall, ceiling, or other surface.

RATIONALE

The many different wavelengths making up white light are bent differentially as a beam of sunlight passes from one medium to another. In the demonstration, at the point where light passes from air to water, each wavelength, representing a different color band, is bent at a slightly different angle. The light strikes against the mirror and is reflected back, whereupon the light beams are bent again as they pass from water to air. The bent rays striking against a surface show as color bands arranged in order of their wavelength, which corresponds to the amount of bending for each.

DISCUSSION AND FOLLOW-UP

- Students should identify the color bands and match them with their corresponding light rays that show relative amounts of bending.

- Those who recall previous demonstrations related to this topic should reinforce their learning by reviewing the concept of the bending of light rays by a prism (producing a rainbow) and the bending of light rays at the surface of a jar of water with a partially submerged pencil (creating the appearance of a bent or broken pencil).

- Having established the bending of light rays by glass and water, other substances should be considered, such as an oil slick that appears iridescent.

- After the discussion has been completed, students should be asked to prepare a labeled diagram of the demonstration in their Science Demonstrations notebooks and to write a short explanation of the demonstration, making proper use of the *key words:* **spectrum, wavelength, light energy,** and **refraction.**

2-10:   CONCENTRATING THE SUN'S LIGHT RAYS*
(elementary level)

INTRODUCTION

On its way to the earth, light from the sun travels in straight lines at a rapid rate. As it gets closer it is slowed down when it passes through air. If it passes through water or a lens as well, it is slowed down even more. When passing from one medium to another, the light rays are bent, as is illustrated when a pencil placed in a glass of water appears to bend at the point where it is viewed entering the water from the air above. Passing light through a hand lens demonstrates how light rays can be bent and brought to a focus with dramatic results.

LEARNING OBJECTIVES

At the end of this demonstration lesson, students should be able to

- understand that light rays are bent when passing from one medium to another.
- understand how light rays can be brought to a focus by a lens.
- relate the demonstration that shows the focus of light rays by a hand lens to the focus of light rays by the lens of the eye on the retina.
- recognize the danger involved in looking directly at the sun or other bright light source.
- show evidence of an understanding of the *key words:* **light rays**, **light energy**, **focus**, and **concentrate**.

MATERIALS REQUIRED

hand lens or reading glass magnifier; area that provides direct sunlight; black construction paper

PRESENTATION

1. On a bright sunny day, set a piece of black construction paper on a window ledge or other area where direct rays from the sun will fall upon the paper.
2. Hold a hand lens above the paper, allowing the sun's rays to pass through the lens onto the paper.

---

* Suitable for teacher-only presentation.

48

3. Adjust the distance between the lens and the paper until the distance is located at which all light rays come to a focus at the same point on the paper.

4. Hold the lens in this position until a hole in the paper appears at the point where the light rays have come to a focus.

5. Continue to hold this position and maintain the focus, allowing the fire to spread to other parts of the paper.

CAUTION: Focusing sun's rays produces sufficient heat to burn delicate living tissue, including human skin.

RATIONALE

The bending of light rays as they pass through a lens produces a likeness of an object when the lens is moved to the correct distance for making the image of the close or distant object clear. Here, light rays are concentrated, producing an image of the sun on the paper. With concentrated light rays producing a picture of the scorching hot sun on the paper, enough heat is produced to burn the combustible paper.

DISCUSSION AND FOLLOW-UP

- Students will observe that the light rays being passed through the lens are concentrated at a very fine point where the hole is burned in the paper. The relationship between light rays from the sun and the heat that they produce when absorbed should be discussed.

- Students should be encouraged to relate the demonstration to other instances in which the familiar use of a lens—in a reading glass magnifier, microscope, telescope, camera, or eyeglasses—is helpful when producing a clear image of a near or distant object.

- Students should also develop an awareness of the presence of a lens in the human eye and of the great harm that could result from looking directly at the sun or other bright light source.

- Student understanding of the key points of the demonstration can be reinforced by their responses made to direct questions:

  — How does a lens concentrate light rays and bring them to a focus?

  — How does the demonstration show that light is a form of energy?

- A short written report of the demonstration, including reasons why one should never look directly at the sun, should then be prepared in the students' Science Demonstrations notebooks.

2–11: MAKING WORK EASIER WITH A RAMP
(intermediate level)

INTRODUCTION

Ancient people discovered that they could use an inclined plane or ramp to make their work easier. We know that the early Egyptians used this kind of simple machine to raise large stones being used to build the pyramids, and today we still employ this method to "lift" a heavy object, by sliding it up a smooth plank placed at an angle. The advantage of using such a simple device has many applications to everyday occurrences and can be easily demonstrated.

LEARNING OBJECTIVES

After having completed this demonstration lesson, students should

- have an awareness of the advantage of using simple machines for doing work more easily.
- recognize the ramp or inclined plane as a simple machine.
- be able to name at least three examples of situations in which a ramp is used as a labor-saving device.
- show evidence of an understanding of the meaning and proper use of *key words:* **simple machine**, **work**, **force**, **energy**, and **inclined plane** (ramp).

MATERIALS REQUIRED

smooth board, 100–120 cm long; spring scale; toy truck; stack of books, 25–30 cm high

PRESENTATION

1. Place a stack of books or magazines on a table top to a height of 25 centimeters or other convenient height to which an object can be lifted.
2. Attach a toy truck to the hook at the lower end of a spring scale.
3. Hold the spring scale upright so that you can determine the amount of force needed to support the toy truck as it is lifted vertically from the table top to the height indicated by the top of the stack of books.
4. Make a ramp by placing a smooth board at an angle from the table top to the top of the stack of books.

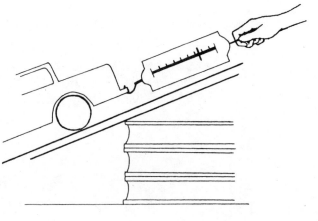

5. Again determine the amount of force needed to lift the toy truck, this time pulling it up the ramp from the table top to the top of the stack of the books.

6. Compare the amount of force needed to lift the truck with and without the use of the ramp.

RATIONALE

The principle of the inclined plane allows us to accomplish useful work with a reduced amount of force merely by moving the force through a greater distance than the weight is lifted. This is possible because the same amount of work necessary to lift a 25-pound sandbag straight up an embankment 4 feet above a trench (25 lb × 4 ft = 100 ft lb of work) can be accomplished with a force of only 10 pounds if we slide the sandbag up a ramp or slanted board that is 10 feet long.

$$\frac{100 \text{ ft lb of work}}{10 \text{ ft distance}} = 10 \text{ lb of force needed}$$

This same principle applies to the demonstration.

DISCUSSION AND FOLLOW-UP

Students should compare the amount of force indicated by the spring scale that was observed in the two methods used to raise the toy truck from the table top to the top of the stack of books.

- A discussion of the advantage of using a ramp in this case can lead to having students suggest other situations in which the work involved in lifting an object is made easier by requiring less force and less of an expenditure of energy. The ramp on a loading platform, the gangplank on a ship's deck, a road or driveway up a hill, and other examples can be cited.

- After the discussion, students should be directed to write a short report, including a diagram and use of the key words relating to the demonstration, in their Science Demonstrations notebooks.

2-12: THE ENERGY OF MOLECULAR MOTION IN A GAS
(elementary level)

INTRODUCTION

We are often tipped off to the presence of an object or event by its odor, detected far in advance of our being close enough to view it firsthand. A favorite food being cooked may be announced by odors emanating from the kitchen, making it unnecessary for us to ask, "What's for dinner?" just as a burning odor sends us scurrying in search of its origin. Simple substances with which we associate distinctive odors can be used to demonstrate the motion of gas molecules as they travel from one place to another in the classroom.

LEARNING OBJECTIVES

At the end of this demonstration lesson, students should be able to

- relate the demonstration to the Molecular Theory of Matter and to the energy level of discrete particles of a gas.
- relate the strength of an odor to the concentration of the molecules of the gas.
- name three occurrences in which the concept of the demonstration is illustrated.
- show evidence of an understanding of the demonstration by describing the event through the use of *key words:* **molecules, diffusion, concentration,** and **molecular energy**.

MATERIALS REQUIRED

bottle of oil of clove or oil of wintergreen; paper fan

PRESENTATION

1. Place a bottle of oil of clove or other nonirritating, highly odorous substance in the front of the room.
2. Remove the stopper from the bottle and fan the area around the mouth of the bottle toward the students.
3. Ask the students to indicate by a show of hands as soon as they detect the odor.
4. Note the developing pattern as students respond.

RATIONALE

Due to their kinetic energy, molecules of clove oil are in constant, random motion, as are those of air molecules in the classroom. As clove molecules escape from the bottle, they move steadily toward the back of the room, intermingling with air molecules and spreading out as they go. The greater the distance from the bottle, the more the spreading, which results in a decrease of their concentration level. An equal distribution of molecules of the two substances may finally be reached as a result of the diffusion, or spreading out, of the molecules.

DISCUSSION AND FOLLOW-UP

- Discussion of the demonstration should focus on how the odor of clove traveled to the back of the room. Students should be encouraged to respond to specific questions:

  — Does the demonstration support the view that clove oil is a continuous substance or that it is made up of individual particles?

  — If the clove oil were not made up of individual particles, could it leave the bottle and travel from the front to the back of the room, as demonstrated?

  — Where do the molecules get the energy required to travel?

  — How do the terms *molecules, energy, diffusion,* and *concentration* relate to the demonstration?

  — Do you predict that the clove odor would reach the back of the room in a shorter or a longer time if the container were gently heated?

- Students should be asked to give examples of other situations in which the energy of molecules causes the diffusion of particles of odorous substances.

- Then, following the discussion, each student should be asked to draw a picture representing the classroom after all students have given a positive response to the detection of the clove odor. By proper placement of twenty red dots on the picture, they should indicate the distribution of the clove molecules, indicating areas in the room in which the concentration is highest, lowest, and somewhere in between. By means of springs, they can show the energy of each molecule that enabled it to travel from the bottle to the various room locations.

CHAPTER 3

Demonstrations Pertaining to Physical Forces

3–1: STOPPING A LEAK IN A SODA BOTTLE
(intermediate level)

INTRODUCTION

On occasion, a liquid may begin to leak from a small hole near the base of the plastic bottle in which it is contained. Although not evident when the bottle was on a shelf or in a cupboard, the leaking becomes very noticeable when the cap is removed and the bottle is opened. The solution, of course, is to transfer the liquid to a nonleaking container; but, as a stopgap measure, people often replace the cap quickly and securely, thus preventing the escape of the liquid, until a more permanent solution can be devised. How the leaking of a liquid through a small hole near the base of the container can be controlled by tightly stoppering the container at the top can be demonstrated with a plastic soda bottle.

LEARNING OBJECTIVES

After this demonstration lesson has been completed, students should be able to

- recognize that more than one force is involved in the removal of a liquid from a container.
- understand how the forces of gravity and air pressure interact when a liquid is removed from a container.
- apply their knowledge of the forces of equalized air pressure to a practical "problem."
- show evidence of an understanding of the meaning and proper usage of *key words:* **air pressure**, **gravity**, and **equalization**.

MATERIALS REQUIRED

clean 1-liter plastic soda bottle or similar container (from household ammonia, laundry bleach, or other product) that is equipped with a screw top cap for tight closure; water; hammer; nail; catch basin or sink

PRESENTATION

1. With a hammer and nail, puncture a small hole in the side of a plastic bottle, about five to six cm from its base.

2. Hold the bottle over a basin and fill the bottle with water.

3. Observe the activity.

55

4. When students discover that water is leaking out of the hole in the bottle, quickly screw the cap on the open mouth of the bottle.

5. Observe.

RATIONALE

In order for water to flow out through the hole near the base of the bottle, something must replace it in the bottle. With the cap off, air can enter the space above the water and allow some water to escape at the bottom. With the cap screwed on tightly, however, no additional air is admitted, and a partial vacuum is created in the bottle. Due to the unequal air pressure, the force of gravity does not act upon the water; therefore, it remains in the bottle. Only if air is allowed to enter the bottle—either by removing the cap or by puncturing a second hole in the wall—will an unequalized air pressure be established, thus allowing the force of gravity to attract the water downward and out through the hole in the container because of the water's weight.

DISCUSSION AND FOLLOW-UP

- Students will no doubt want to be assured that there is indeed a hole in the side of the bottle. The cap can be removed to allow them to check this out and verify its existence by the appearance of water leaking out whenever the cap is removed from the bottle.

- Attention should focus on the interacting forces on the water that would cause the bottle to be emptied. In this regard, consideration should be given to the limitation of air pressure equalization (due to preventing air from entering the bottle), which interferes with the force of gravity that would attract water downward.

- Students should be encouraged to offer suggestions as to why this occurs in a closed container only and to suggest an alternate way of admitting air. They may recall a previous demonstration in which two holes in the lid of a juice can were needed to allow the juice to flow smoothly from the can and identify some of the same principles that were involved in this performance.

- After the discussion has been completed, students should prepare a diagram and explanation of the demonstration in their Science Demonstrations notebooks, using proper terminology and scientific terms: **air pressure**, **equalization of pressure**, and **gravitational force**.

3-2: FRICTION PRODUCED ON ROUGH AND
SMOOTH SURFACES
(intermediate level)

INTRODUCTION

Friction influences almost every moving object. In some instances we may find it advantageous to try to increase this resistance to motion from two objects in contact with each other, while in others we attempt to decrease—or even to eliminate—its influence. For example, baseball players wear shoes with spikes so that their feet do not slip when they run, but skiers wax their skis so that there is less friction with the snow. The friction between two surfaces is determined in part by the nature of the surfaces, a demonstration of which can be performed by two students and observed by their classmates.

LEARNING OBJECTIVES

After this demonstration lesson has been completed, students should be able to

- appropriately apply their skill of comparing as a process of science.
- give an example of an instance in which it is desirable to increase the friction between surfaces and to suggest a practical way to bring about the desired increase.
- give an example of an instance in which it is desirable to decrease the friction between surfaces and to suggest a practical way to bring about the desired decrease.
- understand the relationship between the amount of friction and the nature of the surfaces of the objects involved.
- show evidence of an understanding of the meaning and proper usage of *key words:* **friction** and **moving friction**.

MATERIALS REQUIRED

table top; strip of waxed paper, glass shelf, or other smooth surface; strip of sandpaper, carpeting, doormat, or other rough surface; 2 science books of equal size and weight with smooth paper or plastic covers; 2 spring scales; string

PRESENTATION

1. Prepare each of two science books:
   - Place a length of string lengthwise on the center page near the binding edge. Close the book and, with the ends of the string extending beyond both ends of the binding edge, draw the ends of the string together and tie them, allowing enough slack to form a small loop beyond the edge of the book binding.

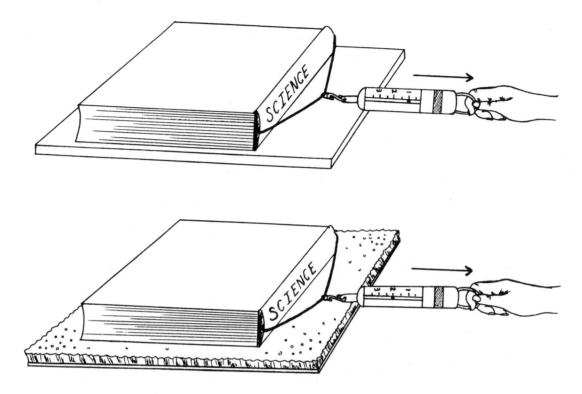

2. Arrange, lengthwise on the table, side-by-side runways, each of which is somewhat wider than the book prepared in step 1: a glass shelf or other smooth surface and a strip of carpeting or other rough surface.

3. Place one book at the far end of each runway.

4. Attach a spring scale to the string loop extending from each book.

5. Ask two students to participate in the demonstration. Each student will pull a spring scale gently and slowly so that the attached book begins to be pulled to the opposite end of the table. While doing so, he or she will take readings on the scale to indicate the amount of force needed to keep the book moving over the surface.

6. Record the force needed in each case and make a comparison.

RATIONALE

Friction is a force that resists motion. It is due to the adhesive forces between the surface molecules of two substances when in contact with each other, as well as to surface irregularities that act as hills and valleys in jamming together two rough surfaces. As such, friction is greater when moving on rough surfaces than on glass, ice, or a waxed or polished surface.

By acting against the direction of a moving object, friction was seen in the demonstration to either reduce the motion or to require that a greater force be applied to move the book.

DISCUSSION AND FOLLOW-UP

- While preparing the table top runways, students should be encouraged to predict the relative amount of force necessary to move a book over the table when in contact with each of the surfaces to be used in the demonstration. After the comparison has been demonstrated, reasons should be suggested and students should cite examples of objects moving over different surfaces:
    - ice skates over "new"/chopped-up ice
    - roller skates over a paved/unpaved surface
    - heavy tread/worn-smooth tires over snow and ice-covered roadways
- In each case, they should identify the ease of moving and the degree of difficulty in stopping the motion once started. Consideration should be given to the desirability of friction, which may prompt us to increase it, and to the disadvantages, which we may want to counteract, with an emphasis on the ways that this may be accomplished.
- Students should then prepare a record of the demonstration lesson, with responses to pointed questions:
    - What is friction?
    - What causes friction?
    - When is friction a friend? When is it an enemy?
    - How can friction be increased and thus improve a situation? How can friction be decreased to gain an advantage?

3-3:   THE INERTIA OF AN OBJECT AT REST
(elementary level)

INTRODUCTION

A magician can produce dramatic effects by pulling a tablecloth from under dishes without disturbing the dishes. The secret of the trick lies in an understanding of the scientific principle of inertia. The inertia of the dishes causes them to remain at rest while the tablecloth is moved very quickly from beneath them. The inertia of objects at rest can be observed in many situations and can be demonstrated easily in the classroom.

LEARNING OBJECTIVES

After having completed this demonstration lesson, students should be able to

- predict the behavior of a stack of several magazines if the one in the lowest position were to be quickly removed.
- relate the demonstration to other activities that they have experienced or heard about.
- name three examples of inertia of objects at rest.
- explain how the demonstration works, using *key words:* **inertia, force, motion, energy,** and **Law of Inertia.**

MATERIALS REQUIRED

sheet of smooth notebook paper; heavy book

PRESENTATION

1. Place a sheet of smooth notebook paper on a table top.

2. Place a science book on top of the paper.

3. Grasp the edge of the paper securely and yank it quickly from the table.

4. Notice what happens to the book as the paper is removed from beneath it.

RATIONALE

If an object is not moving, it tends to remain motionless indefinitely or until it is acted upon by some outside force. This is an important aspect of the Law of Inertia. It applies to many situations in daily life as well as to an important requirement for space travel; an enormous amount of power is required to overcome a spacecraft's inertia of rest when it lifts off a launch pad.

DISCUSSION AND FOLLOW-UP

- Students should be encouraged to describe other examples of inertia of a resting object. A volunteer might demonstrate one example by flicking a card from under a coin resting on its surface from atop an open drinking glass. The demonstrations can then be discussed and, in each case, explanations offered as to why both the book and the coin did not move when the paper or card under them was moved quickly. Students should also be encouraged to describe any observations made of people trying to push a car that has run out of gasoline and the amount of effort required to get it moving, and to comment on the amount of force that is required to overcome a spacecraft's inertia of rest during liftoff.

- If a question arises concerning the inertia of moving objects, it will serve as a good motivator to plan for a demonstration of inertia of motion and of ways to overcome it.

- After the discussion has been completed, students should be asked to state the Law of Inertia of objects at rest and to give one example of the law in operation.

3-4: USING NATURAL FORCES TO EMPTY AN AQUARIUM
(elementary level)

INTRODUCTION

There are many instances in which an understanding of some of nature's forces makes it possible for us to make our work easier. Applying a knowledge of how the combined forces of air pressure and gravity operate, for example, enables us to empty an aquarium tank without having to lift it. The use of a simple siphon system for transferring water from the tank to a sink or bucket can be demonstrated most effectively when a classroom aquarium is scheduled for a routine cleaning.

LEARNING OBJECTIVES

At the end of this demonstration lesson, students should be able to

- identify the two forces of nature that are involved in the demonstration.
- explain the contribution made by each of the two natural forces involved in the operation of a siphon system.
- name two examples of practical uses of a siphon system.
- demonstrate an understanding of the meaning and proper usage of *key words:* **air pressure**, **gravity**, and **siphon**.

MATERIALS REQUIRED

large aquarium tank; sink or catch bucket; plastic airline tubing; water; food coloring or ink (optional)

PRESENTATION

1. Position an aquarium tank on a table top where it can be viewed clearly by all students.
2. Fill the tank to near capacity and add a few drops of food coloring or use a tank that is scheduled for cleaning.
3. Place a catch bucket on the floor near the table.
4. Totally submerge the airline tubing in the water in the aquarium, allowing it to fill completely with water.
5. Keeping one end of the tube underwater, prevent air from escaping

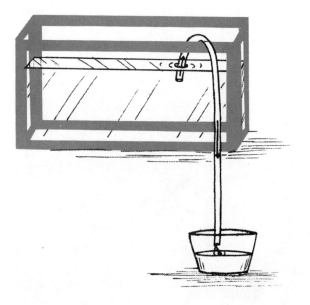

from the other end by placing a thumb securely over the opening or by pinching the end of the tube tightly.

6. Quickly place the plugged end of the tube over the bucket on the floor so that water passing through the tube will pass into the bucket.

7. Release the pressure from the end of the tube and, maintaining conditions—one end of the tube below the surface of the water in the aquarium and the other end at a position lower than the water's surface in the aquarium—observe the activity in the aquarium, in the tube, and in the bucket.

RATIONALE

The combined forces of air pressure and gravity are involved in the operation of a siphon system. Due to the creation of unequal pressure at the water's surface and in the tube, air pressure forces water molecules to move in a steady stream from the container into the tube. Then, because of gravitational forces, water is attracted to a lower level, where it is deposited in the receiving container. As long as no air is allowed to enter the tube and the receiving chamber is positioned lower than the one from which the transfer is being made, these two natural forces will cause the system to continue to operate without interruption.

DISCUSSION AND FOLLOW-UP

- While the demonstration is in progress, discussion should focus on *what* situations:
    - *What* is happening to the water in the aquarium?
    - *What* was removed from the airline tube at the beginning of the demonstration?
    - *What* was the purpose of using food coloring in the water (if that option was exercised)?
- After the demonstration has been completed, attention should focus on the use of *key words:* **air pressure**, **gravity**, and **siphon** in response to
    - *Why* situations:
        - *Why* did water enter the tube from the aquarium?
        - *Why* did water collect in the bucket?
    - *How* situations:
        - *How* can this demonstration be useful in other situations in daily life?
        - *How* can a knowledge of science be useful to help us do things more easily?
    - *What if* situations:
        - *What if* the bucket had been placed on the table top beside the aquarium tank?

- *What if* the airline tubing had not been filled with water at the beginning of the demonstration?
- When the discussion has been completed, students should be asked to write a short description of the demonstration in their Science Demonstrations notebooks, including some reference to the *what, how, why,* and *what if* situations that were a part of the discussion.

3–5: WHY WE USE SEAT BELTS
(intermediate level)

INTRODUCTION

When the car in which you are riding comes to a sudden stop, you are pitched forward, often bumping your head against the windshield; when a horse balks and refuses to jump a fence, his rider is catapulted through the air, even though the horse has come to a dead stop; and when the brakes of a car are applied suddenly, the car comes to an abrupt stop, and any purse or package that happens to be on the seat beside the driver falls to the floor. In each case, the object being carried by a moving object continues in a forward motion because it is not a part of the object that has suddenly stopped. Automotive engineers are well aware of the science involved in these situations. The scientific principle underlying the law of moving objects can be demonstrated in the classroom.

LEARNING OBJECTIVES

After the demonstration lesson has been completed, students should be able to

- recognize the potential dangers accompanying the failure to use seat belts.
- explain to friends and family why it is important to always "buckle up."
- relate the demonstration to an important part of Newton's First Law of Motion.
- show evidence of understanding and the proper use of *key words:* **velocity** and **motion**.

MATERIALS REQUIRED

4-wheel toy truck or cart; slant board runway; brick or other obstruction; books; marbles

PRESENTATION

1. Using a board and a stack of several books on the floor or on a table top, prepare a slanted runway whose length and angle allow the toy selected to travel in a downhill motion at a constant velocity.

2. Position a brick or other object to obstruct the passageway near the end of the runway.

3. Fill the cart or truck with marbles.

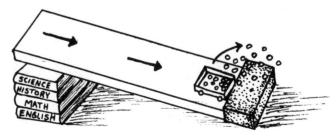

65

4. Carefully place the cart or truck at the top of the runway.

5. Release it and observe what happens when it is stopped by the obstruction which impedes its continued passage.

6. In response to student suggestions, repeat the demonstration, using other loads.

RATIONALE

An important part of Sir Isaac Newton's First Law of Motion states that an object that is moving at a constant velocity along a straight-line path will maintain that motion unless it is acted upon by an outside force. Because only the moving object—a horse, bus, or car—is affected by an outside force that may stop it suddenly, its rider, passengers, and/or cargo (because they are not a part of the moving object that is stopped) continue forward in their motion.

Seat belts fastened around passengers are attached from the frame of the car, to hold passengers firmly in place with the car instead of allowing them to continue in a forward motion when the car stops—or is stopped—suddenly.

DISCUSSION AND FOLLOW-UP

- Discussion may center upon the timeliness of the Law of Motion, first known to Newton nearly 300 years ago. Although not applied in the same context in his day, it can be considered from the standpoint of the value of discovering basic knowledge for which one day a practical application will be found.

- The scientific concept involved in the use of seat belts should be emphasized, and incidents experienced in a bus or car or on a bicycle or horse should be reported and related to the demonstration.

- When the discussion has been completed, students should be asked to explain to at least one other person **how seat belts help to avoid injuries and save lives**, incorporating *key words*—**velocity** and **motion**—and including a well-founded reference to Newton's First Law of Motion.

- For an optional assignment, students should be encouraged to prepare a Safety Belt poster and to research another aspect of this law that relates to objects at rest.

3-6: A LEANING TOWER OF BOOKS
(intermediate level)

INTRODUCTION

From play blocks to large building projects, the most successful and enduring construction designs involve the placement of building components directly above one another in precise vertical columns. However, the Leaning Tower of Pisa has survived since the twelfth century. Although an uneven settling of the ground caused it to tilt when it was less than halfway finished, construction continued anyway, and the eight-story bell tower still stands today. The mechanical equilibrium involved in this building can be demonstrated with a number of books stacked in a leaning formation.

LEARNING OBJECTIVES

After this demonstration has been completed, students should be able to

- relate the demonstration to the stability of a stack of bricks or boxes.
- exhibit an understanding of the concept of the center of balance.
- state a general rule that allows for a stack of objects to resist toppling, despite a gradual overhang.
- show evidence of an understanding of the meaning and proper usage of *key words:* **center of mass, vertical axis, center of balance, equilibrium,** and **mass.**

MATERIALS REQUIRED

table top; hard-cover books of equal size

PRESENTATION

1. Select a table top or other surface that is high enough for all students to view it clearly.

2. Place one book flat on the surface, positioning it so that students can observe it from the side and see that the lower edge of the book is even with the edge of the table top.

3. Place a second book on top of the first, allowing a slight overhang at the table's edge.

4. Continue to build a stack of books, with each book slightly overhanging

the one directly below, gradually increasing the overhang at the edge of the table.

5. When the stack is at the maximum height that can be attained without toppling (to be determined by a practice run), count the number of books and examine the distribution of their mass on the table side and beyond the table's edge.

RATIONALE

A center of balance becomes effective when the center of the mass of all components above any given component is aligned with the vertical axis that cuts through each component. In the case of the books, when the mass of the stack of books is greater on the side of the table top, the stack of books overhanging the table's edge will not topple. When the center of mass shifts, the stack of books will topple onto the floor.

DISCUSSION AND FOLLOW-UP

*   As the demonstration progresses, students should be encouraged to predict the number of books that will be stacked in the pattern established without toppling.

*   At various intervals and after the maximum number has been stacked, attention should be drawn to the distribution of the mass on the table side and on the side where the overhang appears. From this, the relationship between the distribution of mass and the stability of the stack of books should be established and the concept of *center of balance* developed.

*   Thought-provoking considerations, such as, "Suggest reasons that Galileo chose the Leaning Tower of Pisa as the place for conducting his studies to discover the Laws of Falling Bodies," should be used to elicit thoughtful responses from the students.

*   Other key points for students to discuss include the following:

    —   Distinguish between the mass and the weight of an object or collection of objects.

    —   Evaluate the conditions that will determine whether a stack of leaning objects will stand or topple.

    —   Suggest ways to build the tower of books so that more books could be used.

    —   Discuss how the demonstration relates to many common activities and occurrences, such as the way a worker carries a long ladder.

3–7: WATER PRESSURE INCREASES WITH DEPTH
(intermediate level)

INTRODUCTION

The pressure exerted by water is not the same at all depths. In nature, many fish in the sea are crushed to death when they wander to depths where the pressure exceeds the amount their bodies are able to withstand. Deep-sea divers are able to compensate for this increase in pressure on their bodies by wearing pressurized diving suits, which provide them with needed protection for survival. The relationship between water pressure and depth needs to be understood for the success of many activities, including those that involve oceanography and marine biology. This relationship can be demonstrated in the classroom using simple materials that are familiar to all students.

LEARNING OBJECTIVES

After this demonstration lesson has been completed, students should be able to

- recognize that the pressure exerted by water is not the same at all depths.
- state concisely the relationship that exists between the downward pressure of water and its depth.
- describe the demonstration and its application to three activities using *key words:* **pressure** and **depth**.

MATERIALS REQUIRED

heavy plastic bag; food coloring; water; pointed instrument such as a nail or large pin; bucket, basin, or sink; masking tape (2 strips)

PRESENTATION

1. Use a large nail or other pointed instrument to puncture four holes, one above the other, on each side of a heavy plastic bag.

2. Place a strip of masking tape vertically on each side of the bag, covering all holes made in the plastic.

3. Hold the upper part of the bag securely and fill the bag three-fourths full of water to which a few drops of food coloring have been added.

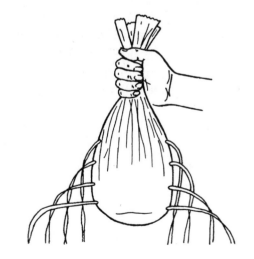

4. Gather the upper part of the bag together and hold it securely in one hand.
5. Hold the bag in position, with both taped sections over a sink, bucket, or catch basin and remove the strips of masking tape.
6. Observe the activity at the point of each hole in the bag.

RATIONALE

The greater the amount of water, the greater the pressure it exerts. Because of this, the weight of water (and air) above the level of each hole in the plastic bag presses down on the column of water with a corresponding amount of pressure. The column of water (and air) pressing on the water is greatest at its lowest level, causing water to shoot out of the bottom holes to reach the farthest distance from the bag, while water coming out of the uppermost holes, where water and the air above it presses the least, appears as little more than a dribble.

DISCUSSION AND FOLLOW-UP

- As students observe the water shooting out of the holes when the masking tape is stripped away from the plastic bag of colored water, attention should be drawn to observations concerning the distance the water shoots out from holes at various heights.
- After they have reported their observations, the discussion should center upon reasons that this is so. At this point, the demonstration can be repeated to confirm the first observation made and to make additional observations concerning changes noted in the distance to which water shoots out of the bottom hole as the demonstration progresses from beginning to end.
- Attention should focus on the kind and amount of matter that is above the water being forced out and on the replacement of the decreasing column of water by air. Students may relate this observation to personal experiences in related matters, such as the change in rate of water flow from a bathtub or swimming pool as the water level decreases, or they may associate the demonstration with observations that dams are built wider at the base to withstand the greater pressure at lower depths.
- After the discussion has been completed, students should prepare a short report, including diagrams and an explanation of the demonstration, in their Science Demonstrations notebooks.

3–8: A MAGNETIC LAZY SUSAN
(intermediate level)

INTRODUCTION

Magnets may attract materials without actually touching them. The earth, acting like a giant bar magnet, attracts certain particles from outer space. The large magnetic field surrounding the earth's "magnet" also influences a magnetized compass needle, making it possible for us to use a compass for telling direction. A magnetic Lazy Susan, whose operation depends upon a magnet with which it never makes direct contact, can be demonstrated in the classroom.

LEARNING OBJECTIVES

After this demonstration lesson has been completed, students should be able to

- relate the demonstration to the concept that magnets exert an attractive force on certain metal objects.
- understand the force of attraction within an area or "field" surrounding a magnet as well as with direct contact.
- recognize that magnetism, like gravity, acts at a distance.
- show evidence of an understanding of the demonstration and of the proper use of *key words:* **magnet**, **magnetic field**, and **compass**.

MATERIALS REQUIRED

small paper plate; paper clips; Styrofoam block or modeling clay; magnet; straight pin; short eraser-topped pencil

PRESENTATION

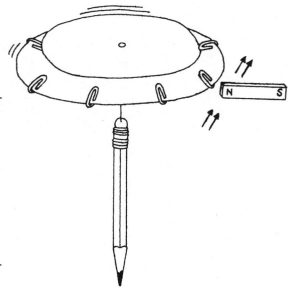

1. Attach eight paper clips at regular intervals to the rim of a six-inch paper plate so that they are distributed evenly around the circumference of the plate.

2. Insert a straight pin through the exact center of the plate so that the point of the pin protrudes from the bottom of the plate.

3. Insert the pinpoint into the eraser at the top of a short pencil.

4. Insert the opposite end of the pencil into a block of Styrofoam, modeling clay, or other material that

will hold it securely in a vertical position.

5. Check to be sure that the paper plate will move freely about the pin acting as a pivot through its center.

6. If necessary, adjust the paper clips to balance the paper plate in a horizontal position.

7. Move a magnet past the rim of the plate in one direction, without touching any part of the plate or paper clips attached to it.

8. Observe the activity.

RATIONALE

A magnet attracts objects containing iron. By moving the magnet past the plate, one after another of the paper clips is drawn to the magnet, causing the plate to move in a manner like that of a Lazy Susan. The magnitude of the magnetic field here is small, and the distance within which it exerts an influence can be measured. The magnetic field of the earth, however, is extremely large, and its influence extends far out into space.

DISCUSSION AND FOLLOW-UP

- Students should concentrate on the manner in which magnetism is used here to cause the plate to move. They should relate the effectiveness of the motion to the magnetic field surrounding the magnet and make predictions about what would happen if the distance between the magnet and the paper clips were to be changed—making them closer together or farther away. A student should then be invited to test these predictions as well as to demonstrate the effect of a stronger magnet or a different number of paper clips positioned around the edge of the plate.

- The basic concept of the demonstration should be reviewed, with students using designated key words, where applicable, in response to direct questions:

  — How is it possible for a magnet to exert an influence on an object without touching it?

  — How could the motion of the Lazy Susan be made continuous without changing the materials or design?

  — In what way is gravitational force like magnetic force?

  — In what way is gravitational force different from magnetic force?

- To evaluate student understanding of the demonstration, each should draw a diagram of the magnetic Lazy Susan and explain how a magnet causes it to be moved without touching it.

3–9: PRODUCING STATIC CHARGES
(elementary level)

INTRODUCTION

Television commercials and magazine advertisements call attention to the problems brought about by static cling and the ways to prevent its occurrence in laundered clothing that has been dried in a clothes dryer. In other instances, we find that bits of Styrofoam packing material tend to cling to the packed objects; freshly shampooed hair is attracted to a hard rubber comb; and individual sheets of paper are difficult to separate from others in a stack. A demonstration of how static charges can be produced in the classroom will help students to understand the nature of static electricity and some of the inconveniences that are associated with it.

LEARNING OBJECTIVES

At the end of this demonstration lesson, students should be able to

- understand the basic nature of static electricity.
- list three examples of static electricity encountered in daily living.
- identify some conditions that favor the production of static charges.
- apply methods for reducing static charges.
- understand the meaning and proper usage of *key words:* **static electricity, electrons, static cling,** and **friction.**

MATERIALS REQUIRED

wire clothes hanger; tissue paper; thread; scissors; hard rubber comb; wool scarf or mitten; fine spray mister or atomizer; warm water

PRESENTATION

1. With scissors, make several tissue paper cutouts of bird figures, each measuring about two inches in length.
2. After tying thread to the top of each bird cutout, suspend two or more of the birds from the cross bar of a wire hanger so that they are several inches apart.
3. Suspend the hanger in an open doorway or from another supporting structure and adjust the positions of the birds so that the entire

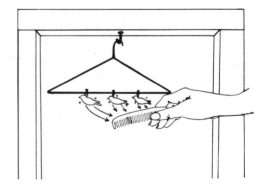

73

assembly is balanced and hangs freely.

4. Using a wool scarf or mitten, vigorously rub a hard rubber comb for about one minute.

5. Hold the charged comb in various positions near the birds and observe the activity.

6. Invite some students to recharge the comb and cause the birds to "fly."

7. Using a fine-mist spray atomizer, mist the area around the birds with warm water.

8. Again, hold a charged comb near the paper birds and observe.

RATIONALE

When two objects are rubbed against each other, their closeness and the heat of friction cause electrons to transfer from one of the objects to the other. In the process, one of the objects gains electrons and becomes negatively charged, while the other loses electrons and is left with a positive charge. In the demonstration, a negative charge was produced on the comb. This caused it to attract the uncharged paper where, by contact, it could pass on the excess electrons and restore its neutral condition.

DISCUSSION AND FOLLOW-UP

• While the comb is being rubbed with wool, students should be reminded of a similar situation in which they may have observed small pieces of paper being attracted to a comb they have just used to comb their hair.

• After this concept has been reinforced by the demonstration, reports of other experiences—the appearance of a slight shock and/or sparks and crackling that accompany the static electricity produced when charges jump from one object to another, as observed when freshly washed long hair is combed, when socks are taken out of a clothes dryer and separated, or when a light switch is touched after shoes have been rubbed on a wool carpet while crossing a room—should be encouraged.

• In each case, an explanation of how the static charges were produced and of the conditions that favored their production should be stressed.

• After the discussion, students should be asked to answer related questions:

   — What is meant by static electricity?

   — Why do clothes taken out of a clothes dryer tend to have static cling, while clothes taken out of a washing machine do not?

   — What are two kinds of products that can be purchased to combat the undesirable effects of static electricity?

3–10:   THE USEFULNESS OF A VACUUM
(elementary level)

INTRODUCTION

When air is removed from an "empty" tube, the partial vacuum created provides for something else to rush into the tube and replace the air that has been forced out. As the Greeks put it, "Nature abhors a vacuum." Evidence of this can be seen whenever we use an atomizer for spraying a fine mist of air freshener or when drinking from a straw. It can also be demonstrated by students with the use of plastic medicine droppers and table salt.

LEARNING OBJECTIVES

After having participated in this demonstration lesson, students should be able to

- understand the nature of a partial vacuum.
- make an inference relating to the creation of a partial vacuum.
- apply the concept of the demonstration to other examples in which the pressure of air can help us to perform simple tasks.
- describe the demonstration and explain how it works, using *key words:* **air pressure** and **vacuum**.

MATERIALS REQUIRED

plastic medicine droppers; baby food jar tops; table salt

PRESENTATION

1. Distribute one baby food jar top and one plastic medicine dropper to each group of four students.
2. Place one teaspoonful of table salt in each jar lid and heap it in the center.
3. Instruct students within each group to take turns as each performs the demonstration:
   — Place the open end of the medicine dropper at an angle, with the opening of the tip below the surface of the heap of salt.
   — Hold the bulb of the medicine dropper between the thumb and forefinger and exert pressure by squeezing.

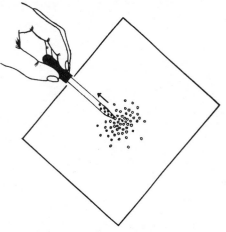

   — Release the pressure on the bulb.
   — Observe the activity of salt grains being drawn into the tube.

RATIONALE

Applying pressure to the bulb of a medicine dropper forces air out of the lower end of the tube, leaving the air remaining in the tube with lesser density and with greatly reduced pressure. The greater atmospheric pressure on the surface of the salt in the jar lid then pushes salt particles into the tube, where they can be observed as they collect. The principle involved is essential to the operation of many common devices, including the vacuum cleaner.

DISCUSSION AND FOLLOW-UP

- As each student in turn performs the demonstration within each group, discussion should focus on the observations made, with attention to the following questions:
    — What was forced out of the medicine dropper when the bulb was squeezed?
    — What entered the tube to replace the air that had been forced out?
    — What caused the upward movement of salt particles in the tube?
    — How could a greater quantity of salt be drawn into the tube using this basic method?
    — What are some devices that illustrate the use of a vacuum to do work?
- When the entire class regroups to review and summarize the main points of the demonstration lesson, attention should focus on the use of the *key words* **air pressure** and **vacuum** to explain the scientific principle involved in the demonstration and to describe some of the ways that applications of this knowledge have proved to be helpful in accomplishing useful work.

3–11: WEIGHT OF AN OBJECT IN AIR AND IN WATER
(elementary level)

INTRODUCTION

A natural reaction in response to seeing an interesting looking object that is underwater is to lift the object out of the water in order to view it better. In the process, we find that the object that was relatively easy to lift while underwater seems to become heavier as it is passed from the water to the air above. The apparent loss of weight of an object when in water can be demonstrated in the classroom.

LEARNING OBJECTIVES

After the demonstration lesson has been completed, students should be able to

- compare the weight of an object in air and in water.
- relate the demonstration to the pressure of water.
- identify the force that pushes upward on objects immersed in water as *buoyancy.*
- describe two personal experiences that illustrate the effect of buoyancy.
- apply science process skills of observing, comparing, and inferring.
- give an explanation of the demonstration, using *key words:* **water pressure**, **weight**, and **buoyancy**.

MATERIALS REQUIRED

large jar; rock (or other heavy object) of suitable size and shape; spring scale; water; string; cork

PRESENTATION

1. Pour water into a tall wide-mouthed glass jar until it is approximately two-thirds full of water.
2. Tie a string around a heavy rock that will fit easily through the mouth of the jar and that can be submerged completely in the water in the jar.
3. Attach the free end of the string to a spring scale.
4. Allow the rock to hang from the scale while a student takes a reading on the scale and records the weight in air on the chalkboard.

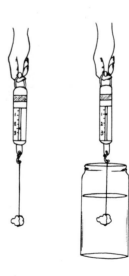

5. Hold the spring scale assembly directly above the jar and gently lower it until the rock is completely submerged in the water.

6. Again have a student read the scale and record the weight of the rock in water on the chalkboard.

7. Observe and make appropriate comparisons and inferences.

RATIONALE

Water exerts pressure on the sides as well as on the bottom of a container in which it is placed. It also pushes in all directions against an object placed in the water, often with enough upward force to make the object float. Although some objects sink because they weigh more than an equal volume of water, all objects submerged in water will weigh less than they do in air because of the buoyant upward force exerted by the water. The apparent loss of weight of the object when in water is equal to the weight of the water that it displaces.

DISCUSSION AND FOLLOW-UP

- After the weights have been recorded for the stone when in air and in water, attention should be focused on the difference. Students should be encouraged to make an inference concerning the cause of the apparent weight loss when the rock was placed in water and to compute the actual loss, as indicated by the recorded weights. They should also be asked to report similar personal experiences they have had in which a similar weight loss has been observed when a submerged object was lifted out of the water in a swimming pool or at the seashore.

- A simple follow-up demonstration can then be performed:

    Float a cork in a basin of water and ask a student to push downward on the cork. Allow all students who wish to volunteer to repeat the operation. Then ask them to describe what they saw and/or felt so that all students can relate the experience to the weight loss of the rock and, using *key words*—**water pressure, weight**, and **buoyancy**—explain the difference in weight of an object in air and in water.

- After all discussion has been completed, students should be asked to write a short report, with diagrams, to indicate their understanding of the demonstration.

3-12: A FLOATING PAPER CLIP
(elementary level)

INTRODUCTION

Most students have some knowledge of magnets and magnetism. They have amused themselves by using a small magnet to attract a variety of small metal objects and they have observed the use of magnetic devices for keeping the doors on small cabinets from swinging open. After a trial run to determine proper distances for the specific magnet being used, a simple classroom demonstration involving student participation will generate interest and elicit student response to a lesson on magnetism.

LEARNING OBJECTIVES

At the end of this demonstration lesson, students should be able to

- identify a magnet as an object that attracts other objects containing iron and/or steel.
- understand the general concept that the force of a magnet operates within the entire magnetic field, which may extend well beyond the outer edges of the actual magnet.
- make an inference that lines of magnetic force from a magnetic field travel through an air space.
- explain how a magnetic force can attract an object without touching it.
- name three uses for magnets in daily life experiences.
- show evidence of an understanding of the meaning and proper usage of *key words:* **magnet**, **magnetic force**, and **magnetic field**.

MATERIALS REQUIRED

bar magnet; paper clip; thread and string; ruler; tape; several books; chalk, file card, or pencil

PRESENTATION

1. Tie a string around the middle of a bar magnet and suspend it from a ruler placed across two stacks of books placed on a table top.
2. Attach a paper clip to one end of a piece of thread.
3. Hold the unattached end of the thread so that the paper clip dangles freely a few inches from the magnet.
4. Slowly draw the dangling paper clip closer to the magnet until a slight pull of the magnet is detected.
5. Make adjustments, as necessary, but without allowing the paper clip to touch the magnet, to find the

distance at which the paper clip is held within the magnetic field.

6. Maintain this distance between the paper clip and the magnet by taping the thread to the table top.

7. Observe the behavior of the paper clip.

8. Invite some students to pass an object, such as a piece of chalk, a ruler, a file card, or a pencil between the suspended paper clip and the magnet.

RATIONALE

As with the gravitational force, magnetic force affects objects at a distance, without actually touching them. In the demonstration, this force can be seen to operate without having the paper clip make contact with the magnet, just as space travelers approaching the earth would probably be aware of the effects of the magnetic force of the earth's giant bar magnet long before they landed on the surface of the earth. The extent of the effectiveness of the magnetic force will, of course, vary with the size and strength of the magnet that is used.

DISCUSSION AND FOLLOW-UP

- Students should be encouraged to volunteer as helpers to demonstrate the magnetic force that holds the paper clip upright, although not in contact with the magnet. They may suggest objects (paper, pencil, ruler, comb, a finger, or another paper clip), which they should then be invited to hold in the space between the magnet and the paper clip.

- They should then make predictions about what would happen if the thread were cut, if the distance or location of the magnet were changed, or if a cork instead of a paper clip had been used in the demonstration. When possible, their predictions should be checked by performing variations of the demonstration and increasing student involvement.

- Students should also relate the demonstration to the effect of the earth's magnetic force on a compass, which also operates without making contact with the earth's magnet.

- They should then be asked to make a list of three objects that are attracted to a magnet and three objects that are not attracted to a magnet.

- When it appears that students understand the basic concept of the demonstration, they should be asked to add the *key words*—**magnet, magnetic field**, and **magnetic force**—to their vocabulary lists in their Science Demonstrations notebooks.

CHAPTER 4

Demonstrations Pertaining to Physical and Chemical Changes

4–1: OXIDATION OF METALS
(elementary level)

INTRODUCTION

The oxidation of metals produces noticeable changes in their appearance. For example, nails become rusted, and the shiny finish on an automobile becomes dulled by the buildup of a surface film. In the case of copper, the oxidized metal forms a green residue at the surface, as can be seen on copper pipes, copper coins, and on the Statue of Liberty. The nature of the changes brought about by this form of oxidation can be demonstrated with simple materials.

LEARNING OBJECTIVES

At the end of this demonstration lesson, students should be able to

- identify oxidation as a process involving a chemical change.
- state some conditions that increase the rate of oxidation of metals.
- tell how the rate of oxidation can be slowed.
- describe how a metal becomes oxidized, using *key words:* **oxidation**, **oxide**, **rust**, **chemical reaction**, and **chemical change**.

MATERIALS REQUIRED

rusty nails, sandpaper, white paper, hand lens (optional)

PRESENTATION

1. Place a well-rusted nail on a piece of white paper.

2. Using fine sandpaper, rub the rust from the surface of the nail.

3. Allow the rust to collect on the paper.

4. Observe the rust and the nail from which it was removed.

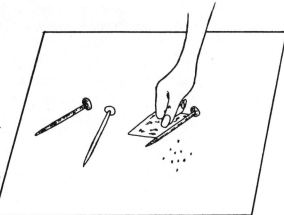

RATIONALE

When oxygen in the air reacts with certain metals, new substances are formed. In the presence of water, the iron in a nail reacts with oxygen to form rust, or iron oxide, whose properties are different from those of either the iron or the oxygen. The chemical reaction is accompanied by an energy change similar to that involved in combustion or rapid oxidation, except that the energy release occurs over a long period of time and is, therefore, hardly noticeable.

DISCUSSION AND FOLLOW-UP

- After students have had an opportunity to examine the scraped rust, they should compare its appearance with that of the clean surface of the nail from which it was removed.
- Their understanding of the demonstration can be developed further by encouraging them to relate the formation of rust to some personal experiences with their bikes, roller skates, and so on, and by asking them to respond to certain guide questions:
  - — What originally caused the nail used in the demonstration to become rusted on the surface?
  - — What is the chemical composition of rust?
  - — What is the chemical name for rust?
  - — How do the properties of rust compare with the properties of iron and of oxygen?
  - — What is another metal that "oxidizes"?
  - — Does the formation of an oxide illustrate a chemical or a physical change?
  - — What is an appropriate way to remove an oxide buildup from your family car?
  - — How does keeping nails, steel wool, and so on, dry retard the formation of rust?
  - — What is the meaning of the scientific terms *oxidation, oxide, rust, chemical reaction,* and *chemical change,* and how do they apply to the demonstration and related situations?
- To summarize, students should be asked to write a recipe for making rust, indicating ingredients, necessary conditions, the kind of change involved, and the resulting product.

4–2: USING A CHEMICAL INDICATOR
(intermediate level)

INTRODUCTION

Many chemical tests to detect the presence of a specific substance have been devised for use in both laboratory procedures and situations encountered in daily activities. Test papers for determining the acidity level of a substance and easy-to-use procedures for detecting the presence of moisture, nutrients, and indicators of water pollution are among those that depend upon color changes brought about by chemical reactions. An iodine solution can be used to demonstrate a color change that occurs only in the presence of a starch.

LEARNING ACTIVITIES

At the end of this demonstration lesson, students should be able to

- infer that the color change of iodine from amber to blue-black was due to its reaction with starch.
- associate the color change demonstrated with a chemical reaction.
- name three chemical tests in which a color change is involved.
- describe the demonstration and the effective use of a chemical indicator using *key words:* **chemical reaction, chemical change,** and **chemical complex.**

MATERIALS REQUIRED

mayonnaise or peanut butter jar; baby food jar; iodine solution; corn starch or flour; medicine dropper

PRESENTATION

1. Prepare an iodine solution in a baby food jar: Add iodine, drop by drop, to a jar half full of water, until the iodine-water solution is deep amber in color.

2. Prepare a starch mixture in a mayonnaise jar: Add one tablespoon of corn starch to a jar two-thirds full of water, stirring the mixture to distribute the starch uniformly in the water.

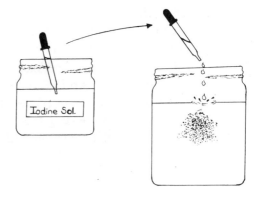

3. Using a medicine dropper, add several drops of the prepared iodine solution, drop by drop, to the starch mixture in the mayonnaise jar.

4. Observe as a new color appears, spreads throughout the iodine-starch complex, and persists with its intense blue-black appearance.

RATIONALE

The production of color molecules associated with chemicals does more than signify a chemical change. If the color is produced only when a specific substance combines with a given chemical, that chemical becomes useful as a chemical indicator. In the demonstration, for example, the distinctive blue-black color produced by the iodine-starch complex is not formed by the addition of iodine to any other substance. This makes iodine a useful indicator when testing for the presence of a starch.

DISCUSSION AND FOLLOW-UP

- As students observe the demonstration, they should report all changes noted, or they can respond to leading questions:
    - What is the color of the iodine solution?
    - What is the color of the starch mixture?
    - What happens when iodine is added to the starch?
    - What is responsible for the color change?
    - What can you tell about a substance that turns blue-black when iodine is added to it?
    - What can you tell about a substance that does not turn blue-black when iodine is added to it?
    - Does the positive action of an indicator depend on a chemical or a physical change?
    - In the demonstration, what was the "new" substance formed when iodine was added to starch?
- Discussion of the demonstration should include other chemical indicators with which students may be familiar. Some may have used litmus paper or seen color-change tests used for the detection of moisture in the air or sugar in the blood or urine. It should be noted that these convenient tests are based on chemical changes that are specific.
- As a follow-up, students should be asked to apply the *key words:* **chemical reaction, chemical change, chemical indicator**, and **chemical complex** to an explanation of the demonstration, and to discuss the suitability of a chemical as an indicator if it reacted in the same manner when brought in contact with two different substances.

4–3: CONSERVATION OF MATTER
(elementary level)

INTRODUCTION

No substance serves better than water to illustrate change in the physical form of matter. Responding to changes in temperature, ice melts, water evaporates, water vapor condenses, and water freezes. Usually observed as natural phenomena, these changes are also initiated by people as they incorporate them appropriately in devices for cooking and refrigerating foods; for heating, cooling, humidifying, and dehumidifying the air; and for operating certain engines. The water is changed from one physical form to another, but none is actually lost. This can be demonstrated in the classroom using simple and easy-to-obtain materials.

LEARNING OBJECTIVES

After having completed this demonstration lesson, students should be able to

- recognize the change demonstrated as a physical change.
- name the characteristics by which a physical change can be identified.
- understand the basic concept of the Law of Conservation of Matter.
- name three substances that can be changed physically, with no gain or loss in the amount of the substance.
- show evidence of an understanding of the meaning and proper use of the *key word:* **mass.**

MATERIALS REQUIRED

baby food jar; aluminum foil; weighing balance; crushed ice

PRESENTATION

1. Place crushed ice in a baby food jar until the jar is two-thirds full of loosely packed ice.

2. Cover the jar with aluminum foil.

3. Place the covered jar on a weighing balance in a position where all students can view it clearly.

4. Determine the weight in grams of the combined jar, ice, and aluminum foil.

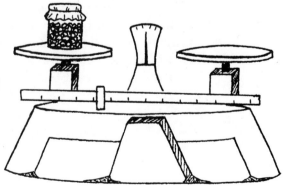

5. Have students prepare a diagram of the demonstration setup, in balance, including labels on all structures and materials used and a record of the weight in grams. They should designate this diagram as a *before* situation.

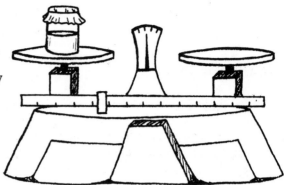

6. Observe closely for evidence of change.

RATIONALE

Depending upon the temperature, many substances can exist in more than one physical state. Water, for example, may exist as a solid, a liquid, or a gas, and, although changed from one form to another, the chemical makeup of its molecules remains the familiar H_2O. The mass of a given amount of water also remains unchanged when water changes from a liquid to a solid or a gas. The total number of its molecules is the same, for none are lost and none are gained. Collecting the water formed when a piece of ice melts, therefore, introduces students to the Law of Conservation of Matter, which states that "Matter can neither be created nor destroyed; it may, however, be converted from one form to another."

DISCUSSION AND FOLLOW-UP

- As students prepare their diagrams of the demonstration setup, they will note that some of the ice begins to melt, eventually forming water within the jar. They should identify the physical change that is occurring.

- Attention should also focus on the weight of the jar containing ice/water, and on the balance that is maintained throughout the demonstrated physical change. A second diagram showing the demonstration *after* the ice melts should be prepared to accompany the *before* diagram. Students should then write a statement expressing the constancy of the *mass* when the measured amount of ice was melted in the jar.

- Students should be encouraged to volunteer information about how other examples of physical change, such as melting a block of paraffin, crushing a piece of chalk, cutting a piece of paper, or shredding a head of cabbage illustrate the Law of Conservation of Matter. They should then formulate a general statement of the law and write it in their Science Demonstrations notebooks.

4-4: BOUNCING BALLS IN WATER
(intermediate level)

INTRODUCTION

Chemical reactions often produce dramatic effects that appear to be unexplainable. When featured in science centers, they attract the attention of observers of all ages. Using a similar approach in the classroom, a demonstration involving a relatively simple chemical reaction can be performed to capture the attention of students and motivate them to want to learn how the effects are achieved.

LEARNING OBJECTIVES

At the end of this demonstration lesson, students should be able to

- infer that the unusual activity observed in the demonstration is due to a chemical reaction between the substances added to the water.
- identify one new product formed by the chemical reaction involved in the demonstration.
- relate the up-and-down movement of objects in water to changes in their density.
- describe the demonstration, including an explanation of what causes mothballs to bounce in water and the use of *key words:* **density**, **carbon dioxide**, and **chemical reaction**.

MATERIALS REQUIRED

baking soda; white vinegar; food coloring; glass cylinder or tall jar; water; table salt; mothballs

PRESENTATION

1. Place a tall jar that is one-fourth full of water in a location where it can be viewed clearly by all students.
2. Add a few drops of food coloring, one tablespoonful of baking soda, and one teaspoonful of table salt to the water in the jar.
3. Stir the contents of the jar and, when all components have been dissolved in the water, add one tablespoonful of white vinegar and sufficient water to bring the level of the liquid in the jar to three-fourths of its capacity.

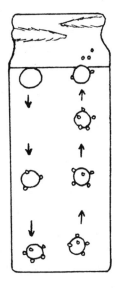

4. Place several mothballs in the liquid mixture.

5. Observe the activity.

RATIONALE

Due to their density, mothballs sink to the bottom of a container of tap water. However, this density can be changed temporarily by the addition of vinegar and baking soda to the water. A chemical reaction between the two chemicals produces carbon dioxide bubbles which adhere to the surface of the mothballs, reducing their overall density. Then, aided by the buoyant force of salt dissolved in the water, the collected gas bubbles cause the balls to rise to the surface. For a period of time they float, but, as the mothballs lose their carbon dioxide to the atmosphere, their original density is restored and they sink again. Until all chemical reactants are spent, the process continues, and the accompanying activity can be seen to recur repeatedly, thus creating an effect of mothballs bouncing in the water.

DISCUSSION AND FOLLOW-UP

- Students should be allowed to observe the demonstration in action for a period of time while they make close observations and reflect on previous demonstrations that were somewhat similar. They should be encouraged to offer comments relating to their observations and to suggest explanations for the activity witnessed.

- Discussion should pinpoint specific events in the demonstration, with guidance for student thought and interpretation being supplied by directed questions:

  — What signs of chemical activity were noted?
  — What chemicals used are known to react with each other in water?
  — What gas is produced by this chemical reaction?
  — What do you observe clinging to the surface of the mothballs?
  — Why do the gas bubbles cling to the surface of the mothballs?
  — What causes the mothballs to rise?
  — What happens to the gas bubbles when the mothballs reach the surface?
  — Why do the mothballs sink again?
  — Why do the mothballs upon reaching the bottom not bounce immediately to the top?
  — Why was table salt used in the demonstration?
  — If salt and food coloring did not take an active part in the chemical reaction, why were they used in the demonstration?

- If, after a period of time, the demonstration activity comes to a stop, students may be asked to suggest ways to reactivate the system and be given an opportunity to test their hypotheses.

- Also, variations in the amounts of baking soda and vinegar may be tried as well as alternate objects such as beads or corn seeds, to alternately collect and release carbon dioxide as they are caused to bounce in the water.

- After the discussion has been completed, students should explain the demonstration, using the *key words:* **density, carbon dioxide (CO_2),** and **chemical reaction** and to prepare a descriptive summary of the demonstration in their Science Demonstrations notebooks.

4–5: THE ANATOMY OF A CHEMICAL REACTION
(elementary level)

INTRODUCTION

Mixing chemicals together often produces observable results—energy may be given off in the form of heat or light; a change in the color, odor, mass, or form of the reactants may occur; or smoke and/or other gaseous materials may be produced and released. Some of these events, signaling that a chemical change is taking place, can be demonstrated with the use of common materials as the reactive chemicals.

LEARNING OBJECTIVES

At the end of this demonstration lesson, students should be able to

- relate a chemical change to the formation of products that are different from the reactants.
- recognize the involvement of energy in a chemical reaction.
- tell how a chemical change can be distinguished from a physical change.
- name three situations in which a chemical change is involved.
- analyze the events occurring in the chemical change demonstrated, with proper usage of *key words:* **chemical change, chemical reaction, chemical energy**, and **reactants**.

MATERIALS REQUIRED

baking soda; teaspoon; vinegar; tall jar; paper toweling

PRESENTATION

1. Place several thicknesses of paper toweling on the surface of a table or workbench.

2. Set a tall jar on the protected table top in a position where all students can view it clearly.

3. Pour household vinegar into the jar until a one-half inch layer is deposited in the jar.

4. Add one teaspoonful of baking soda to the vinegar in the jar.

5. Observe the activity.

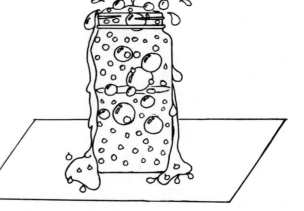

RATIONALE

When an acid reacts with another substance, a salt and at least one other substance are formed. In the case of vinegar (acetic acid) and baking soda (sodium bicarbonate), the other substances formed are water and carbon dioxide gas, with the carbon dioxide being primarily responsible for the exertion of pressure on the solid component, causing the substance to foam.

DISCUSSION AND FOLLOW-UP

- It may be necessary to repeat the demonstration several times to allow all students to make close observations of the reaction, which is immediate and dramatic. They should then be asked to describe the foaming activity and explain reasons for using a tall jar and for placing paper toweling on the table.

- Students should be encouraged to consider whether similar results would be expected to occur in other cases involving the mixture of a liquid with a dry substance. Those making workable suggestions, such as adding an Alka Seltzer tablet to water or mixing salt with lemon juice, should be allowed to test their mixtures and to present their demonstrations to the class. The association of chemical action between specific combinations of substances and the production of carbon dioxide gas can then be established.

- When discussing the demonstration, students should make use of the *key words:* **chemical change**, **chemical reaction**, **chemical energy**, and **reactants** as they analyze and explain the chain of events that was traced in the demonstration.

- After all discussion of the demonstration has been completed, students should write a short report about chemical reactions in their Science Demonstrations notebooks.

4–6: THE BROWNING OF BRUISED FRUIT
(elementary level)

INTRODUCTION

There is a basic similarity between the practice of treating diced raw apple for salads with lemon juice and of keeping slices of raw potatoes immersed in water. Both prevent the rapid change in color and taste that occurs when these foods are peeled and exposed directly to air. With sufficient exposure, the banana peel or the apple we bite into shows the same darkening that accompanies the injury of a fruit when it becomes bruised. Any one of a number of fresh fruits and/or vegetables can be used to demonstrate this kind of change.

LEARNING ACTIVITIES

At the end of this demonstration lesson, students should be able to

- infer that something in the air reacted with something in the exposed fruit to cause it to change color.
- recognize the change in color of the fruit used in the demonstration as a chemical change.
- relate the demonstration to the browning of other foods, such as meat when it is cooked and bread when it is baked.
- understand the basic concept of the demonstration and explain it, using *key words:* **oxidation, chemical change,** and **chemical reaction.**

MATERIALS REQUIRED

selected raw fruits and/or vegetables, such as apple, banana, pear, potato, and so on; paring knife; saucer

PRESENTATION

1. Cut several fresh raw fruits and vegetables, and place slices of each on a saucer.

2. Allow the foods to be exposed directly to air.

3. Observe.

RATIONALE

Cuts and other injuries that damage the living cells of raw fruits and vegetables are responsible for initiating certain chemical changes. When the oxidative enzymes

94

released by the damaged tissue react with oxygen in the air, they become actively involved in a chemical breakdown of the cells, which is accompanied by a "browning" of the tissue. Although this enzyme activity can be slowed by preventing oxygen from combining with the enzyme and can be interfered with by introducing a highly acidic environment, it is generally not completely destroyed without exposure to high heat.

DISCUSSION AND FOLLOW-UP

- As students observe the demonstration, they should be encouraged to relate it to a personal experience—such as taking a bite out of an apple—and to predict what will happen to the food slices in the demonstration.

- Attention should focus on the observations made and on the meaning attached to them:
    - What changes are detected?
    - Under what conditions did the changes occur?
    - What evidence is provided to indicate that the food slices have been changed chemically?
    - How do the *key words*—**oxidation**, **chemical change**, and **chemical reaction**—help to describe what happened in the demonstration?

- Other examples of changes in the color of food should be considered and compared with those demonstrated to illustrate differences as well as similarities.

- In a related situation, reasons should be offered to explain why a grilled steak may be brown on the outside but red in the center.

- After the discussion has been completed, students should be asked to prepare a list of three foods that change color when they are exposed to oxygen and two ways to prevent this chemical reaction from occurring.

4–7: LOWERING THE TEMPERATURE AT WHICH ICE MELTS
(elementary level)

INTRODUCTION

Under normal conditions, pure water freezes and ice melts at a temperature of 0°C. There are times, however, when lowering this temperature becomes desirable. The addition of antifreeze preparations to the water in car radiators, for example, prevents freeze-ups during cold weather, and salt is spread over icy roads and walkways to melt the ice without raising the temperature. Lowering the temperature at which ice melts can be demonstrated with ice and ordinary table salt.

LEARNING OBJECTIVES

At the end of this demonstration lesson, students should be able to

- recognize 0°C as the temperature at which water freezes and ice melts.
- relate the lowering of the melting point of ice to the addition of a suitable substance.
- name two practical situations in which the concept of the demonstration can be applied.
- identify two physical changes that are involved in the demonstration.
- explain the demonstration, using *key words:* **temperature**, **melting point**, **freezing point**, and **solute**.

MATERIALS REQUIRED

ice; 2 laboratory thermometers; 2 stirring rods, 2 glass peanut butter jars; table salt or rock salt

PRESENTATION

1. Label and prepare two peanut butter jars to be used in the demonstration:

   #1—Fill with crushed ice until it is three-fourths full of ice.

   #2—Fill with crushed ice until it is three-fourths full of ice and add one tablespoonful of table salt.

2. Place the jars in a location where they can be easily viewed by students.

3. Select two student volunteers to stir the contents of the jars.

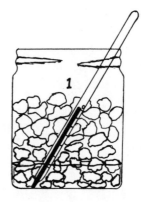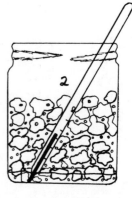

4. Observe closely and, when the ice begins to melt, take temperature readings.

5. Record the temperature readings indicating the temperature at which ice melts under both conditions demonstrated.

RATIONALE

The ability of a substance to lower the temperature at which ice melts and/or water freezes is due largely to its solubility in water. Alcohol and ethylene glycol are commonly added to water to prevent freeze-ups in car radiators, and rock salt is spread on icy roadways to lower the freezing point of the salt solution formed to below that of the surrounding temperature, thus causing the ice to melt.

DISCUSSION AND FOLLOW-UP

- Discussion of the demonstration should allow for students to make predictions about what they expect to happen in the two jars.
- After the temperature readings have been taken and attention focuses on the differences noted, students should respond to pertinent questions:
  — At what temperature did the ice melt?
  — How did the addition of salt affect the temperature?
  — What is the relationship between the freezing point of water and the melting point of ice under the conditions that were demonstrated?
- Consideration of how the demonstration relates to some everyday situations should include:
  — What the buildup of salt deposits on cars in winter indicates about the kind of change that occurs when the salt spread on icy roads combines with the melting ice.
  — How the addition of antifreeze preparations prevents freeze-ups in car radiators during cold weather.
  — Why rock salt is commonly added to the bucket of an ice cream maker when making homemade ice cream.
- Students should then summarize the key points of the demonstration by preparing a list of *solutes:—ethylene glycol, alcohol,* and *salt*—and telling how each is related to the lowering of the temperature at which water freezes.

4-8: COLLECTING A GAS PRODUCED BY A CHEMICAL CHANGE
(elementary level)

INTRODUCTION

Chemical changes may be fast and dramatic—a huge bonfire or an exploding fire-cracker—or they may be slow and almost imperceptible—the rusting of iron or the discoloration of a newspaper exposed to bright light. However, each is one of many chemical changes that are taking place around us all the time. In each case, the chemical change rearranges the atoms and molecules of the original substances to produce new and different substances. Unless such a reaction can be reversed, it is permanent and is classified as a chemical change.

LEARNING OBJECTIVES

After having completed this demonstration lesson, students should be able to

- understand the concept of the change in composition of a substance and the production of new ones during a chemical change.
- apply and reinforce previous learning about relative densities of liquids and gases and the displacement of one substance by another.
- infer that the gas formed in the demonstration was brought about by a reaction between the original substances.
- relate the demonstration to other occurrences in which a gas is formed by reacting substances.
- describe the demonstration and its events, using *key words:* **chemical change** and **chemical reaction**.

MATERIALS REQUIRED

glass baby bottle; Alka Seltzer tablet; water; clear plastic shoe box or refrigerator dish; piece of glass; tongs

PRESENTATION

1. Fill a glass baby bottle with water and place a piece of glass over the mouth of the bottle.

2. Fill a transparent plastic refrigerator dish or shoe box with water to within one inch of the top.

3. Invert the bottle in the dish or shoe box so that the mouth, covered by the glass plate to prevent any water from escaping, is below the surface of the water in the dish. Then remove the glass plate, taking care to prevent any air bubbles from entering the bottle.

4. Set the bottle, mouth down, on the bottom of the dish or box, so that it tilts very slightly.

98

5. Using tongs, lower an Alka Seltzer tablet into the water so that it rests on the bottom of the dish or box, directly beneath the mouth of the bottle. Then, quickly but carefully, straighten the bottle so that it rests securely on the bottom of the dish.

6. Hold the bottle in this position and observe the activity.

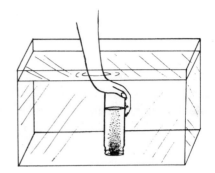

RATIONALE

Alka Seltzer contains many active ingredients, among which is sodium bicarbonate, an important source of carbon dioxide gas. When a chemical reaction occurs between the tablet and water, this gas, which can be seen in the form of bubbles rising through the liquid, can be collected by displacement of water in an inverted container. The pressure exerted by the gas rising to the top of the bottle presses down on the water, forcing it out of the bottle. Some of the solid reactant material from the tablet becomes dissolved in the water, while the newly formed carbon dioxide gas escapes from the chemical composition of the original component.

DISCUSSION AND FOLLOW-UP

- As the demonstration progresses, attention should be drawn to the materials used and the manner in which they are assembled.
- Points for discussion should include:
    — Why does water stay in the bottle when placed upside down in the dish or box full of water?
    — What evidence is there that a reaction is taking place?
    — Where do the bubbles come from?
    — Why do the bubbles rise?
    — What causes the water to be pushed out of the bottle?
    — If the bottle of water had not been placed over the Alka Seltzer tablet in the water, where would the bubbles have gone?
    — In what way does the demonstration resemble a bottle of soda that has just been opened or just poured into a glass?
    — What is the clue to the kind of change that is involved in this demonstration?
- If the opening presents itself, advantage should be taken of the opportunity to motivate student interest in a future demonstration designed to identify the gas produced and to show some of its properties.
- Students should then be asked to write a short report in which they describe the demonstration and identify the activity that indicates a *chemical reaction*, resulting in a *chemical change*.

4-9:   MIXING OIL AND WATER
(intermediate level)

INTRODUCTION

Although water is the primary substance used in household laundry and dishwashing activities, water alone cannot do these jobs satisfactorily. As we are reminded by television commercials and other media advertisements, soap and/or detergent preparations are needed as well. Just how these products act to "lift out grease" and "cause dirt and grime to float away" can be demonstrated by students in science class on two successive days.

LEARNING OBJECTIVES

At the completion of this demonstration lesson, students should be able to

- understand the basic concept illustrated in the demonstration and give three examples of its application to everyday life activities.
- explain how soap or detergent acts to remove oil and grease from surfaces of soiled skin, clothing, and dishes.
- show evidence of an understanding of the meaning and proper usage of *key words:* **soap, detergent, emulsion, emulsifying agent,** and **dispersing medium**.

MATERIALS REQUIRED

2 transparent baby bottles with caps; water; cooking oil or salad oil; "soapy" water prepared from powdered or liquid soap or detergent

PRESENTATION

Day 1

1. Partially fill a baby bottle with tap water and add 12 to 15 drops of cooking oil. Then add more water, sufficient to nearly fill the bottle to its capacity. Finally, screw the bottle cap on tightly.

2. In a similar manner, prepare a second baby bottle, using soapy water in place of plain tap water.

3. Select two students to participate; ask each to shake one of the bottles vigorously.

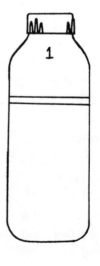 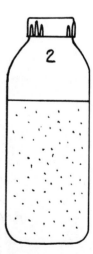

100

4. Set the two bottles, properly identified, on a shelf where they can remain undisturbed until the following day.

Day 2

1. Observe the contents of the two baby bottles.
2. Compare the two situations and consider the reasons for the differences noted.

RATIONALE

Large liquid globules of oil do not naturally distribute themselves uniformly with droplets of water. However, due to the presence of an emulsifying agent, this third component acts to break down the large globules to smaller size and form a protective coating around the droplets, thus preventing them from grouping together again. In the process, the globules are physically "lifted" from the object on which they may have been present and, in their small droplet form, are spread evenly throughout the system, where they are ready to be floated away with the rinse water.

DISCUSSION AND FOLLOW-UP

Discussion of the demonstration should be reserved for the second day when the students who prepared the bottle mixtures can show the results to other members of the class. When students have noted the difference in appearance between the two preparations, they should focus their attention on the reasons why it is only in bottle #1 that the oil and water layer out and do not mix. They should infer that the soap present in bottle #2 is responsible for the distribution of fine oil droplets throughout the suspension formed in that bottle, and that this action has a practical application in household laundry matters. Several students should be encouraged to trace the events, starting with grease on a pair of jeans, through the wash and rinse cycles of a washing machine. *Key words*—**soap**, **detergent**, **emulsion**, **emulsifying agent**, and **dispersing medium**—should be used to check for a basic understanding of their meaning and proper usage. A final windup can involve volunteers; two students who place a greasy substance on their hands will proceed to wash their hands—one using a basin containing plain tap water, the other using soapy water—and, relating the experience to the original demonstration, describe the results and explain how success or failure in getting their hands clean depended upon the method used.

4–10:   THE MANY COLORS IN FOODS
(intermediate level)

INTRODUCTION

Package labels on many foods list "artificial coloring" as an ingredient. To achieve just the right color corresponding to orange, cherry, raspberry, or lemon gelatine or to the various flavors of powdered drink mixes, soft drinks, jams, jellies, and candies, a mixture of many pigments is generally used. The pigments found in a colored food substance can be demonstrated with food coloring and a strip cut from white paper toweling or a coffee filter.

LEARNING OBJECTIVES

At the end of this demonstration lesson, students should be able to

- identify the color bands that result from a separation of pigments in a sample of food coloring.
- apply the technique demonstrated to other separations of pigment mixtures found in other color products, such as inks, dyes, paints, and crayons.
- identify the separation of pigments in a color substance as a physical change.
- describe the nature of the process demonstrated, including proper usage of *key words:* **pigment**, **chromatography**, **mixture**, and **physical change**.

MATERIALS REQUIRED

mayonnaise jar; white paper toweling, napkin, or coffee filter; green food coloring; toothpick or medicine dropper; water; paper clip; scissors

PRESENTATION

1. Cut a piece of white paper toweling, napkin, or coffee filter to form a strip that is one inch wide and 10 to 12 inches long.

2. Place a faint pencil mark about midway between the two sides of the paper strip and about one inch from one end.

3. With a toothpick or small-bore medicine dropper, transfer a small drop of green food coloring to the location on the paper strip indi-

cated by the pencil mark. Allow the food coloring to dry on the paper strip.

4. Place water to a depth of one half inch in the bottom of the mayonnaise jar.

5. Position the paper strip in the jar so that, without touching the bottom of the jar, one end makes contact with the water while keeping the spot of food coloring above the water level.

6. Bend the upper end of the paper strip over the rim of the jar, allowing the paper to hang freely without touching the bottom or sides of the jar, and hold it in this position by attaching a paper clip at the point where the paper strip bends over the rim of the jar.

7. Observe the activity and, when the water has risen more than halfway up the paper strip, remove the strip from the jar and allow it to dry.

8. Observe the developed chromatogram.

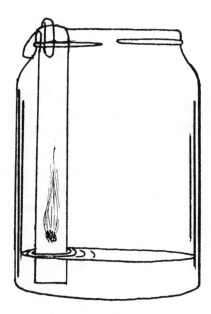

RATIONALE

The separation of a color mixture into its component pigments by the chromatography method depends upon the migration of molecules of the mixture through the paper. Different components of the mixture are deposited at different levels, depending primarily on their comparative weight and degree of solubility in the solvent used. The resulting chromatogram, showing a separation of the components of the mixture into distinct color bands, furnishes a useful analysis of the coloring material.

DISCUSSION AND FOLLOW-UP

- Students should analyze the events of the demonstration as they occur, relating them to familiar situations:
  - Relate the manner in which water molecules move up the paper strip to the absorption of a water spill by paper toweling.
  - Relate the layering out of different color bands on the paper strip to the order in which pebbles of different size and weight are deposited at different locations along a swift-flowing stream or river.
- After the paper strip has been removed from the jar, attention should focus on the chromatogram and on the employment of the key words associated with the concept of the demonstration, as students respond to questions:
  - How many color bands are identified?
  - What does this indicate about the food color sample used?
  - What does the order of the color bands tell about the relative weight of the particles making up each pigment?

— Would the same color bands be expected to be present on a chromatogram showing the separation of pigments in a different color sample?

— Why did no color particles travel as far as the particles of water along the paper strip?

— Would the demonstration have worked if the paper strip had been cut from a piece of smooth notebook paper?

— What adjustments in the demonstration design would be necessary in order to separate the pigments in a drop of waterproof red ink?

- Variations of the demonstration, using different food colors and/or different substances, should be discussed. Then, interested students should be encouraged to perform such a demonstration on their own and to display the resulting chromatograms on the bulletin board for all to see.

- When the discussion has been completed, students should prepare a record of the demonstration in their Science Demonstrations notebooks.

4-11: SEPARATING THE COMPONENTS OF A SALTWATER SOLUTION
(elementary level)

INTRODUCTION

The solutions we find useful in our daily life activities are many and varied: a mixture of sugar, water, and lemon juice forms lemonade, a solution that we enjoy as a refreshing drink; alcohol and water form an antifreeze solution that we use to prevent freeze-ups in cold weather; and oil paint and turpentine form a solution that cleans paintbrushes when we place used brushes in the turpentine solvent. Although not always easily detected, solutions can be separated into their original solvent and solute components. A saltwater solution can be used to demonstrate this separation.

LEARNING OBJECTIVES

At the end of this demonstration lesson, students should be able to

- describe what happens when molecules of a solid substance are placed in a "friendly" liquid.
- name three examples of solutions and their components.
- prepare a diagram showing how molecules of a solvent and a solute intermingle in a solution.
- identify the change that is illustrated by the demonstration as a physical change.
- suggest one way to separate a solvent from a solute in a water solution.
- describe the demonstration, using *key words:* **solution, solute, solvent,** and **evaporation.**

MATERIALS REQUIRED

clean, empty baby food jar; saucer or clean lid from a baby food jar; table salt; water; teaspoon; warm area near radiator or other heat source; toothpicks

PRESENTATION

1. Place water in a baby food jar until it is one-fourth filled with water.
2. Add one teaspoonful of table salt to the water in the baby food jar and stir until the mixture is clear, with no visible evidence of salt.
3. Using a clean toothpick, touched first to the salt water and then to

the tip of the tongue, verify that salt is indeed present.

4. Invite volunteer students to use the same procedure and make the same verification.

5. Pour some salty water into a saucer or lid of a baby food jar.

6. Place the saucer containing salt water on a shelf or windowsill near a radiator or other heat source.

7. Allow the demonstration to remain, undisturbed, until the next day.

8. Observe and make inferences.

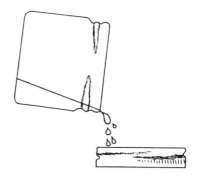

RATIONALE

In a glass of salty water, the salt crystals are separated by the water into extremely small particles. When stirred, these particles become evenly distributed throughout the liquid, forming a solution made up of dissolved salt (the solute) and water (the solvent). Of the two, only the water will evaporate; therefore, the salt is left behind as a residue when the solution is separated into its original parts—salt and water vapor. The changes involved are physical only.

DISCUSSION AND FOLLOW-UP

- Although part of the discussion of the demonstration must be reserved until its completion on the second day, opportunities should be provided for students to make predictions about what they expect will happen and to research and review the concept of *solutions, solutes,* and *solvents* as they apply to the demonstration.

- On the second day, students can be asked to name as many solutions as they can and, in each case, identify the solute and solvent portions.

- Information about what students have learned about *how* a solution is made should then be reviewed, and a diagram showing the formation of the salt solution—salt particles intermingle with particles of water, causing them to become uniformly distributed as they spread into the spaces between water particles—should be prepared on the chalkboard.

- Attention should then focus on the saucer in which the salt solution had been placed on the previous day. After students have observed the residue in the saucer, they should be encouraged to make comments and to give answers to leading questions:

  — What is the substance in the saucer?

  — How can you identify it?

— What happened to the water?

— In what form did it escape?

— What is the name of the process by which it escaped?

— What kind of change was illustrated by the demonstration?

- To establish the relationship between the two parts of the demonstration, students should prepare diagrams showing (1) the arrangement of particles in the solution prepared and (2) the separation of solvent and solute, as indicated by the second-day observation.

4–12:   MAKING A BLUEPRINT
(intermediate level)

INTRODUCTION

The effect of light on photographs, newspaper, and clothing can be seen in many instances: if not protected from light, photographs fade and newspapers yellow; when exposed to bright sunlight, the colors of many articles of clothing fade; a common treatment used for bleaching a stain on a white laundry item is to place it, while wet, in direct sunlight. In another application, the sensitivity of a chemically treated paper to radiant energy serves as the basis for blueprint making. Because the chemical action involved occurs quickly, the making of blueprints can be demonstrated in the classroom.

LEARNING OBJECTIVES

At the end of this demonstration lesson, students should be able to:

- explain why some areas of a blueprint are blue, while others are white.
- identify the making of a blueprint as a process involving a chemical change.
- relate the demonstration to other copy processes that make use of chemicals and light.
- describe the process by which a blueprint is made, using *key words:* **light energy** and **chemical reaction**.

MATERIALS REQUIRED

blueprint paper*; frame and glass plate of suitable shape and size; shallow tray; water; sunny windowsill or other bright light source; leaf, fern frond, or other interesting flat object

PRESENTATION

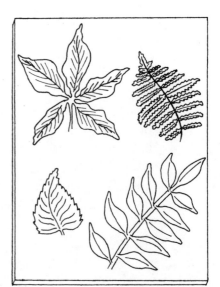

1. Position a leaf, fern frond, or other interesting flat object on the sensitized surface of a piece of blueprint paper* placed in a picture frame with backing.
2. Place a plate glass over the object to keep it flat and in contact with the paper.
3. Place the assembled materials in an area of direct sunlight or a strong artificial light source.

---

* Solargraphic™ paper may be used.

4. Allow the assembled materials to remain undisturbed for a period of five to seven minutes, depending upon the intensity of the light.

5. Disassemble the materials and quickly transfer the exposed paper to a shallow tray of tap water for a one-minute rinse.

6. Lay the paper on a flat surface and allow it to dry.

7. Examine the "blueprint."

RATIONALE

When a piece of blueprint paper with a leaf placed on its surface is exposed to bright light for a short time, then washed with water and allowed to dry, a print of the leaf appears on the paper. It occurs because radiant energy converted to chemical energy changes the chemicals with which the paper was treated to an insoluble substance. This remains on the exposed surface area, placing it in sharp color contrast with the shielded areas, which remain unaffected, therefore still soluble and easily removed from the paper by a water wash.

DISCUSSION AND FOLLOW-UP

- While the demonstration is in progress, students should observe the fading of the treated paper being exposed to light and make the inference that the color change that is occurring is due to light.

- As the demonstration progresses, continued observation should be accompanied by student responses to leading questions:

  — Why was it necessary to protect the treated paper from exposure to light before everything was ready for use?

  — Why is it necessary to wash the paper in water after the period of light exposure?

  — What kind of change is illustrated in the making of a blueprint?

- Discussion of the demonstration should focus on the chemical change involved—chemical reactions between the chemically treated paper, initiated by energy from light which was converted to chemical energy. In their responses and explanations, students should make use of the *key words:* **light energy, chemical energy, chemical reaction, soluble,** and **insoluble.**

- The demonstration should also be discussed in relation to photographic processes and other copy devices, with a determination of the role of light, energy conversions, and chemical reactions in bringing about the "copies."

- When the discussion has been completed, students should be asked to write a report of the demonstration in their Science Demonstrations notebooks.

PART II

ENVIRONMENTAL SCIENCE

Environmental Science-based demonstration lessons encourage students to become aware of the value of simulations in the classroom as a practical method of gaining knowledge about the real earth and the way in which living things interact with it. Many concepts presented and the processes employed in the demonstrations will be somewhat familiar to students, enabling them to develop their ability to make new application of previous learning and to reinforce their understanding of it.

Demonstrations in the areas of Earth Science and Ecology help students to establish a recognition of the interrelationship between living and nonliving factors that is necessary for maintaining an ecological balance. Through involvement in the demonstration lessons, they will be afforded opportunities to develop critical-thinking and problem-solving skills and to become active participants in school and local events, such as Earth Day events, anti-litter projects, recycling programs, and anti-pollution campaigns.

CHAPTER 5

Demonstrations Pertaining to Earth Science

*Suitable for teacher-only presentation.

5-1:   CHEMICAL WEATHERING OF ROCK
(elementary level)

INTRODUCTION

The appearance of rust-colored material on some exposed rock surfaces is related to the flaking off of thin rock layers from rocks on which a mosslike plant called lichen is growing. Both are examples of chemical weathering, which occurs slowly and causes rock to crumble. Recently, there has been a noticeable increase in the rate at which this type of weathering is taking place. A much speeded-up version of the process can be demonstrated in the classroom.

LEARNING OBJECTIVES

At the conclusion of this demonstration lesson, students should be able to

- describe the action of acids on rock.
- name two sources of acids that are responsible for chemical weathering of rock.
- give two examples of specific locations in which there is evidence of chemical weathering.
- apply the concept of the demonstration to chemical weathering of the earth's rock materials, using *key words:* **atmospheric gases, volcanic gases,** and **chemical weathering**.

MATERIALS REQUIRED

mayonnaise jar; piece of limestone; white vinegar

PRESENTATION

1. Place a mayonnaise jar on a table top where all students can view it clearly.
2. Place a piece of limestone in the jar.
3. Pour white vinegar into the jar until the limestone is covered completely.
4. Observe the limestone for signs of activity brought about by contact with the acid substance.

RATIONALE

The action of vinegar or other weak acid on limestone dissolves out the calcite mineral content of the stone, causing the residue to crumble. Other weak acids also increase the dissolving action of water considerably and are harmful to many rock formations. Weak solutions of carbonic acid are formed when carbon dioxide combines with water, and both sulfur dioxide and nitrogen oxides also combine with moisture in the atmosphere and fall to the earth in various forms of precipitation known as "acid rain." It has been estimated that 90 percent of all sulfur dioxide production entering into this formation comes from the combustion of fossil fuels. This carries with it an important message for people who are interested in preventing runaway chemical weathering of earth rock materials. This is an added incentive to find an alternative to fossil fuels as an energy source.

DISCUSSION AND FOLLOW-UP

- As students observe the demonstration, they should identify the crumbling of limestone as a chemical change caused by its chemical reaction with an acid substance.
- Discussion should focus on guide questions:
  - What effect did the vinegar have on the limestone?
  - Is vinegar an acid or a base type of substance?
  - What kinds of acids are likely to be present in acid rain?
  - How is acid rain formed?
  - What is the primary source of toxic gases that combine with water to form these dilute acids?
  - How do volcanic eruptions contribute to the natural introduction of toxic gases into the atmosphere?
  - How does ground water become "acid"?
- Students should compare the processes of mechanical and chemical weathering, relating them to physical and chemical changes of matter. They should be encouraged to describe the appearance of some exposed rock formations, cemetery tombstones, monuments, statues, and public buildings that show signs of weathering, and to make a determination of the type of weathering that is illustrated by each.
- After the discussion has been completed, students should be asked to write an account of How Chemical Weathering Is Changing the Earth, in their Science Demonstrations notebooks.

5-2: MECHANICAL WEATHERING OF ROCK
(elementary level)

INTRODUCTION

Nothing stays the same forever. Mountains have been made smaller by glacial action that has removed some of their rock formations and carried them to other locations; rough edges on stones have been smoothed and rounded by the action of water passing over them; rocks have been reduced to sand particles by the pounding action of waves on a shore; and the noses and facial features of some famous statues have gradually become less distinct. Each represents a change in size and shape of a rock, due to a wearing-away process. Normally a slow process taking place over a period of time, a speeded-up version of mechanical weathering can be demonstrated in the classroom.

LEARNING OBJECTIVES

After having participated in this demonstration lesson, students should be able to

- identify the characteristics of mechanical weathering.
- name two agents of mechanical weathering.
- name three specific examples of earth change due to mechanical weathering.
- apply the concept of the demonstration to the mechanical weathering of earth rock materials, using *key words:* **mechanical weathering, physical change,** and **erosion.**

MATERIALS REQUIRED

small stones or pebbles; jar with screw cap lid; water; paper toweling; small vial or jar; tray

PRESENTATION

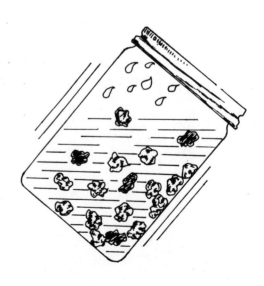

1. Wash pebbles or small stones and discard any debris.
2. Fill a jar about one-fourth full of washed stones or pebbles.
3. Add sufficient water to cover the pebbles completely.
4. Screw the cap on the jar to make a tight closure with no leaks.
5. Shake the jar and swirl the contents.
6. Allow each student who wishes to participate to shake the jar vigor-

ously for one to two minutes, swirling the contents after each shaking.

7. Place a layer of paper toweling on a tray.

8. Swirl the jar once more and quickly pour the water into a vial

or clean jar and transfer the stones or pebbles to the paper toweling on the tray.

9. Allow the water in the vial to settle.

10. Examine the stones and the material that has settled out in the water in the vial.

RATIONALE

Mechanical weathering breaks down rock into smaller pieces. It involves a physical change and is brought about by a variety of agents, such as running water, wind, rain, glaciers, and earthquakes. Physical weathering changes a rock's size and shape as it breaks down but does not bring about any changes in its minerals or chemical composition. Although it generally takes place over a long period of time, its effects add up, resulting in mountains that have become worn down and rock material that has been reduced to sand.

DISCUSSION AND FOLLOW-UP

- Discussion should focus on the activity involved in the demonstration as well as the appearance of the resulting materials.
- Student comments concerning their observations should be encouraged, with the inclusion of answers to pertinent questions:
  — How do the stones at the end of the demonstration compare with their appearance at the beginning?
  — Where did the particles in the water at the end of the demonstration come from?
  — What caused small particles of stone to break off?
  — Does this represent a physical or a chemical change of matter?
- Students should be asked to report familiar examples of mechanical weathering, such as water-worn pebbles in a stream or beach area and difficult-to-read names and dates on old tombstones in cemeteries.
- After the discussion has been completed, students should be asked to write an account of the demonstration, in which they explain how mechanical weathering of rock brings about changes in the earth's surface.

5–3: FORMATION OF A CLOUD IN A JAR*
(elementary level)

INTRODUCTION

Often our attention is drawn to a cloud formation that appears to resemble some familiar object. While this fleeting image has no basis in fact, cloud shapes and patterns can be used as a source of scientific information. In addition to helping us to forecast the weather, they supply us with information about the direction of the wind and the rate at which it is blowing, and about the amount of moisture that is present in the air. Demonstrating the formation of a cloud in a jar simulates the process by which natural clouds are formed in the earth's atmosphere.

LEARNING OBJECTIVES

At the end of this demonstration lesson, students should be able to

- state the conditions under which clouds are formed.
- recognize cloud formation as a process involving a physical change of matter.
- identify the role of cloud formation in the larger sphere of nature's water cycle.
- describe the events involved in cloud formation, using *key words:* **evaporation**, **condensation**, **water vapor**, and **water droplets**.

MATERIALS REQUIRED

glass jar with mouth of suitable size to support an ice cube; hot water; ice cube

PRESENTATION

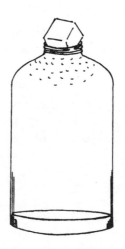

1. Pour a small amount of hot water into a jar.

   NOTE: Take proper precautions to protect students from possible harm due to contact with hot water.

2. Place an ice cube at the opening in the top of the jar.

3. Observe the changes occurring within the jar.

---

* Suitable for teacher-only presentation.

RATIONALE

The formation of a cloud in the jar requires energy to bring about a change in the physical state of the water. Heat energy enables the rapidly moving molecules of hot water to move farther apart and evaporate into the air space above the hot water. Being less dense, the vapor rises to the upper part of the jar. Here the molecules come in contact with cool air near the ice, causing the water vapor to lose energy, become more dense, and condense to form minute droplets of water. The accumulated droplets of water near the top of the jar can then be seen as a cloud. In a similar pattern, which involves energy and change of the physical state of water, water evaporates from the surface of the earth and forms clouds, as a part of nature's water cycle.

DISCUSSION AND FOLLOW-UP

- As the demonstration progresses, students should recognize the familiar processes of evaporation and condensation, which are associated with the changes observed in the physical change in the state of water.
- Attention should focus on specific events, highlighted by student answers to pertinent questions:
  - What was happening to the hot water in the jar?
  - What was observed near the ice cube?
  - What happened when the moist air came in contact with the cold region at the top of the jar?
  - Where did the cloud form?
  - What caused the cloud to form?
  - How does the demonstration illustrate the formation of clouds in nature?
- When the discussion has been completed, students should be asked to prepare labeled diagrams showing how a cloud is formed.

5–4: SEPARATING COMPONENTS IN A SOIL SAMPLE
(intermediate level)

INTRODUCTION

Separating objects in a mixture is relatively simple if, as in the case of a bag of apples and oranges, the fruits are large in size and easily distinguished from each other. In other instances, ingenuity and applications of scientific knowledge may be helpful. Japanese macaque monkeys, for example, have been observed to scoop up mixtures of sand and seeds from the ground, drop them into a nearby body of water, and then to eat the seeds picked easily at the water's surface where they had floated free of the sand which dropped to the bottom.

Separating components of a soil mixture by allowing them to settle out in layers according to their density is a useful technique for developing an insight into an important way in which earth materials are built up.

LEARNING OBJECTIVES

At the end of this demonstration lesson, students should be able to

- recognize that soil can be separated into its components when placed in water and allowed to settle.
- relate the formation of distinct layers to the settling of different components of a mixture according to their densities.
- understand the usefulness of the technique employed for separating substances in a mixture.
- apply information from the demonstration to an explanation of how deposits of sediment build up the earth.
- plan an investigation for comparing the composition of two different soil samples, employing the demonstrated technique and using *key words:* **mixture, density, organic, inorganic, sediment,** and **sedimentary rock**.

MATERIALS REQUIRED

soil sample containing sand, clay, small pebbles, and fragments of organic debris; tall glass jar with cap; water

PRESENTATION

1. Mix well a suitable soil sample, distributing the organic and inorganic components throughout the mixture.

2. Place a handful of the soil mixture into a tall narrow jar or wide-mouthed bottle nearly full of water.

120

3. After capping the jar and checking for tightness of fit, shake the jar so as to distribute the soil components uniformly throughout the water.

4. Set the jar on a table top or other area that is clearly visible to all students and allow it to remain undisturbed until the solids can be seen to be separated from the water.

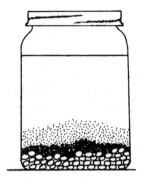

RATIONALE

The soil mixture in the water is composed of materials of different particle size. This has an effect on the settling of the materials, which are heavier than the water in which they were placed. They settle out according to particle size and density:

- *pebbles* settle out quickly because of their comparative large size and heavier weight, forming the bottom layer.
- smaller sized *sand grains* settle out in a layer on top of the layer of pebbles.
- *clay particles*, because of their small size and light weight, are held longer by the water before they are dropped to form a layer on top of the clay.
- bits of organic matter, being less dense than the water, float to the surface.

Sedimentary rock forms when layers of sediment exert pressure on layers below them, pressing them into solid rock.

DISCUSSION AND FOLLOW-UP

- Discussion should focus on the process employed as well as the layering out of different earth materials.
- Students wishing to repeat the demonstration should be allowed to reshake the jar to confirm the validity of the results obtained. They should then be asked questions relating to the demonstration and to its application to earth composition and formation:
    - In what order did the materials in the soil mixture settle out?
    - What factors determined the order in which the materials settled out in layers?
    - How does this demonstration relate to the layers seen in rock formations such as those in the Grand Canyon?
    - What does this suggest about the original location of the Grand Canyon when it was formed?
    - How can we account for the present location of the Grand Canyon above sea level on dry land?

— What kind of rock is formed by the process involved in the demonstration?

- After the discussion has been completed, students should be asked to prepare a labeled diagram of the demonstration and an explanation of how it relates to the formation of layers of earth such as those in the Grand Canyon.

5–5:   EARTHQUAKE ACTIVITY AND ITS EFFECTS
(intermediate level)

INTRODUCTION

Although a slight trembling occurs somewhere on earth many times each day, we occasionally hear news reports of intense earthquake activity, in which land areas are dislocated, buildings are toppled, and, in some cases, people are injured or killed. Sometimes these earth tremors can be felt at a considerable distance from the center of the 'quake. The damage to a structure close to the epicenter can be demonstrated with vibrations simulating those caused by an earthquake.

LEARNING OBJECTIVES

After the demonstration lesson has been completed, students should be able to

- understand how earthquake shocks occurring at one location can affect property at a different location on earth.
- predict the comparative damage to property at far and close distances from the center of an earthquake.
- gain some insight into how scientists make use of available information to formulate theories about the earth's interior and the forces that act to change the earth's shape.
- describe the nature of earthquake activity and its effects, using *key words:* **earthquake**, **epicenter**, and **vibrations**.

MATERIALS REQUIRED

sturdy piece of wood $2'' \times 4'' \times 24''$; deck of playing cards; hammer or similar tool

PRESENTATION

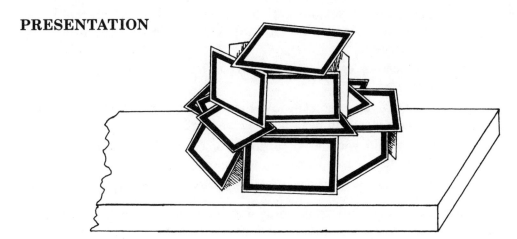

1. Position the wood on a table top where all students can view it clearly.
2. Construct a simple house of cards fairly close to one end of the wood.

123

3. Using a hammer to deliver hard blows, hit the surface of the wood six times at the end that is farther from the house of cards.

4. Using the hammer again, deliver six blows to the wood at the end that is closer to the card house.

5. Observe the activity.

RATIONALE

Forces within the earth are constantly exerting pressure in all directions. Rock layers may be caused to bend and fold, and, if the pressure continues to build, the rock may eventually break, thus relieving the pressure and setting up shock waves that radiate outward from the source. As a result, the earth's crust moves and its surface vibrates noticeably. In the demonstration, vibrations traveling through the wood are observed to cause the unanchored, unreinforced structure in the form of a house of cards to topple.

DISCUSSION AND FOLLOW-UP

- Discussion of the demonstration should focus on the reasons why a disturbance at one location of the board caused the collapse of the house of cards at a slightly different location, and should be related to an actual earthquake and the intensity of the vibrations felt at various distances from the epicenter.

  The discussion can be guided by leading questions:
  - Why did the house of cards collapse when the source of the disturbance was close but merely vibrate when a similar disturbance originated at a greater distance?
  - How does the demonstration relate to conditions of a real house or building, depending on its distance from the epicenter of an earthquake?
  - What causes earthquake activity to be felt at a distance from its source?
  - What do you predict would happen to the house of cards if the hammer blow had been harder? weaker?
  - How would you design a house of cards that would withstand vibrations such as those in the demonstration?
  - How could you test the effectiveness of your design?

- Methods used by scientists in collecting information about earthquakes should be researched and reported. This information should then be discussed. The data collected should acquaint students with the forces within the earth that are responsible for the shaping of the earth as we know it and that are continuing to effect changes on an ongoing basis.

5–6: WAVE ACTION ON A SHORELINE
(elementary level)

INTRODUCTION

All shorelines are not alike. In the United States alone, we see distinctive features of the different coastal regions along the Gulf of Mexico as well as along the Atlantic and Pacific oceans. All shorelines are affected to some degree by the wave action of water on the earth materials at their outer edge. Some of these effects can be demonstrated with the use of a stream table.

LEARNING OBJECTIVES

When this demonstration lesson has been completed, students should be able to

- recognize the advantage of using a demonstration in a simulation setting for gaining information about an occurrence in a real situation concerning the earth.
- relate the work of waves to the energy of moving water.
- describe the effect of wave action on a shoreline, using *key words:* **wave**, **energy**, and **shoreline**.

MATERIALS REQUIRED

stream table, long rectangular baking dish, or pan; water; sand-pebble mixture; plastic or rubber tubing; large sponge; block of wood

PRESENTATION

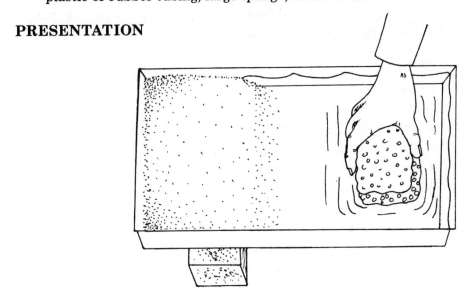

1. Fill one end of a large rectangular pan or a stream table with a two-inch layer of sand-pebble mixture.

2. Place a block of wood under this end to elevate the "beach" about two inches.

3. Using a length of plastic or rubber tubing attached to a water faucet, carefully add water to the lower part of the pan until the bottom edge of the sand-pebble mixture becomes covered with water.

4. Holding a large sponge securely in one hand, place it in the water at the end opposite the sandy shore and apply downward pressure. Repeat this activity at intervals of about two seconds for a period of about five minutes.

5. Allow the water to remain undisturbed for a few minutes.

6. Observe the effects that were produced by the action of waves on the shoreline.

7. Examine the water at the lower edge of the pan for evidence of sand deposits.

RATIONALE

Energy carried to the shoreline by waves originates as energy transferred to the water by wind and other storm activity, sometimes many miles out at sea. Waves pounding against the shoreline transfer this energy to the shore materials, where it is used to erode the earth materials. Here, sand particles are carried away by the water, leaving the pebbles exposed. In a rocky terrain, the energy is used to wear down large rock formations, and it may take a long period of time for the gradual process to be noticed.

DISCUSSION AND FOLLOW-UP

- Students should observe that the waves generated by the sponge travel from the point of their generation toward the shore. They should then relate the action of the waves to the energy of motion generated by the moving sponge and be encouraged to repeat the demonstration, varying the amount of wave energy by applying greater and/or lesser amounts of pressure to the sponge wave generator.

- Students should be asked to respond to questions:
  — What happened to the sand over which the waves passed?
  — What happened to the pebbles over which the waves passed?
  — What do you predict would happen to a beach during a severe storm such as a hurricane?
  — What evidence of wave action on an actual shoreline have you witnessed?

- After the discussion has been completed, students should be asked to write a paragraph in which they describe the action of waves on a shore with which they are familiar or in which they have a special interest.

5–7: GYROSCOPIC STABILITY OF THE EARTH
(intermediate level)

INTRODUCTION

A spinning top, a circus clown's unicycle, and a student's bicycle have a very important characteristic in common—all are stable systems as long as their rotation continues; when allowed to slow down appreciably or stopped, however, the stability is destroyed, causing the affected system to topple. The earth, too, is a stable system, rotating on its axis, which is tilted 23 ½ degrees from the plane of its orbit. Its gyroscopic stability, whose force keeps it from tumbling into space, can be demonstrated with the use of a toy gyroscope.

LEARNING OBJECTIVES

After having participated in this demonstration lesson, students should be able to

- recognize the stability of a gyroscopic system.
- name the factors that contribute to the stability of a gyroscopic system.
- identify the factors that counteract gyroscopic stability.
- name two gyroscopic systems and explain their stability.
- predict what might happen to the earth if its gyroscopic stability were destroyed.
- express an understanding of *key words:* **stability**, **rotation**, **axis**, **gyroscope**, **inertia**, and **friction**.

MATERIALS REQUIRED

toy gyroscope

PRESENTATION

1. Arrange a suitable support on a table top where all students can view clearly the activity of the gyroscope.

2. Start the gyroscope wheel spinning vertically, with the axis oriented in a north-south direction. Then, slowly and carefully, turn the supporting structure to complete a 360-degree turn. Note the direction in which the axis of the spinning gyroscope points at all times. Observe what eventually happens to the gyroscope.

3. Start the gyroscope wheel spinning horizontally. Encourage students to suggest ways to tip the axis out of its up-and-down position while in motion, and allow several students to demonstrate their suggestions while the gyroscope is spinning rapidly.

4. Note any effect on the spinning gyroscope. Observe what eventually happens to the spinning gyroscope.

5. Repeat the demonstration several times to allow students to observe the activity and to analyze the stability of the system.

RATIONALE

An object that spins achieves stability because of its two unique properties:

1. While spinning, its axis tends to point continuously in the direction in which it is set, thus resisting any change in direction.

2. As long as the object continues to spin, it remains in an upright position and does not topple.

This applies to a toy gyroscope as well as to the earth, which is really a giant gyroscope whose spinning allows it to maintain its position by preventing it from flying out into space and by keeping one end of its axis at an angle of 23 ½ degrees as it points in the direction of Polaris, the North Star.

DISCUSSION AND FOLLOW-UP

- Discussion of the demonstration should focus on factors that contribute to the stability of the system, to counteracting forces such as friction that slow it down and cause it to come to an eventual stop, and to other gyroscopic systems.

- Students should be encouraged to make comments about the demonstration and to respond to pertinent questions:
    - What caused the gyroscope to eventually stop spinning?
    - How does the action of the gyroscope relate to your experiences while riding a bike?
    - How does the gyroscope activity illustrate the rotation of the earth on its axis as it revolves about the sun?
    - What makes it possible for the earth to maintain its spinning activity without interruption?
    - What prediction would you make concerning the earth if its gyroscopic activity were to be interrupted?

- After the discussion has been completed, students should be asked to write a report in their Science Demonstrations notebooks in which they indicate how the demonstration relates to the earth as a giant gyroscope.

5–8: DENSITY CURRENTS IN THE SEA
(intermediate level)

INTRODUCTION

Oceanographers have identified cold water currents flowing beneath warmer surface waters in parts of the Atlantic Ocean as well as the in the Pacific Ocean. Swimmers, too, are aware of the temperature difference at the surface and at greater depths in a body of water. How water of two different temperatures tends to remain separated despite the mixing of the two can be demonstrated with simple materials.

LEARNING OBJECTIVES

At the conclusion of this demonstration lesson, students should be able to

- understand the role of color as a "tracer" in scientific investigative work.
- relate the formation of distinct layers of water of different temperature with differences in their density.
- name three different ways that density currents can be produced.
- tell how an underwater density current affects the earth and its physical features.
- explain why colder water is found below warmer water in seas and oceans, using *key words:* **density**, **current**, and **density current**.

MATERIALS REQUIRED

waxed paper or Styrofoam cup; food coloring; ice pick or large nail; rectangular glass or clear plastic aquarium tank or sweater box; crushed ice; warm water

PRESENTATION

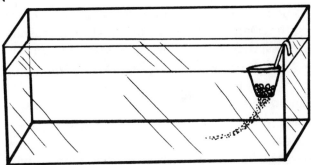

1. Pour warm water into a clear rectangular aquarium tank or sweater box until it is about two-thirds filled with water.
2. Use a nail or an ice pick to pierce several holes in the bottom of a large paper or Styrofoam cup.

3. Tape the cup to one corner of the tank or box at a level that positions the bottom of the cup slightly below the surface of the water.
4. Carefully fill the cup with crushed ice to which several drops of food coloring have been added.
5. Observe the water for signs of activity.

RATIONALE

When cold water meets warm water it sinks below the warmer water and continues for a period of time as a subsurface current. This can be seen as the colored ice water escapes from the cup and, because of its greater density, forms a current below the lighter, less dense warm water. Density currents, produced by differences in temperature, salt concentration, and turbidity of the water are common in many sea and ocean waters of the earth.

DISCUSSION AND FOLLOW-UP

- Students should observe the demonstration closely, noting the appearance of a colored water density current below the uncolored warm water in the aquarium.
- Discussion of the demonstration should be guided by pertinent questions:
    — Why did the cold water sink beneath the warm water?
    — What was the purpose of adding food coloring to the crushed ice?
    — Why is the current formed called a *density current*?
    — Can you predict the outcome of the demonstration if salt water instead of crushed ice had been placed in the cup?
- Students should be encouraged to plan variations of the demonstration, using salt, sand, or silt to create a density current and to research the effects that such currents have on the modifications of temperature and physiographic features of the earth.
- They should also be asked to predict the outcome of the demonstration if it is allowed to remain undisturbed overnight, and then be permitted to check out their predictions by a follow-up observation on the next day.
- Specific density currents in the Atlantic and Pacific oceans, as well as one occurring where the Mediterranean Sea waters flow into the Atlantic Ocean should be researched and reported to the class for discussion.
- As a follow-up study, students can be presented with an interesting challenge in the form of an actual application of the concept of the demonstration. They can be asked to write a paragraph in which they explain the rationale of World War II submariners who "rode the density current" past the Strait of Gibraltar from the Mediterranean Sea to the Atlantic Ocean without being detected.

5–9:   THE FORMATION OF DEW
(elementary level)

INTRODUCTION

Water is all around us—in oceans, lakes, rivers, and streams; in the soil and on rocks at the surface of the earth; in plant and animal bodies; and in the air. Although colorless, tasteless, and odorless, the water vapor in the air can be detected when certain temperature changes occur within our weather patterns and cause the vapor to condense in the form of dew on rocks and grass at the earth's surface. This can be demonstrated in the classroom.

LEARNING OBJECTIVES

After having completed this demonstration lesson, students should be able to

- name the source of the moisture from which dew is formed.
- recognize the process of condensation as an example of a physical change.
- identify the relationship between temperature and the amount of water vapor in the air.
- develop an insight into the effects of moisture in the air on personal comfort, weather patterns, and climates of the world.
- explain how the demonstration relates to the formation of dew and frost, using *key words:* **condensation, dew, frost, dew point,** and **saturation level.**

MATERIALS REQUIRED

metal juice can; crushed ice; lukewarm water; swizzle stick; thermometer

PRESENTATION

1. Remove the label from a clean, empty juice can.
2. Pour lukewarm water into the can until it is filled with water to the halfway mark.
3. Add crushed ice to the water and use the swizzle stick to mix the ice-water mixture.
4. Place a thermometer in the can.
5. Observe the outside of the can.
6. When a film of moisture begins to form on the outside of the can, ask a student to take a temperature reading and record it on the chalkboard.

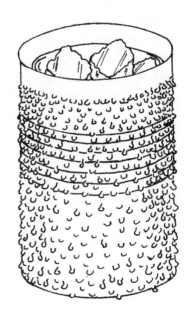

RATIONALE

Warm air can hold more moisture than cold air. Consequently, when ice water cooled the can and the can cooled the air surrounding it, the amount of moisture that the air could hold at its lowered temperature was reduced. Excess water vapor in the surrounding air condensed and collected as water droplets on the cold surface of the juice can. When this occurs in nature, dew is formed on a cool surface at a temperature level that is appropriately termed the *dew point*.

DISCUSSION AND FOLLOW-UP

- As students observe the demonstration, they should respond to direct questions:
    - What is observed forming on the side of the can?
    - Where did the water droplets come from?
    - Why did they form on the can?
    - At what temperature did they form?
    - How does this remind you of water droplets formed on a pitcher of ice-cold lemonade on a hot summer day?
    - What form would the condensation take if the temperature within the can was lowered below the freezing point of water?
    - Does the formation of dew illustrate a chemical or a physical change of matter?

- Attention should focus on the way the demonstration relates to a similar occurrence in nature, with consideration given to the formation of dew and frost when air close to the ground is cooled at night and to what happens to these formations as the sun rises the next morning and then moves higher in the sky.

- Reasons that the dew point is not the same at all times or at all locations on earth should then be discussed, with attention to the importance of scientific data for reporting weather conditions.

- Diagrams of the demonstration, with an explanation of how it applies to the formation of dew and frost should then be recorded by students in their Science Demonstration notebooks.

5–10: FORMATION OF UNDERGROUND CAVES AND CAVERNS
(intermediate level)

INTRODUCTION

Some of the most visited scenic wonders are the product of a slow, steady action of ground water on certain rock formations. Over thousands of years this action hollows out the rock to form limestone caves with many interesting features. Long icicles hanging from the ceiling and others building beneath them from the floor often meet to form continuous columns in formations that are equally interesting to visitors and to scientists who study cave formations.

LEARNING OBJECTIVES

At the end of this demonstration lesson, students should be able to

- identify the physical change and the chemical change involved in stalactite and stalagmite formation.
- understand the chemical reactions that are involved when acid rain water seeps through cracks in limestone layers.
- have an appreciation of the long, slow process that is involved in many earth formations.
- explain why caves are formed in limestone layers of rock and distinguish between different formations in caves, using *key words*: **limestone, calcium carbonate, acid rain water, stalactite,** and **stalagmite.**

MATERIALS REQUIRED

2 peanut butter jars; 1 jar lid; water; 2 nails or weights; Epsom salts; string; tray

PRESENTATION

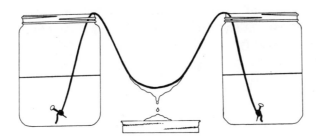

1. Prepare a supersaturated solution of Epsom salts by adding Epsom salts to heated water until no more of the salt will go into solution.
2. Pour the Epsom salt solution into two peanut butter jars, with equal amounts of the solution in each of the jars, positioned on a tray.

3. Tie a nail to each end of a piece of string and position the string so that an end is immersed in the Epsom salts solution in each jar and the middle of the string hangs down loosely between the two jars.

4. Place a lid below the dip in the string.

5. Allow the demonstration setup to remain undisturbed on the tray until the next day.

6. Observe over a period of several days.

RATIONALE

Ground water containing carbon dioxide is a weak acid that dissolves limestone and, over a period of thousands of years, hollows it out to form caves and caverns. As water seeps through a cave ceiling, it carries dissolved calcium. Then, carbon dioxide from the air unites chemically with the calcium in the water, forming calcium carbonate. As this water drips from the ceiling of the cave, some of the water evaporates, leaving particles of calcium carbonate on the ceiling of the cave. Another drop of water forms around each particle and the water again evaporates, leaving more calcium carbonate deposited over the previous particles. Molecule by molecule, drop by drop, this is repeated over and over again to form a stalactite. But not all of the water evaporates. Some of the water drops from the end of the stalactite and falls on the floor below. This may undergo some evaporation and build up to form a stalagmite. If and when stalactite and stalagmite meet, a column is formed which may become a part of an intricate feature in a cave.

DISCUSSION AND FOLLOW-UP

- As students observe the demonstration they should gain some insight into the long, slow process that is a part of cave formation. During this time, they should be encouraged to report any personal experiences they have had during visits to caves and/or caverns, and to discuss them in relation to the demonstration.

- Daily observations of the demonstration should be made, during which time each new observation should be considered as it contributes to the answers to pertinent questions:
  - What is the difference between a stalactite and a stalagmite?
  - How do you account for the fact that stalagmites and stalactites feel cold to the touch?

- After relating the demonstration to the natural phenomenon of cave formation, additional questions can be posed:
  - How do you account for the fact that it takes thousands of years for a natural cave to form?
  - What is the chemical composition of naturally formed stalactites and stalagmites?

— What would you infer about the kind of rock formation of the earth in areas where caves are found?

• As a follow-up activity, students should be asked to write a report about the demonstration, in which they indicate how caves and caverns are formed and the physical and chemical changes that are involved in the formation of stalactites and stalagmites.

5–11: HEATING AND COOLING OF LAND AND WATER
(elementary level)

INTRODUCTION

Swimmers are quick to note that the land surface is warmer than the water on a bright, sunny day. The water temperature may be too cold for swimming, even though the sand on the beach feels hot to the soles of the feet.

The difference in the rate at which soil and water temperatures rise, while receiving radiant energy from the same source, can be demonstrated in the classroom.

LEARNING OBJECTIVES

After having participated in this demonstration lesson, students should be able to

- understand the value of precise data for use in a comparative study.
- recognize an important difference in the characteristics of earth materials.
- analyze data and establish a relationship between factors involved.
- explain the relationship of the demonstration to an actual earth situation, using *key words:* **temperature**, **heat**, and **thermometer**.

MATERIALS REQUIRED

garden soil or potting soil; 2 stand-up thermometers; 2 plastic containers from margarine; bright light source; water

PRESENTATION

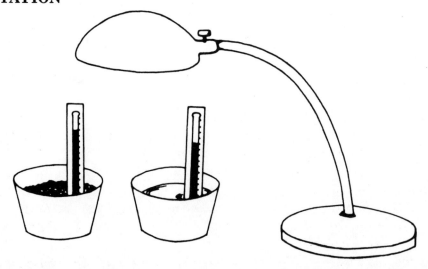

1. Place supplies of soil and water in separate containers and allow them to remain overnight in the same location in the classroom to equalize their temperature levels.

2. Pour water into one margarine container until it is two-thirds full of water.

3. Place soil in a second margarine container until it is two-thirds full of soil.

4. Place a stand-up thermometer in each container so that the thermometer bulb is positioned just below the surface of the soil or water.

5. Place a bright light source above the two containers so that each container receives the same amount of light.

6. Have students take temperature readings of both materials and record the initial readings on the chalkboard.

7. Take and record additional temperature readings at two-minute intervals.

8. Continue temperature readings until a difference in the temperature of the two materials is noted.

9. Analyze the data collected.

RATIONALE

Heat energy can be transferred from one place to another, causing the material to which it is transferred to become warmer. However, the rate at which the substance becomes warmer depends upon its physical features. Molecules of soil, being darker, readily absorb light energy and convert it into heat, while water molecules, being light and shiny, reflect some of the light back into the atmosphere. This causes a land surface to become warmer than water on a bright, sunny day at the seashore.

DISCUSSION AND FOLLOW-UP

- At specific intervals during the demonstration, students should be given turns for taking temperature readings and recording them on a chart maintained on the chalkboard where all can see. Between temperature readings, temperature and heat should be distinguished and discussed, and students should be encouraged to predict what they think the outcome of the demonstration will be.

- After about six readings, or whenever a difference in the temperature of the two substances has been noted, the data collected should be analyzed and a determination made as to the comparative rate of heating of soil and of water.

- Students should be encouraged to report personal experiences at the seashore or other swimming area and to relate the demonstration to an actual situation, with attention given to differences in the rate of heating of different earth materials.

- The demonstration should be reviewed, with attention focused on summary statements:

  — The temperature of matter changes when the amount of heat in it changes.

— Heat energy travels from a warmer to a cooler location.

— A thermometer is used to measure the temperature of a substance.

— When exposed to the same source of heat, soil heats at a faster rate than water.

- After the demonstration has been discussed and summarized, students should be asked to apply what they have learned by preparing a written response to the question, Why is the land warmer than the water on a bright, sunny day at the seashore?

5–12: EROSION DUE TO GLACIER ACTIVITY
(elementary level)

INTRODUCTION

Although little is known about the cause of the four great glacial periods that took place about two million years ago, there is much evidence of the changes the glaciers made in the surface of the earth. In addition to many glacier-formed lakes, there are some regions that have been gouged out by glacial activity and others in which the earth materials have been relocated after having been transported by rivers of snow and ice. A model "glacier" can be used to demonstrate some of the characteristics of real glacier activity.

LEARNING OBJECTIVES

After participating in this demonstration lesson, students should be able to

- understand how the use of a model can provide some information about a real change in the earth's surface.
- name three specific ways that glaciers can change the surface of the earth.
- describe how glaciers cause erosion of the earth's surface.
- show evidence of an understanding of the meaning and proper use of *key words:* **glacier** and **erosion**.

MATERIALS REQUIRED

ice cubes; sand and small pebble mixture; large bars of laundry soap; plastic table cloth or protective cover

PRESENTATION

1. Prepare a work area on a table top where all students can view the activity clearly.
2. Cut bars of laundry soap lengthwise to form several thin, rectangular slabs.
3. Arrange ice cubes, the sand-pebble mixture, and a few slabs of laundry soap, in sequence from left to right, on a plastic tablecloth.
4. Applying gentle downward pressure, move an ice cube in a left-to-right direction, through the sand-pebble mixture and over the soap.

5. Examine the surface of the soap.

RATIONALE

Glaciers, for the most part, move at a slow and steady pace, eroding the land areas over which they pass. When a glacier presses against the earth's surface, sand, gravel, stones, and loose rocks become frozen into the bottom layers of ice. Then, as the glacier continues to move, these materials are carried along, scratching, scraping, and digging into the land over which they pass. Some of the greatest erosion of the mountains of North America and Europe was caused by this type of glacial action during a period in the earth's history known as the Ice Age.

DISCUSSION AND FOLLOW-UP

- After the first run of the "glacier," the soap layers should be distributed to students for an examination of the surface over which the ice and its load has passed, and for a comparison of the appearance of soap sections from different locations along the glacier's pathway. Individual students should then be encouraged to investigate the effects produced by applying greater pressure, different mixtures of loads carried, and/or different rates of passing over the unused soap surfaces provided.

- Students who have difficulty in understanding how accumulated snow turns to ice at the bottom should be reminded of their experiences in making snowballs, where pressing and squeezing on the outside results in the formation of ice at the center.

- A discussion of the demonstration should focus on some important points:
  - the effect of increasing the amount of pressure applied to moving ice
  - the effect of particle size of the load being carried by the ice
  - evidence of three different ways the soap eroded
  - evidence that some material taken from the sand area was relocated by the glacier's action

- Students should then relate the demonstration to erosion caused by real glaciers by writing a brief report in their Science Demonstrations notebooks, in which they describe how glaciers cause erosion of the earth's surface.

5-13: ENERGY RECEIVED FROM THE SUN IN WINTER AND SUMMER
(intermediate level)

INTRODUCTION

Energy received from the sun is not distributed evenly over the earth's surface. In different locations on the earth, there are different amounts of heat and light, which can be seen to vary as the earth tilts on its axis and causes our changing seasons. An understanding of the difference between direct and slanting rays of the sun and how they are produced can be developed with the use of light rays from an artificial light source as they strike against a surface in the classroom.

LEARNING OBJECTIVES

At the end of this demonstration lesson, students should be able to

- understand how a scientific method can be useful for gathering information about an earth study.
- identify the relationship between the concentration of light rays and the amount of energy per unit of surface over which the light is distributed.
- relate the concept of the demonstration to the different amounts of heat derived from light energy from the sun received on the earth's surface during summer and winter seasons, using *key words:* **light rays**, **energy**, **heat**, **concentration**, and **surface area**.

MATERIALS REQUIRED

2 identical flashlights; large poster paper or the reverse side of a wall map or chart; colored marking pens or pencils

PRESENTATION

1. Tape a large piece of plain construction paper, poster board, or a reversed wall map or chart to the chalkboard or a wall area where it will be clearly visible to all students.

2. Standing at a distance of about three feet from the "surface" and with a flashlight in each hand, hold one flashlight in a position that is horizontal to the floor and aimed directly at the wall chart. At the same time, tilt the second flashlight so that it is directed to a different location on the wall, slightly higher and to one side of the first.

3. While holding the flashlights steady in these positions, press the switches with your thumbs and shine light on the two locations.

   NOTE: A trial run will enable you to estimate proper positions and target points so as to avoid

any danger of crossing pathways of light rays or overlapping light areas. It is important that the flashlights used be identical for simultaneous production of direct and slanting rays. If this is not possible, it is better to produce them one at a time, using the same flashlight for both direct and slanting rays.

4. Ask one student to draw an outline around the lighted area produced by the direct beam of light, while, similarly, but with a contrasting color, a second student marks the outline of the lighted area produced by the slanting rays.

5. Encourage all students to participate in performing measurements and calculations of the size of the two lighted areas, as well as in the discussion of their comparative brightness.

RATIONALE

Direct light rays produce a relatively small, concentrated circle of light on a surface, thus providing more energy per unit of area than do slanting rays received from the same source. The rays that slant spread over a larger area, thus providing comparatively less energy per unit of surface affected.

Light may be spread over a large earth surface that receives slanted sun's rays as the earth turns on its axis and tilts away from the sun. This energy, converted into heat when it is absorbed by the earth, produces a lower temperature level than another earth surface receiving direct light rays, because of its position in relation to the sun at the same time.

DISCUSSION AND FOLLOW-UP

- Students should measure the outlines that were drawn of the lighted surfaces produced by the direct and slanting rays, and relate their size to the relative brightness observed when the light was being shone.

- A basic understanding should be developed: the direct rays, in producing a smaller, more concentrated circle of light on the paper, provided more energy per unit of area; while slanting rays received from the same source were spread over a larger area, thus providing less energy per unit of surface affected. This can be related to actual experiences that students can be asked to recall:

    — During which season is the temperature the highest in your area?

    — During which season is it easiest for you to get a suntan or a sunburn?

- With reference to studies of relative positions of the sun and the earth, and of the tilting of the earth on its axis, the nature of light rays and associated heat energy being received during summer and winter months on other parts of the earth should also be discussed.

- After these concepts and applications have been developed, students should be asked to write a short report of the demonstration in their Science Demonstrations notebooks.

5–14: EFFECTS PRODUCED BY WATER TRAVELING IN A CURVED PATH
(elementary level)

INTRODUCTION

Water flowing over the surface of the earth does not always travel in a straight line. Often, water bypasses obstructions in its pathway, causing bends in a river or stream and affecting the surrounding area in observable ways. Some of the effects of water traveling in a curved path can be demonstrated in the classroom and related to natural occurrences where most rivers and streams are seen to move through a number of curves.

LEARNING OBJECTIVES

After completing this demonstration lesson, students should be able to

- name at least one reason that water might be prevented from traveling in a straight-line pathway.
- understand that water traveling in a curved path affects the surrounding area differently from water traveling in a straight pathway.
- identify specific effects produced on the inside and on the outside of a curve in a stream in which water is moving in a curved pathway.
- demonstrate an understanding of the meaning and proper use of *key words:* **curved pathway, deposit, sediment,** and **erosion.**

MATERIALS REQUIRED

large jar with flat bottom; colored sand; spoon; water

PRESENTATION

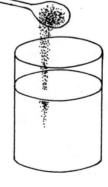
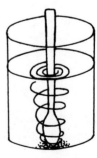

1. Pour water into a large flat-bottomed jar until it is two-thirds full of water.

2. Add a spoonful of colored sand to the water in the jar.

3. Create a rapid swirling action in the jar by stirring the contents vigorously in one direction.

4. Discontinue the stirring and note what happens to the sand when the swirling stops.

RATIONALE

Sand that is closer to the center of the swirling water current moves a relatively short distance with each cycle and therefore moves slowly during each swirling cycle. But water around the outside edge must move at a faster rate to cover the longer distance. Consequently, slower-moving water drops its sand, which is seen to pile up in the center of the jar. This same effect can be seen in the deposit of sediment on the inside curve of a river bend, where the water moves at its slowest rate; while along the outer part of the curve, the water—moving fast enough to keep the sediment from settling out—also erodes the outer bank as the river rounds the bend.

DISCUSSION AND FOLLOW-UP

- Students should note the swirling action of the sand and water and relate it to a fast-moving wheel in which the outside edge must travel a greater distance—therefore, at a faster rate—than the hub at its center.

- As they observe the swirling sand and water and the eventual deposit of sand building up in the center of the jar, they should respond to direct questions:

  — In what region does the swirling water travel the greater distance?

  — In what region does the swirling water travel the shorter distance?

  — What effect does the distance traveled have on the rate at which the sand and water particles must travel to complete one swirling action?

  — Do you expect the settling out of sediment to be greater when carried by a fast-moving or a slow-moving current?

  — Does water travel at a faster rate at the inner or the outer part of a bend in a stream or river?

  — How does this relate to deposits of sand and erosion of earth material on the outer and inner part of each bend in a river?

- After the discussion of the demonstration and its application to water flowing in a curved path in a stream has been completed, students should be asked to draw a diagram that shows the action of water moving in a curved path in a stream or river.

CHAPTER 6

Demonstrations Pertaining to Ecology

6–1: THE ACID RAIN PROBLEM
(intermediate level)

INTRODUCTION

Damage due to acid rain is varied and widespread: crumbling of buildings and monuments; acidification of ground water; and both immediate and long-range harm to plants, animals, and humans have been linked to its presence. Although the condition of acid rain was identified in England during the early part of the Industrial Revolution, the problems associated with it have been increasing at a steady rate over the past one hundred years. Ways to bring our activities into harmony with nature are being sought in an effort to solve the problem.

LEARNING OBJECTIVES

At the end of this demonstration lesson, students should be able to

- name three specific examples of the harmful effects of acid rain on living and/or nonliving substances.
- give the names of two toxic gases responsible for the formation of acid rain.
- apply a scientific test to determine if a substance is an acid.
- identify the cause-and-effect relationship illustrated in the demonstration.
- suggest ways to solve the problem of acid rain.
- show evidence of the meaning and proper use of *key words:* **acid rain, precipitation, combustion,** and **fossil fuels.**

MATERIALS REQUIRED

small crayfish; mayonnaise jar; litmus or pH paper; club soda

PRESENTATION

1. Place a mayonnaise jar on a table top where all students can view it clearly.
2. Place a small active crayfish in the mayonnaise jar.
3. Use litmus or pH paper to determine the acidity of a freshly opened bottle of club soda.
4. Pour club soda into the jar until the crayfish is completely covered.
5. Observe the crayfish.

6. Rescue the crayfish from its acidic environment if and when it becomes severely distressed or gives any indication that the situation is life-threatening.

RATIONALE

The behavior of aquatic animals, such as crayfish, changes when placed in an acid environment—such as that provided by club soda, a carbonic acid. Similarly, when acidic rain or snow falls to earth, lakes, streams, forests, and fields become contaminated, with serious threats to the affected members of the natural world. Primarily in the form of weak solutions of sulfuric and nitric acids, formed when sulfur dioxide and nitrogen oxides from volcanoes and combustion of fossil fuels are dissolved in moisture in the atmosphere, these acids are harmful to the delicate membranes and tissues of living organisms. Because the poisonous nature of some chemical substances—such as chlorine, mercury, lead, and iodine—is increased at low pH levels, acid rain provides the conditions for magnifying the damage inflicted by these substances as well as bringing harm to living things directly.

DISCUSSION AND FOLLOW-UP

- Students can become actively involved in this demonstration. One student can be asked to test the club soda with litmus or pH paper, and another can rescue the crayfish if its behavior indicates that its life is becoming threatened. Students should observe the behavior of the crayfish when placed in carbonic acid and discuss the demonstration by responding to direct questions:
    - What effect did the club soda have on the crayfish?
    - What would have happened to the crayfish if it had not been rescued?
    - Is carbonic acid normally found in nature?
    - What is the source of other acids that would contaminate ponds and lakes and find their way into water supply systems?
    - Why is acid rain harmful?
    - How may the dangers to living things from acid rain be reduced?
- After the discussion has been completed, students should be asked to write a report of the demonstration in their Science Demonstrations notebooks.

6–2:   DETERGENTS AND SURVIVAL OF FISH
(elementary level)

INTRODUCTION

Detergents do not disappear when discarded after being used for washing laundry or dishes—foam floating down a river and the frothing of tap water give very real evidence of their lingering presence. Because they do not decompose readily, detergents pollute the water and exert a harmful effect on aquatic forms of life. This effect can be demonstrated.

LEARNING OBJECTIVES

After completing this demonstration lesson, students should be able to

- analyze a cause-and-effect relationship that occurs over a period of time.
- recognize that the observable action of some pollutants may not be immediate.
- make inferences concerning the effect of detergents on plants, animals, and people.
- relate observations of the demonstration to the overall "ecological crisis."
- describe the effects of detergents on fish, using *key words:* **detergent**, **biodegradable**, and **nonbiodegradable**.

MATERIALS REQUIRED

large glass jar; medicine dropper; water; colored liquid detergent; 2 small active fish; fish net; jar of fresh water

PRESENTATION

1. Fill a large jar about three-fourths full of water.
2. Place two small active fish in the water.
3. Observe the activity of the fish.
4. Using a medicine dropper, add one drop of a colored liquid laundry detergent to the water.
5. Again, observe the activity and behavior of the fish.
6. On each of three or four succeeding days, add one additional drop of liquid detergent to the water.

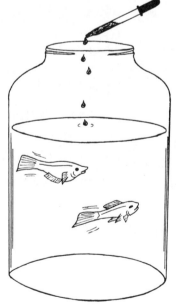

7. Observe the activity and behavior of the fish each day for a period of one week.
8. As soon as the fish are observed hovering near the surface in search of a fresh air supply, transfer them to a jar containing fresh water.

NOTE: Students should recognize the similarities between this temporary interference seen in the fish breathing pattern and that of a "fish out of water." Normal breathing is restored when the fish are quickly placed in fresh, unpolluted water.

RATIONALE

When detergent is added to an aquatic environment, it affects the fish living in that environment. It causes them to swim in erratic patterns near the surface and affects their gills by causing them to enlarge. In small concentrations, it interferes with their breathing and impairs their general state of health; while in larger concentrations or during prolonged periods of exposure, it may cause death.

DISCUSSION AND FOLLOW-UP

- Students should observe the effect of the detergent on the activity and behavior of the fish and describe any changes noted in their pattern of swimming.
- Observations, made over a period of several days, should enable them to respond to questions:
  — How did the behavior of the fish change when the detergent was added to the water?
  — How were the gills of the fish affected by the detergent?
  — What was the effect of an increased concentration of detergent on the behavior of the fish?
  — What do you predict would eventually happen to the fish if the concentration level of the detergent were increased still more?
  — Is it reasonable to expect that detergents would have a harmful effect on other forms of life?
- Students should be asked to write a short report in their Science Demonstrations notebooks, in which they explain why detergents should be considered to be dangerous water pollutants and suggest a plan for preventing harmful effects of detergents on fish.

6–3: RECYCLING MATERIALS
(intermediate level)

INTRODUCTION

There is a finite amount of matter on earth that must be used and reused over and over again in order to maintain the abiotic world and serve the needs of the biotic factors. Nature's plan of recycling materials is seen in the nitrogen cycle, the carbon cycle, and the water cycle, where matter undergoes both physical and chemical changes. People can take some of the pressure off the limited natural resources by recycling materials—such as paper, rubber, and glass—in a manner that allows them to reuse materials without the necessity of having them reduced to their basic elements first.

LEARNING OBJECTIVES

After students have participated in this demonstration lesson, they should be able to

- recognize nature as the originator of recycling programs.
- understand how people who participate in recycling programs help to preserve our ecological balance.
- relate the demonstration to current programs and their effectiveness.
- name three substances that are being recycled in the community.
- become actively involved as participants in a recycling program sponsored by the school or community.
- show evidence of an understanding of the meaning of *key words:* **recycling**, **conservation**, and **natural resources**.

MATERIALS REQUIRED

newspaper; scissors; paint tray; window screen; waxed paper; water; flour; small bucket; wooden paint mixer; rolling pin or tall jar

PRESENTATION

1. Pour water into a small bucket until it is about half full.
2. Cut several pages of a newspaper into small squares and immerse them in the water in the bucket.
3. Allow the newspapers to become thoroughly wet.
4. Use a wooden paint stirrer to stir the paper-water mixture until it forms a consistency of gruel.

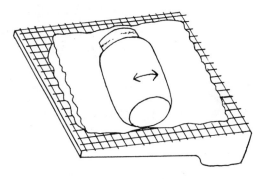

5. Add two tablespoonfuls of flour to the mixture and continue stirring.

6. Lift the pulpy mass out of the bucket and press out the excess water.

7. Place the mass on top of a piece of window screen on a paint tray and allow the remaining water to run off.

8. Place a sheet of waxed paper over the pulp mass and, using a rolling pin or a glass jar, roll the pulp out into the form of a sheet of paper.

9. Remove the waxed paper and allow the newly formed sheet of paper to dry thoroughly before writing on it.

RATIONALE

Paper is one of the leading materials that is recycled for the production of new products from old ones. For example, old newspapers can be recycled for the manufacture of boxes, packing material, newsprint, stationery, and greeting cards. The recycling of newspaper is accompanied by significant savings; for each ton recycled, seventeen trees are spared from being cut down for their pulp value, and the energy required for manufacturing the new paper products is cut in half when recycled sources are used.

DISCUSSION AND FOLLOW-UP

- There are many opportunities for students to become actively involved in the performance of the demonstration. Cutting newspaper into small squares, stirring the pulp, and rolling out the pulp into a thin layer are tasks that can be performed by different individuals and used as discussion points about the demonstration.

- An awareness of the current nature and ecological importance of the recycling process should be developed, using guide questions:

  — What paper products do you use that are made from recycled paper?

  — How many trees could be saved if ten tons of paper used each year by your school were produced from recycled newspaper?

  — Why is it more crucial to recycle paper today than it was one hundred years ago?

  — What materials are collected in your school or community as a part of a recycling program?

  — How are scientific processes involved in the recycling of materials?

- Special efforts should be made to involve students in any existing recycling programs that are sponsored by the school or community.

- After the discussion has been completed, students should be asked to write a report about the demonstration and the relationship between recycling practices and ecology.

6–4: ANATOMY OF AN ECOSYSTEM
(elementary level)

INTRODUCTION

An ecosystem is concerned with a community and its environment. There are interrelationships in terrestrial, aquatic, woodland, desert, bog, and marine ecosystems, in which the organisms engage in give-and-take interrelationships with each other and with physical factors of the environment that lead to an eventual overall balance. Creating a balanced aquarium in the classroom presents an opportunity for developing important insights into a world in miniature, in which the drama of life is enacted within a sealed container.

LEARNING OBJECTIVES

After having participated in this demonstration lesson, students should be able to

- identify the living and the nonliving components of an ecosystem.
- understand how various elements of an ecosystem are interrelated.
- have an awareness of the long-range aspects of establishing and maintaining a balance within an ecosystem.
- name five different ecosystems.
- describe two different ecosystems, using *key words:* **ecosystem, balanced aquarium, biotic factors, abiotic factors,** and **interrelationship**.

MATERIALS REQUIRED

large pickle jar with a screw-cap top; spring water or aged tap water; washed sand and gravel; 4 guppies or other small fish; 3 aquatic snails; elodea or other aquatic plants; daphnia

PRESENTATION

1. Place a large wide-mouthed jar in an area in which there is sunlight for a major part of the day.

2. Arrange a base layer of gravel, covered by a layer of sand in the bottom of the jar.

3. Add tap water and allow to settle overnight.

4. Position plants appropriately; anchor rooted plants in the soil layer and allow others to float freely. Then allow the plants to adjust to the new environment.

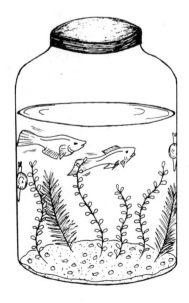

5. Introduce three aquatic snails, four minnows or guppies, and some daphnia to the prepared environment.

6. Allow sufficient time for the plants and animals to become adjusted to their surroundings.

7. After two or three days, close the jar by screwing the cap on tightly.

8. Observe the aquatic ecosystem over a period of one week.

RATIONALE

A balanced freshwater aquarium simulates conditions found in a pond in nature, where the watery environment favors the plant and animal forms of life that are present. Water protects the plants from drying out, facilitates the unique forms of locomotion of water animals, and acts as a medium for holding substances and making them available to the organisms. The organisms engage in give-and-take activities—plants produce food for animals and replenish the supply of oxygen needed for their respiration; animals, in return, exhale carbon dioxide to be used by plants in their food-making process; and snails, acting as scavengers, keep the water clean and free of debris and fish excrement. As long as these activities continue in over-and-over-again cycles, the ecosystem maintains its balance.

DISCUSSION AND FOLLOW-UP

- Sustained interest in this demonstration will be in evidence for several months after the initial observations are made.
- Throughout this period, students should be encouraged to discover new evidence that will enable them to answer certain questions:
    - Which factors in the ecosystem are classified as living?
    - Which factors in the ecosystem are classified as nonliving?
    - What contributions are made by the plants in the ecosystem?
    - What contributions are made by the animals in the ecosystem?
    - Why is it necessary for both plants and animals to be present in this ecosystem?
    - What do you predict would happen if the plants were removed from this ecosystem?
    - What do you predict would happen if the snails were removed from this ecosystem?
    - What evidence of a food chain is observed in this ecosystem?
- Discussion of the demonstration should focus on other ecosystems, including that of the earth as a giant ecosystem and plans for the building of a model, *Biosphere II,* as a preliminary for developing a space colony for the future.
- As a follow-up activity, students can be asked to draw a picture of the earth as a giant ecosystem in which many smaller ecosystems interrelate with each other in maintaining a natural balance.

6-5:   THE EFFECTS OF THERMAL POLLUTION
(intermediate level)

INTRODUCTION

Some industries pose a serious threat to aquatic ecosystems even though they do not pollute the nearby waterways with the usual form of toxic chemicals or other industrial waste. Instead, they take water from a stream, use it as a cooling agent, and return it in a heated condition to the normally cooler source. There is evidence to indicate that many fish are killed by the elevated water temperature that results.

LEARNING OBJECTIVES

After having completed this demonstration lesson, students should be able to

- analyze the demonstrated chain of events, starting with the elevation of water temperature and ending with the effects on the affected organism.
- interpret the information gathered via observations and apply it to a natural setting.
- discuss the immediate and long-range effects of thermal pollution, with an awareness and understanding of the interrelationship that exists between people and nature.
- apply properly and in correct context the *key words:* **thermal pollution** and **aquatic ecosystem**.

MATERIALS REQUIRED

small aquarium bowl containing an active goldfish in water at room temperature; peanut butter jar; thermometer; hot water; water at room temperature

PRESENTATION

1. Assemble needed materials on a table top where all students can view them clearly.
2. Mix hot and room-temperature water in a peanut butter jar until the temperature of the resulting mixture is approximately 45°C.
3. Ask a student to use a thermometer to take accurate temperature readings of the water
   (a) in the aquarium bowl containing the goldfish.
   (b) in the peanut butter jar.

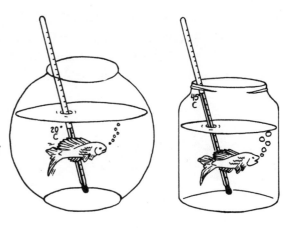

4. Transfer the small active goldfish from the aquarium bowl to the peanut butter jar.

5. Observe the activity of the goldfish in heated water.

6. Allow a student to rescue the goldfish if it appears that the difficulties it experiences in heated water become too severe for its survival.

RATIONALE

Many industries, including nuclear fission plants, dump hot water waste into nearby rivers and streams, causing a rise in the temperature of the water. This sets into motion a chain of events: in its heated form, water can hold less oxygen than at its normal temperature; aquatic forms of life, lacking sufficient oxygen for their normal rate of functioning, are slowed down in the rate at which they perform their life activities; and, in the extreme, death of organisms in the aquatic ecosystem results.

DISCUSSION AND FOLLOW-UP

- As students observe the demonstration, discussion can be guided by key questions:
    - How does the activity of the goldfish in the heated water compare with the activity noted when it was in the aquarium?
    - How does the temperature of the water in the peanut butter jar compare with the temperature of water in the aquarium?
    - What difficulties does the goldfish appear to be having in the heated water?
    - What do you predict would happen if the goldfish were left in the heated water for more than thirty minutes?
    - How does thermal pollution threaten aquatic forms of life?
    - What are the causes of thermal pollution?
    - What can be done to overcome the problem of thermal pollution?
- After the discussion has been completed, students should be asked to prepare diagrams showing the behavior of the goldfish both in water at a normal temperature and in heated water.

6–6: IS DILUTION THE SOLUTION TO POLLUTION?
(elementary level)

INTRODUCTION

It has been a common practice of many industries to discharge their chemical wastes into a nearby waterway. Eventually, this polluted water reaches the sea, where it becomes highly diluted. The theory seems to be that dilution on a large scale will eliminate the highly toxic materials and the dangers that are associated with them. The fallacy of this "solution" can be demonstrated quite dramatically in the classroom.

LEARNING OBJECTIVES

At the end of this demonstration lesson, students should be able to

- recognize the process of dilution, demonstrated here and in an earlier lesson.
- apply scientific skills to the evaluation of a problem situation.
- understand that toxic materials do not disappear when diluted in a large amount of water.
- evaluate the overall effectiveness of the practice of dumping wastes offshore or of carting them out to sea.
- describe the event demonstrated, using *key words:* **pollution**, **dilution**, and **concentration**.

MATERIALS REQUIRED

mayonnaise jar; water; food coloring; medicine droppers; white cloth; swizzle stick

PRESENTATION

1. Place a mayonnaise jar on a table top where all students can view it clearly.
2. Pour water into the jar until it is three-fourths full of water.
3. With a medicine dropper, add one drop of food coloring to the water and stir until all molecules of the color substance have been distributed uniformly throughout the water.
4. Observe the mixture for signs of any tinge of color.

5. With a clean medicine dropper, place one drop of the diluted food coloring on a clean white handkerchief or square of cloth.

6. Place the cloth near a heat source or in an area of moving air and allow the water to evaporate.

7. When the cloth is completely dry, examine again for signs of the coloring substance.

RATIONALE

When a drop of food coloring is added to a jar of water, it loses some of the intensity of its color by spreading the color molecules between molecules of water until there are very few of them at any one place. This gives a much lighter appearance to the color. When a sample of this dilution is then placed on a white cloth, the water evaporates but the color molecules remain behind in the form of a color residue on the white cloth. The contaminant in the water has become less concentrated but does not disappear.

DISCUSSION AND FOLLOW-UP

- Students should observe both aspects of the demonstration closely for evidence of what happens to the color material. They should be encouraged to report their observations and to answer a series of guide questions.

  — What happened to the food coloring when one drop was placed in water?

  — What caused the color to fade?

  — What is the appearance of the dried water spot on the white cloth?

  — Where did the color come from?

  — Did the "pollution" disappear when it was diluted in water?

  — What do you predict would happen if the food coloring material were a toxic chemical?

    Would the water be safe to drink?

    Would the water have a harmful effect on fish?

- After the discussion has been completed, students should be asked to prepare diagrams which indicate the continued presence of a pollution material after it has been diluted in a large body of water.

6–7: A TEMPERATURE INVERSION
(intermediate level)

INTRODUCTION

Tiny solid particles from automobile exhaust and soot from factory smokestacks are largely responsible for the formation of the haze that can be seen hovering over many large cities and industrial areas. Many people who breathe this air experience some discomfort and suffer some health problems. The severity of this form of pollution is increased when local weather conditions and/or the unique topography of a region cause the pollutants to be trapped in a layer of still air that prevents them from moving away from the area.

LEARNING OBJECTIVES

After having completed this demonstration lesson, students should be able to

- describe how a temperature inversion occurs.
- name two primary sources of air pollutants that can become trapped in a temperature inversion.
- understand how the activities of people interact with natural events concerning the air in our environment.
- apply information from the demonstration model of a temperature inversion to such an occurrence in the real world, using *key words:* **pollutant**, **air pollution**, **temperature inversion**, and **smog**.

MATERIALS REQUIRED

wide-mouthed gallon jar, with cover; plastic bags; chilled sand bags; hot water; funnel; incense; plastic tubing; twisties; masking tape

PRESENTATION

1. Place a wide-mouthed gallon jar on a table top where all students can view it clearly.
2. Place one or more very cold sand bags in the bottom of the jar.
3. Fill one or more small plastic bags with very hot water and use twisties to close the tops.
4. Suspend the plastic bags containing hot water inside the jar by taping their closed top edges to the rim of the jar.

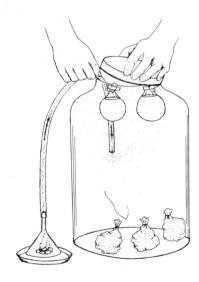

5. Attach one end of a length of plastic tubing to a funnel stem and place the free end in the jar.

6. Position the mouth of the funnel over a small container of burning incense.

7. Hold the jar top securely in place atop the jar and direct smoke from the incense through the funnel and tube and into the jar.

8. Observe the activity in the jar.

RATIONALE

Usually, air that is close to the ground is warmer than that which is found at higher altitudes. When the air is especially still, however, the cooler air, because of its greater density, settles close to the ground, and the warmer air forms a blanket above it. Pollutants in the air, such as smoke and soot, are also trapped close to the ground when this type of temperature inversion occurs. Fog, formed when moisture in the cool air condenses close to the earth's surface, becomes *smog* when combined with these pollutants.

DISCUSSION AND FOLLOW-UP

- While observing the demonstration, students should report their observations and respond to direct questions:
    - How does the temperature in the upper part of the jar compare with the temperature of air in the lower section?
    - How does this compare with the temperature you would expect to experience as you left the ground and traveled to the top of a high mountain or to a high altitude in an airplane?
    - Are there any currents of air moving in the jar or are any currents of air circulating from the jar to the air in the room?
    - Why is this called a *temperature inversion*?
    - What happens to the smoke from the incense when it enters the jar?
    - In what way would the situation be different during a natural temperature condition?
    - Why is air pollution in cities more serious during a temperature inversion?

- Students should be allowed to vary the demonstration by using other sources of smoke, such as a punk or a smoke generator. They should also be encouraged to report any personal experiences involving contact with smog and to suggest ways that the smog created by a temperature inversion is finally cleared.

- Discussion should focus on the importance of understanding how wastes produced by some technology interact with a natural phenomenon of the weather to create conditions that are harmful to plants, animals, and people.

- As a follow-up activity, students should be asked to prepare posters showing how a catastrophe due to a temperature inversion occurs and how it can be avoided.

6–8: PURIFYING DIRTY WATER
(elementary level)

INTRODUCTION

Much of the water we use was at one time unclean and unsuitable for use in drinking, bathing, cooking, washing dishes, and doing the laundry. By removing unwanted materials from water, nature routinely recycles water, making it safe for us to use. One of nature's methods can be demonstrated in the elementary classroom.

LEARNING OBJECTIVES

At the end of this demonstration lesson, students should be able to

- identify some soluble and insoluble substances that make water impure.
- name three methods by which impurities get into our water supplies.
- make a list of six substances that can be filtered out of dirty water.
- name two substances that cannot be removed from dirty water by the process of filtration.
- relate the process of filtration to both natural processes and those used in water purification systems.
- explain how the method of filtration, used in the demonstration, removed some but not all impurities from the dirty water. The explanation should make proper use of *key words:* **filtration, soluble,** and **insoluble.**

MATERIALS REQUIRED

large mayonnaise jar; spoon; jar with screw-cap top; medicine dropper; coffee filters; aquarium filter floss; food coloring; paper clips; washed sand; small clean pebbles; water; garden soil with bits of grass and leaf matter

PRESENTATION

1. Enlist the aid of a student to prepare some dirty water by adding a spoonful of garden soil and several drops of food coloring to a jar of water. Tightly screw the cap on the jar and mix the contents well by vigorously shaking it.
2. Prepare the filtration system:
   - Place a double coffee filter at the top of a clean mayonnaise jar so that the edges of the filters are turned down over the

rim of the jar. Then position the paper clips at intervals to hold the filters in this position.

- Line the filter with a layer of aquarium filter floss, then a layer of washed sand, and top it with a layer of washed pebbles.

3. Shake the dirty water mixture once more and slowly pour it into the prepared filtration system.

4. Have students watch closely and observe the appearance of the water as it passes through the filtration system and collects in the mayonnaise jar.

RATIONALE

Muddy water usually passes through layers of earth materials and is eventually stored in layers of rock called aquifers. In the process, the small water molecules pass easily through the layers of sand and pebbles, while larger particles are trapped and held back by the rocks and sand. In the demonstration filtration system, soluble materials, such as food coloring, do pass through the filter with the water. However, the system does remove particles of soil and fragments of grass and leaves and other insoluble materials from the water.

DISCUSSION AND FOLLOW-UP

- Students can become actively involved in the performance of this demonstration. There are opportunities for them to bring in soil samples, mix the dirty water, and pour the mixture through the filtration system.

- As the filtration system is being assembled, the components that are used and their placement should be discussed, with attention given also to the size difference in particles used to make the dirty water mixture. As water collects in the mayonnaise jar, it should be examined for evidence of the substances that were used to make the mixture.

- Questions concerning where the solid materials went should be encouraged, and an examination should be made of the filtration system to identify the point at which specific materials were held back. Students should recall an earlier demonstration in which it was observed that larger spaces between pebbles and successively smaller spaces between particles of sand, fibers in filter floss, and pores in a coffee filter trapped particles that were graduated from larger to smaller size. From this, students might infer the relatively small size of the particles of food coloring that were allowed to pass through all parts of the filtration system along with the molecules of water.

- Concern about whether the filtered water is safe to drink should present an opening for the introduction of a concept dealing with the removal of soluble substances from water and for providing motivation for planning another demonstration that focuses on this aspect of water purification.

- Both natural and people-made purification systems should be discussed in relation to our dependence upon recycling water for personal and industrial uses and, in the process, introducing impurities that render it unfit for reuse unless treated.

- After the discussion has been completed, students should be asked to write a report on the topic of clean water, including a diagram that shows how a filtration system operates to remove insoluble impurities.

6-9: A GREENHOUSE EFFECT
(intermediate level)

INTRODUCTION

When the sun shines on an automobile with the windows closed, the air inside the car becomes considerably warmer than the air outside. The same effect is produced in a greenhouse (where the increased temperature helps plants to grow) and in some solar heating systems. It also occurs naturally in the atmosphere, making the earth a giant greenhouse. When excess heat becomes trapped by certain pollutants in the atmosphere, the earth's ecological balance becomes seriously threatened.

LEARNING OBJECTIVES

Upon completion of this demonstration lesson, students should be able to

- identify how the cause-and-effect principle is illustrated in the demonstration.
- relate the demonstration to global conditions and predict the possible consequences of an increased warming trend.
- name two primary causes of an increased greenhouse effect on a global scale.
- explain the scientific principle applied in the demonstration, using *key words:* **greenhouse effect**, **long waves**, and **short waves**.

MATERIALS REQUIRED

dark-colored modeling clay; 2 thermometers; glass mayonnaise jar; tray

PRESENTATION

1. Construct two small mounds of clay, spaced about six inches apart, on a flat tray.
2. Support a small thermometer in an upright position in each mound of clay, taking care to keep the thermometer bulb above the level of the clay.
3. Place the tray in an area that receives direct sunlight.
4. Ask a student to take temperature readings, as shown on both thermometers.
5. When the temperature readings are at the same level on both thermom-

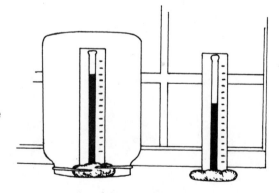

164

eters, place a mayonnaise jar over one of the mounted thermometers. Do not disturb the thermometers or their bases and be sure that both thermometers still receive direct sunlight.

6. Observe what happens to the tem-

perature readings, as indicated by the thermometers in each case.

7. After fifteen minutes have elapsed, ask a student to take another set of temperature readings and compare the two situations.

RATIONALE

Glass walls of the jar allow short waves from the sun to enter the jar and warm the air and clay base within but reflect long waves radiated by the heated clay so that these waves are reflected back to the interior. When the heat is prevented from escaping, conditions in the jar become hotter than those in the similar setup beside it on the tray. The same effect is produced in a greenhouse and in the atmosphere of the earth. When long waves cannot penetrate large amounts of carbon dioxide and water vapor in a polluted atmosphere, excess heat waves are trapped and global temperatures rise.

DISCUSSION AND FOLLOW-UP

- As the demonstration progresses, students should be encouraged to comment about observations made and to respond directly to questions:

    — Under which conditions did the thermometer record a greater rise in temperature?

    — How were short waves from the sun treated by the glass?

    — How were long waves radiated by the heated clay treated by the glass?

    — How do carbon dioxide and water vapor influence the greenhouse effect?

    — Why are ecologists concerned about an increase in pollutants in the atmosphere?

    — What effect would an increase in the greenhouse effect have on the polar ice cap and, consequently, on many of the earth's coastal areas?

    — What steps should be included in a program designed to reduce the amount of carbon dioxide and water vapor in the atmosphere?

- After the discussion has been completed, students should be asked to

    — Draw a diagram showing the greenhouse effect in action, as illustrated by an actual greenhouse or a classroom terrarium.

    — In terms of the greenhouse effect, account for the difference in temperature on Earth and on Mars.

6–10: DESALINATION OF SEA WATER
(intermediate level)

INTRODUCTION

The needs for fresh water for use in generating electricity, for industry and agriculture, and for human consumption are growing at a rapid rate. At the same time, the available supplies of fresh water on earth are decreasing. Many of the usual sources—rivers, lakes, and streams—are becoming infiltrated by sea water, and even the salt used in the salting of icy roads is finding its way into ground water and building up in water supply systems. Practical methods for removing salt from our abundant sources of sea water are being investigated as a solution to the problems posed by the shortage of fresh water.

LEARNING OBJECTIVES

At the end of this demonstration lesson, students should be able to

- identify the process of desalination of sea water as one involving a physical change.
- recognize the model demonstrated as a copy of nature's water cycle.
- develop an awareness of the ecological crisis brought about by shortages of fresh water.
- describe the method by which salt water may be converted to fresh water, using *key words:* **evaporation**, **condensation**, and **desalination**.

MATERIALS REQUIRED

large rectangular piece of Styrofoam; 2 rectangular pieces of glass; 2 triangular pieces of glass; dark enamelware rectangular baking pan; strong tape; aluminum foil; baby food jar; 2 heat lamps; X-acto® knife; salt water; toothpicks

PRESENTATION

1. Construct a working model of a solar still:

   — Set a dark enamelware rectangular baking pan on a slightly larger rectangular piece of Styrofoam. Then, using an X-acto® knife, carve a shallow channel in the surface of the Styrofoam, one-half inch beyond the perimeter of the pan. At one end, extend a small outlet from the channel to the outside edge.

   — Tape two rectangular pieces of glass to two triangular pieces of glass to form an A-frame that can be mounted on the Styrofoam rectangle.

   — Place the A-frame over the baking pan on the Styrofoam and supply the outlet with one end of a folded aluminum foil trough whose other end makes contact with a baby food jar.

2. Place sea water or a saltwater solution, made by dissolving three tablespoonfuls of salt in one quart of water, in the enamelware pan.

3. Direct a heat lamp on either side of the A-frame still.

4. Observe the activity in the still and in the trough.

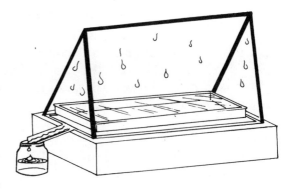

RATIONALE

The ecological crisis of diminishing supplies of fresh water on earth is being met by technology that copies nature's natural desalination as a part of the hydrological cycle. In the working model, light from the heat lamps is absorbed by the dark surface of the pan and converted to heat energy that is passed on to the water in the pan, causing it to evaporate. Upon striking the cooler surface of the glass, the water vapor condenses on the glass, trickles down the inside surface of the A-frame, and is deposited in the channel, from which it is conducted through the outlet, via the trough, to the baby food jar, where it is collected. Since only the water evaporates, salt is left behind, where, in time, it will be seen to form a salt deposit on the pan, and a quantity of fresh water accumulates in the baby food jar.

DISCUSSION AND FOLLOW-UP

- As students observe the demonstration, they should be encouraged to make comments and respond to questions:
  - What caused the water vapor to collect inside the roof of the A-frame?
  - Where did the water collected in the channel come from?
  - How can you determine if the water collected in the baby food jar is salt water or fresh water?
  - How does this demonstration resemble the hydrological cycle in nature?
  - By what more familiar name is the hydrological cycle known?
- Students should be allowed, if they wish, to taste the water collected by touching an unused toothpick first to the collected water in the baby food jar and then to the tip of the tongue.
- They should evaluate the merit of using this method of converting salt water to fresh water in areas that are close to an ocean, in a desert region, and in places where fresh water is not available. Specific places on earth

where people successfully employ desalination and/or other practical methods of obtaining fresh water from the sea should be explored.

- When the discussion has been completed, a brief report on the importance of maintaining an ecological balance between living organisms and their activities and the availability (by natural or technologically developed methods) of fresh water should be written in students' Science Demonstrations notebooks.

PART III

LIFE SCIENCE

Demonstration lessons in Life Science have their own built-in motivation for learning—most students are fascinated by the activities of organisms that live and grow and respond to external stimuli. They are also concerned with their own physical well-being and respond enthusiastically to demonstrations that involve matters of personal physical fitness.

Many demonstrations that focus on matters relating to plants, animals, humans, and health and physical fitness provide opportunities for students to apply previous learning of basic concepts to situations involving Life Science. Many are also open-ended, providing enrichment for students who become involved in the raising of pets, growing of gardens, maintaining of aquaria and/or terraria at home or in the classroom, and in activities that help them to enjoy good health and improve their personal physical fitness.

CHAPTER 7

Demonstrations Pertaining to Plants

*Suitable for teacher-only presentation.

7-1: SEEDS THAT "POP"*
(elementary level)

INTRODUCTION

Many new snack foods are developed and marketed every year. While these new products are designed to appeal to the palate, popcorn—with or without salt, butter, and sweeteners—continues to be an all-time favorite. This variety of corn was first cultivated by the American Indians, who later introduced it to the early American settlers. A demonstration showing how popcorn "pops" can be concluded with an enjoyable mid-morning or afternoon treat for all students.

LEARNING OBJECTIVES

After having participated in this demonstration lesson, students should be able to

- identify popcorn kernels as seeds of plants that are related to those that produce ordinary sweet corn.
- estimate the total increase in mass of popcorn when the kernels have been popped.
- explain the importance of moisture during the popping process, using *key words:* **kernel**, **water**, **steam**, **pressure**, **starch**, and **shell**.

MATERIALS REQUIRED

unpopped kernels of popcorn; hot plate; heatproof glass cooking vessel with handle and transparent lid; small paper cups

PRESENTATION

1. Obtain a quantity of popcorn kernels and note the very tough outer coat that covers each kernel.
2. Place the kernels in a heatproof glass cooking vessel and place the cover in position.
3. Heat the vessel on an electric hot plate.
   CAUTION: Do not allow students to come too close to the hot plate.

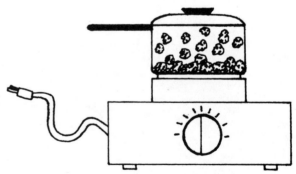

---

* Suitable for teacher-only presentation.

172

4. Shake the cooking vessel at intervals, while continuing to apply heat until the popcorn "pops."

5. Observe the appearance and the volume of popped corn.

RATIONALE

Due to its popping when heated, popcorn kernels expand to as much as 30 to 40 times their original size. The hard waterproof seed coat prevents the escape of moisture within the kernel until heat is applied. Then, as the water inside is converted to steam, pressure builds from within, causing the kernel to explode and push the stored starch out through the split kernel in the form of delicious white fluff.

DISCUSSION AND FOLLOW-UP

- As the corn kernels are heated, students will be alerted to the activity within the cooking vessel by the extremely active kernels and the sounds they make as they pop and hit against the top and sides of the container. They should be encouraged to comment on observations they make and to answer questions concerning the activity:
  - What was observed forming on the cover of the cooking vessel?
  - Where did this moisture come from?
  - What caused the kernels to pop?
  - How does popped corn differ from the unpopped kernels?
  - How does the space occupied by the popped corn compare with the amount of space it occupied before it was popped?
  - What caused this increase?
  - Where did the white fluff come from?
  - What do you think would happen if a pinhole had been made in each kernel before being placed in the cooking vessel and heated?
- After the discussion has been completed, the popcorn can be divided into small portions and distributed in individual paper cups to students to sample and enjoy.

7-2: TRANSPORT OF MATERIALS UPWARD IN STEMS*
(elementary level)

INTRODUCTION

The placement of plant stems in a strategic position between the roots and leaves enables them to perform important functions related to photosynthesis. They support leaves to receive air and sunlight, and they transport soil water obtained by roots to the food-making cells in leaves. Many physical forces are involved in the movement of water upward through stems. The effects of these forces at work and the structure of stems which makes them continuous with roots and leaves can be demonstrated.

LEARNING OBJECTIVES

After having participated in this demonstration lesson, students should be able to

- trace the pathway of water from lower to upper parts of a plant.
- identify the tubular structures that conduct fluids in plants.
- infer that the water rising in tree trunks may be explained as being due to the same forces as shown in the demonstration.
- understand the use of a colored substance as a "tracer" in scientific inquiry.
- show evidence of the ability to understand the meaning and use of *key words*: **conduction**, **transport tissue**, **xylem**, and **capillary tubes**.

MATERIALS REQUIRED

crisp celery stalk with leaves; razor blade; water; bowl; food coloring; baby food jar; medicine dropper

PRESENTATION

1. Place three drops of food coloring in a baby food jar that is one-fourth full of water.
2. Holding the bottom end of a celery stalk under water in a bowl, use a razor blade to cut across the stalk and expose fresh tissue.
3. Place the cut end of the celery stalk in the colored water in the baby food jar.

---

* Suitable for teacher-only presentation.

174

4. Allow the celery to remain in the colored water for several hours or until the next day.

5. Observe the appearance of the leaves at the upper end of the stalk.

6. With a razor blade or knife, cut across the stalk to make several pieces, each about one inch in length.

   CAUTION: Do not allow students to handle sharp instruments.

7. Distribute celery sections to student groups for observation of the cut ends.

RATIONALE

Although many physical forces interact to move water upward in a plant stem, the structure of the stem itself provides the very narrow capillary tubes that facilitate the rise of liquids. Evidence of these structures is seen in the cut sections of celery, which show the presence of colored water at higher levels than its point of entry at the cut end immersed in the liquid in the jar. Each cut end of celery sections and the veins in the leaves trace the pathway of water through distinct tubes as it rises in stems and reaches the leaves of the plant.

DISCUSSION AND FOLLOW-UP

- Students should be encouraged at the beginning of the demonstration to predict its outcome and to check out their predictions when they observe the appearance of the celery stalk and leaves.

- After the overall effects have been noted, student groups should examine and discuss the individual cut sections, with attention to questions relating to their observations and to the usefulness of methods used in the demonstration:
  - What is the appearance of the cut end of the celery section?
  - How did the colored water get into the tubes?
  - What is the value of using colored water in the demonstration?
  - What is water used for in the leaves of plants?
  - Is there evidence to indicate that colored water actually traveled from the water in the jar to the leaves?
  - Why was it necessary to wait several hours or until the next day to complete the demonstration?

- After the discussion period, students should be asked to draw a diagram showing the structure of a stem which allows liquids to rise to the leaves.

7-3: THE STRENGTH OF GERMINATING SEEDS
(elementary level)

INTRODUCTION

The tiny embryo plant wedged in a seed is left pretty much to its own devices when we plant it in the soil. It must emerge from the seed, send outgrowths through the soil for the development of root and stem systems, and push above the ground surface to unfold its leaves and make its appearance as a young seedling. To do all of this a plant must be amazingly strong. Its strength begins to build from the moment the seed is provided with conditions that favor its germination, and continues to increase as the plant grows and matures.

LEARNING OBJECTIVES

At the end of this demonstration lesson, students should be able to

- relate the effects of pressure exerted by germinating seeds to the increase in size that occurs when they imbibe water.
- recognize the relationship between the strength of germinating seeds and their success in producing new plants.
- predict what would happen to a seed sprout that could not exert enough pressure to push its way through hard, packed-down soil.
- describe how the structure of a seed contributes to the survival of a plant species, using *key words:* **imbibition, volume, pressure, stored food,** and **energy**.

MATERIALS REQUIRED

viable lima bean or pea seeds; water; small plastic food container, with lid

PRESENTATION

1. Fill a small plastic food container with viable bean or pea seeds.
2. Add water to fill the spaces between individual seeds and to bring the water level to the top of the container.
3. Snap on the plastic cover and check the container to be sure that it is closed tightly.
4. Place the container in an area where it can be viewed periodically.
5. Report observations of any changes.

RATIONALE

Water is needed to initiate the germination of the seeds. As the water is "imbibed" to activate the enzyme action that will convert the stored food to usable form by the plant embryo within the seed, each seed swells up and occupies more space. The effect of many seeds germinating in the closed container is seen in the upward pressure that is exerted, causing the cover to be pushed up and forced off the container.

DISCUSSION AND FOLLOW-UP

- Students should be encouraged to make periodic observations of the demonstration and to report signs of change, such as:
  - — swelling of the seeds.
  - — apparent disappearance of the water.
  - — increase in volume within the container.
  - — upward push of seeds that forces the lid off the container.
- Attention should focus on the advantage offered to a plant as it exerts pressure to push its way through the soil. Students should be asked to predict what would happen if the seed were planted in soil that was closely packed or if a rock or other object obstructed the pathway taken by the developing plant during its root and shoot formation.
- As a follow-up of the demonstration, students should be asked to consider the effect of pressure exerted by plants throughout their lifetimes. They should search the area near their homes and school grounds for specific examples, such as rocks that have been split, pavements that have been uplifted and cracked, and drainage pipes that have been broken by root pressure. These should be listed on the chalkboard and discussed in terms of their effects on nature and on people and their activities.

7–4: FORMATION OF A SPORE PRINT
(elementary level)

INTRODUCTION

Not all plants are green, nor do they all produce seeds. The mushroom plant, for example, lacks chlorophyll and, instead of seeds, it produces tiny spores from which new mushroom plants can be grown. A spore print, made from an edible mushroom, reveals the location, appearance, and pattern of arrangement of the spores within its cap.

LEARNING OBJECTIVES

After having participated in this demonstration lesson, students should be able to

- distinguish "green" from "nongreen" plants.
- name a common nongreen plant that is used for food.
- identify spores as reproductive cells produced by certain plants.
- relate differences in kinds of plants to differences in their structure.
- describe the basic structure of a mushroom plant, using *key words:* **cap**, **gill**, **stipe**, and **spore**.

MATERIALS REQUIRED

well-opened fresh mushroom; white paper; bowl; tray

PRESENTATION

1. Place a piece of white paper on a tray so that it forms a smooth, flat surface.
2. Remove the cap from the stipe of a well-opened mushroom.
3. Set the mushroom cap, gill surface down, on the paper.
4. Without disturbing the mushroom cap, cover it with a bowl.
5. Set the assembled tray in an area where it can remain undisturbed overnight.
6. Carefully remove the bowl and lift the mushroom cap from the paper.
7. Observe the print that has formed on the paper and identify the tiny

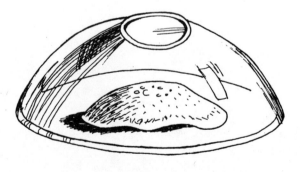

spores that outline the pattern of gill arrangement on the underside of the cap.

RATIONALE

There are important differences between the familiar green plants and fungi such as mushrooms. Mostly, the mushroom plant grows underground, where its food requirements are supplied by humus in the soil. However, to release its spores for use in reproduction, the mature plant must send a fruiting body above the ground level. Here, as the cap matures, spores are developed and eventually released when gills on the underside of the cap open and make possible their escape. The print made by released spores from a single cap reveals the pattern of the gill arrangement and gives a good indication of the extremes of size and number of spores produced.

DISCUSSION AND FOLLOW-UP

- Students should be encouraged to report observances of mushroom caps that appear to pop up in a lawn or meadow and to associate their rather sudden appearance with conditions that favor their growth and method of reproduction.

- The spore print developed should be examined and discussed, with attention to specific features:
    - What is the general pattern of the spore print?
    - What was released by the cap to form the print?
    - How were the spores released?
    - What is the function of a spore?
    - What can you determine about the size of a spore?
    - What can you determine about the number of spores produced?
    - Why does the mushroom plant send its cap above ground level?

- The spore as a reproductive structure should be compared with the seed of other plants, with differences in structure and formation as well as similarities in function noted.

- After the spore print has been examined and discussed, students should be asked to draw a labeled diagram of the undersurface of a mushroom cap, based on the pattern revealed by the spore print.

7–5:   THE ACTIVITY OF YEAST CELLS
(elementary level)

INTRODUCTION

From ancient times people have made use of some very simple organisms called yeasts. Early peoples depended upon collecting yeasts from wild grapes and other fruits to supply themselves with agents that would make bread dough rise and convert grape juice to wine. Although we have more convenient sources and know more about the processes by which these activities occur, the uses of yeasts today are still basically due to the products they produce during their cellular respiration—carbon dioxide bubbles, which cause bread dough to rise, and alcohol, which is an essential ingredient in wine.

LEARNING OBJECTIVES

At the end of this demonstration lesson, students should be able to

- identify yeast cells as living organisms that engage in basic life processes.
- name the products that are formed when yeasts engage in cellular respiration.
- name the carbohydrate used by yeasts for their nutrition.
- name two important industries whose products are formed as a result of the activity of yeasts.
- explain the activity involved in the demonstration, using *key words:* **fermentation**, **respiration**, **sugar**, **carbon dioxide**, and **alcohol**.

MATERIALS REQUIRED

dry yeast; water; peanut butter jar; table sugar; spoon; rubber band; plastic wrap or plastic sandwich bag

PRESENTATION

1. Pour slightly warm water into a peanut butter jar until it is about halfway filled with water.

2. Add one tablespoonful of sugar to the water and stir the mixture until the sugar becomes dissolved.

3. Crush the dried yeast grains and add them to the sugar-water mixture.

4. Cover the jar with a plastic sandwich bag or a piece of plastic wrap.

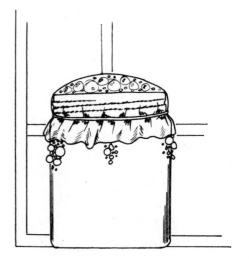

5. Turn the edges of the plastic down and place a rubber band around it where it covers the rim of the jar.

6. Place the jar close to a bright light or on a warm radiator or windowsill.

RATIONALE

Yeast cells become activated when they are provided with conditions of suitable food, oxygen, temperature, and moisture. In the process, they secrete enzymes that break down sugar to carbon dioxide and ethyl alcohol, utilizing only the energy released from the molecules to engage in their growth and reproduction. The effects of one of the breakdown products, however, can be observed in the demonstration—carbon dioxide bubbles rise to the top of the jar, carrying a frothy sugar water-yeast mixture with them as they spill over the sides of the overflowing jar. In a similar manner, bubbles of carbon dioxide cause bread dough to expand and rise, making the bread light and fluffy. Alcohol, the second breakdown product, evaporates and is driven off in the baking process.

DISCUSSION AND FOLLOW-UP

- Students should observe the demonstration closely and make note of
  - the conditions that were provided to activate the yeasts.
  - the formation of gas bubbles that cause the yeast-sugar water mixture to expand and rise to the top of the jar.
- Similar conditions provided for the making of bread should be reported, with an explanation of the chemical action that is responsible for breaking sugar molecules into smaller molecules and for the release of energy when the chemical bonds are broken.
- Students should be encouraged to report any personal experiences they have had for observing the baking of bread and/or the making of wine and to comment on the processes involved as well as the materials used and the products produced.
- After making close observations and participating in the discussion, students should be asked to draw a diagram representing the activity of yeasts and the products produced as a result of the activity. Then, as a follow-up activity, they should be encouraged to bake some bread at home and report to the class about how this home activity relates to the demonstration.

7–6: HOW PLANTS OBTAIN WATER FOR LIFE PROCESSES
(intermediate level)

INTRODUCTION

Plant parts may be equipped to perform more than one function. For example, in addition to anchoring a plant in the soil, a root system is specialized for obtaining water, which is necessary for the plant to engage in its various life activities. The effectiveness of thin membranes, which allow water molecules to pass from one side to the other, illustrates the special fitness of plant roots to obtain water from the soil.

LEARNING OBJECTIVES

After completing this demonstration lesson, students should be able to

- identify the structure/function relationship between plant parts and the work they do.
- develop an awareness of different concentration levels of water molecules and of the effect these differences have on the amount of pressure exerted on a membrane.
- relate a simulation to an actual situation in a plant.
- gain some insight into the uses of thin membranes in living tissues.
- practice, with understanding, the watering of soil around the root systems of plants.
- describe the activity observed in the demonstration, using *key words:* **membrane**, **concentration**, and **pressure**.

MATERIALS REQUIRED

peanut butter jar; water; small plastic sandwich bag; heavy syrup; thread or twistie

PRESENTATION

1. Partially fill a plastic sandwich bag with a very concentrated sugar solution, such as a heavy syrup, and twist the open end closely around the content.
2. Tie a thread around the tightly twisted section of the plastic sandwich bag and check to be certain that the closure is tight and completely leak-proof.

3. Immerse the bag in a jar containing tap water and again check for leaks.

4. Note the appearance and approximate volume of the material in the bag.

5. Allow the demonstration to remain undisturbed for several hours or until there is a noticeable difference in the appearance and an increase in the volume of the bag.

6. Examine the distended bag and the water in the jar.

RATIONALE

The content of the plastic sandwich bag increases when water molecules pass from the jar, through pores in the membrane, and into the "plant root." This is due to the greater pressure built up by water molecules in the jar, where they are at a concentration of 100 percent, than by water molecules in the plastic bag, where sugar molecules are present also. The greater pressure exerted by the water molecules on the membrane causes more water molecules to leave the area of their greater concentration and to locate on the other side of the membrane. It represents an attempt to equalize the pressure on both sides of the membrane and results in the intake of water by plant roots.

DISCUSSION AND FOLLOW-UP

- Students should observe the demonstration closely and report any changes noticed in the size and shape of the plastic bag. Discussion of the demonstration should focus on specific guide points:

  — a comparison of the concentration levels of water molecules on either side of the membrane-walled bag

  — the relative pressure exerted by water molecules at different concentration levels inside and outside the bag

  — the structures, materials, and activity in an actual plant root that are represented by the materials and activity involved in the demonstration

- After all key factors involved in the demonstration and its application to the intake of water by plant roots have been reviewed, students should be asked to reinforce their understanding of the important scientific concept relating to the passage of water molecules through a membrane by writing a report about the demonstration in their Science Demonstrations notebooks.

7–7: PRODUCTION OF OXYGEN BY GREEN PLANTS
(intermediate level)

INTRODUCTION

Green plants are unique among living things in that they are capable of engaging in the process of photosynthesis. By this process they produce basic food for themselves as well as for the human and animal forms of life that are present. Simultaneously they replenish the oxygen supply in the environment, where it becomes available to all living things for use in their respiration. The survival of life as we know it depends upon the production of oxygen by both aquatic and terrestrial species of green plants.

LEARNING OBJECTIVES

At the end of this demonstration lesson, students should be able to

- understand the importance of green plants to animals and people.
- relate the demonstration to the energy cycle.
- make inferences that involve the role of green plants that live on land as well as those that live in water.
- make predictions concerning the effects to be expected if conditions in the demonstration were to be altered.
- show evidence of an understanding of the meaning and proper use of *key words:* **photosynthesis**, **light energy**, **oxygen**, and **respiration**.

MATERIALS REQUIRED

sprigs of fresh elodea; glass rod or wooden applicator stick; thread; baking soda; aquarium water; mayonnaise jar; tablespoon

PRESENTATION

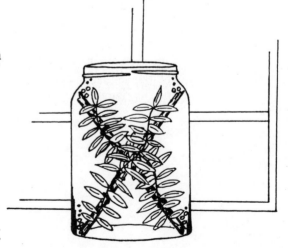

1. Fill a mayonnaise jar with aquarium water that has been boiled and allowed to cool to room temperature.
2. Add one tablespoonful of baking soda to the water in the jar and stir slowly until all of the material is dissolved.
3. Cut the ends of two to three sprigs of fresh elodea and, using soft thread, tie the sprigs loosely to a glass rod or wooden applicator stick.

4. Place the supported elodea sprigs upright in the jar, with all plant parts completely covered with the solution.

5. Place the jar in an area that provides bright sunlight or under a bright artificial light source.

6. Observe the activity in the jar.

RATIONALE

Small bubbles of gas can be seen rising in the water from the cut ends of the elodea sprigs. This is gaseous oxygen, the byproduct of photosynthesis, which becomes dissolved in the water. Here it may be obtained easily by fish and other forms of aquatic life for use in their respiration. Oxygen gas that is not utilized by the water dwellers rises to the surface and escapes, replenishing the supply of oxygen in the atmosphere for use by organisms that breathe air.

DISCUSSION AND FOLLOW-UP

- While the demonstration is in progress, students should focus attention on the activity in the jar. They should be encouraged to report observations made and to respond to related questions:
  - What can be seen coming from the elodea stems?
  - What kind of bubbles are they?
  - What is the name of the process by which the oxygen bubbles are produced?
  - Does it indicate that a physical or a chemical change is taking place?
  - Why is light needed?
  - What would happen if the jar were removed from the area of bright light?
  - What was the purpose of boiling the aquarium water?
  - Why was baking soda added to the boiled and cooled aquarium water?
  - Why is elodea used in fish aquaria?
- After the discussion, students should be asked to write a report in which they tell how the demonstration helps to explain the importance of oxygen production by green plants to the survival of life on earth.

7–8: PRODUCTION OF HEAT BY GERMINATING SEEDS
(intermediate level)

INTRODUCTION

The heat that is produced when food is oxidized by living cells can be detected in many instances—in heat waves rising from organic matter that is being decomposed by bacteria, in the warmth of a breath that is being exhaled, and in the steady body temperature that is maintained by birds and mammals. Plant embryos also produce heat when they use the stored food in their seeds for growth and development. This can be demonstrated and measured when sprouting seeds are placed in a closed container.

LEARNING OBJECTIVES

After having completed this demonstration lesson, students should be able to

- associate the oxidation of food with the release of energy for life processes.
- identify the interaction of food and oxygen with the process of respiration.
- predict the relative success of seeds planted in loose soil and in packed-down soil.
- identify the oxidative process as one involving a chemical change.
- describe the events in the demonstration, using *key words:* **oxidation, cell respiration, energy,** and **heat.**

MATERIALS REQUIRED

viable pea seeds; vacuum bottle with one-hole stopper to fit; long thermometer; absorbent cotton; jar; water

PRESENTATION

1. Place a handful of viable pea seeds in a jar and fill the remaining space in the jar with water.
2. Allow the seeds to soak in water overnight.
3. Transfer the soaked seeds to layers of wet absorbent cotton arranged in "rag-doll" fashion, and maintain the wet rolls until sprouts can be seen emerging from the seeds.
4. Place a layer of wet absorbent cotton in the bottom of a vacuum bottle.

5. Carefully arrange sprouting seeds on top of the cotton, filling the vacuum bottle almost all the way.

6. Insert the thermometer through the hole in the rubber stopper and adjust its length so that it will reach down into the sprouting seeds.

7. Place the stopper in the mouth of the vacuum bottle and check all connections to be sure that there are no leaks and that all parts fit tightly.

8. Ask a student to take a beginning temperature reading and record it on the chalkboard.

9. Take additional temperature readings and note any changes in temperature during a 24-hour period.

RATIONALE

The young plant embryos engaged in respiration, combining oxygen with stored food in the seed and making available both the material and energy needed for the pea plants' growth. In the process heat was generated also, which, trapped in the container, was detected and recorded by the thermometer. While some heat generated by the oxidative process during cell respiration is useful in maintaining the body temperature of some organisms such as birds and mammals, much of the heat generated normally escapes into the surroundings.

DISCUSSION AND FOLLOW-UP

- Students should be allowed to examine the sprouting seeds and to discuss how a seed produces a new plant.

- Individual students can be selected to take temperature readings at intervals during the day, plus a next-day reading, if necessary.

- When a temperature rise is noted, discussion should focus on the nature and importance of the life process involved in the demonstration:
  - What happened to the temperature in the vacuum bottle?
  - What was the source of the heat produced?
  - Does this indicate the involvement of a physical or a chemical change taking place in sprouting seeds?
  - What would happen to the heat generated by the sprouting seeds if the container had not been closed?

- Students can then be asked to test an exhaled breath against a hand to detect its warmth. They should discuss this as an extension of the demonstration, noting evidence of the generation of heat by respiration of cells within their own bodies and of the release of unused heat energy by an organism.

- When the discussion has been completed, students should be asked to write a report of the demonstration, including the source, nature, and importance of energy released when living things engage in the process of respiration.

7–9: PLANT LEAF PIGMENTS*
(intermediate level)

INTRODUCTION

The color of plant leaves is due to the presence of color pigments which, acting together, produce the distinctive color we generally associate with different kinds of plants such as grass, spinach, lettuce, cabbage, and geranium. The specific color pigments present in any one kind of leaf can be determined by a scientific method of separation known as chromatographic analysis.

LEARNING OBJECTIVES

At the end of this demonstration lesson, students should be able to

- identify the chlorophyll pigments present in a specific green leaf that make up its shade of the color "green."
- understand the scientific principle involved in the chromatographic process.
- name other color substances that might be analyzed by using this method of separation.
- understand the precautionary measures to be taken when using a strong solvent.
- describe the demonstrated technique for separating components in a mixture, using *key words:* **chromatogram**, **chlorophyll**, **solvent**, and **solute**.

MATERIALS REQUIRED

fresh leaf from a geranium plant; alcohol; coin; jar; white absorbent toweling; pencil; tape; scissors

PRESENTATION

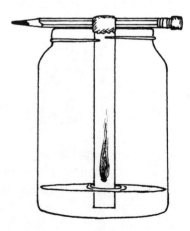

1. Cut a strip of paper, about three fourths of an inch wide, from a sheet of white paper toweling.
2. Remove a leaf from a geranium plant and lay it across one end of the paper strip.
3. Make a mark of leaf color on the paper strip by rubbing the edge of a coin against the leaf so that color rubbed off the leaf forms a narrow

---

* Suitable for teacher-only presentation.

streak across the paper strip, about one inch from the end. Repeat the process, using additional sections of the leaf to darken the streak on the paper.

4. Roll the opposite end of the paper strip around a pencil and, after adjusting its length so that it will hang freely when the pencil is placed across the top of the jar, tape the paper strip to the pencil.

5. Carefully place alcohol to a depth of one-half inch in the jar.

   NOTE: Caution must be exercised to prevent alcohol from spilling or from coming in close contact with students.

6. Set the pencil atop the jar so that the end of the paper strip is in contact with the alcohol in the jar and the ridge of green leaf material is held above the alcohol level.

7. Observe the activity for about ten minutes or until there is evidence that "color" has risen about two-thirds of the way up the strip.

8. Remove the strip from the jar and allow it to dry.

9. Examine the chromatogram.

RATIONALE

Alcohol can be observed as it travels upward along the paper strip, picking up and carrying with it materials comprising the ridge of transferred leaf pigment. Bands of different shades of green and yellow are then formed as molecules in the mixture are separated and deposited according to their molecular weight and degree of solubility in alcohol. The solvent carries molecules of small molecular weight to a higher level on the paper before depositing them in a visible color band at a distance beyond a different color band made up of molecules of a greater molecular weight.

DISCUSSION AND FOLLOW-UP

- As students observe the demonstration they may be reminded of the activity of a river in which rocks, stones, and sand particles are picked up, carried a distance, and deposited at different locations by water traveling the length of the river.

- The value of the chromatographic technique as a scientific tool as well as the specific knowledge gained about the geranium leaf pigments should be discussed:

  — How many different pigments were separated from the leaf streak made by the geranium leaf?

  — Why was alcohol used in the jar?

  — Which color band reached the highest level on the chromatogram?

  — What does this tell you about the weight of the molecules making up this pigment?

  — What is the color of the band that is located at the lowest level of this chromatogram?

— What does this tell you about the weight of the molecules making up this pigment?

— What is the name of the green pigment found in leaves?

— What other leaves or plant parts could be used in a similar demonstration?

• Asking students to recall incidents in which water proved to be ineffective for removing grass stains from white sneakers will help them to develop the concept of the use of other solvents such as alcohol and dry cleaning fluids.

• After discussing the demonstration and its applications, students should be asked to write a short report in their Science Demonstrations notebooks. A labeled diagram of the chromatogram developed should be included.

7–10: THE AUTOBIOGRAPHY OF A TREE
(intermediate level)

INTRODUCTION

Trees, which are among the oldest living things on earth, have much information recorded in their annual growth rings. An examination of the cut end of the trunk of a tree that has been cut down reveals an autobiographical account of many of the tree's experiences due to climate and weather conditions, and the number of rings that can be counted in this cross cut tells us the number of years the tree has lived.

LEARNING OBJECTIVES

At the end of this demonstration lesson, students should be able to

- identify the tissues that make up an annual growth ring.
- understand how physical factors and environmental conditions affect the uniformity and thickness of a growth ring formation.
- determine the age of a woody twig or tree trunk specimen.
- associate the presence of growth rings with woody tissue in perennial plants.
- show evidence of an understanding of the manner in which growth rings are formed in a woody plant, using *key words:* **annual ring**, **xylem tissue**, **heartwood**, and **sapwood**.

MATERIALS REQUIRED

cross-sectional cut from a tree trunk or woody branch showing several years' growth

PRESENTATION

1. Obtain a cross section of a tree trunk or of a branch of considerable size and age.
2. Examine the cut end surface and note the appearance of concentric rings.
3. Distinguish the light and dark bands that alternate in concentric ringlike formation.
4. Identify a light ring followed by a dark ring at its outer edge as comprising one year's growth.
5. Count the number of annual rings.

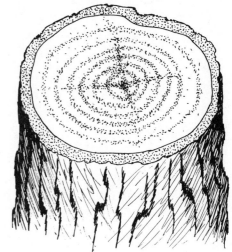

6. Note any irregularities in the width of the rings.

191

RATIONALE

As trees grow taller they also increase their diameter, adding a new ring of growth to the outer edge of their circumference each year. Each summer, xylem cells form a dark-colored band of small cells adjacent to the lighter colored band of larger cells grown the previous spring. Together these two bands constitute an annual ring whose width is influenced by conditions of temperature, sunlight, rainfall, space, and minerals in the soil. The alternating light and dark rings counted on the cut end of a tree trunk provide a fairly accurate record of the age of the tree when it was cut.

DISCUSSION AND FOLLOW-UP

- As students observe the specimen being demonstrated, their attention should be drawn to the manner in which it was formed and the information that it reveals. This can be guided by posing pertinent questions:
    - How many years old was the tree when its trunk was cut?
    - Why does it take two growth bands to make one annual ring?
    - How can early spring growth be distinguished from the later growth of summer?
    - Is the older wood located closer to the center or to the outside edge?
    - Is there any growth band that is unusually narrow?
    - What could account for an unusually narrow growth band?
    - How does this method of studying a tree's age and growth pattern reveal information about rainfall and weather patterns during any given year or period of time?
- When all discussion relating to the tree trunk specimen has been completed, students should be asked to draw a diagram of a ten-year-old tree trunk that experienced poor growing conditions during the third year of its life. The year that each of the growth rings was formed should be indicated on the diagram, assuming that the tree was cut down during the current year.

7–11: TRANSPIRATION IN PLANTS
(intermediate level)

INTRODUCTION

Not all of the water taken into a plant root system is used by the plant in performing its life functions. Some plants, such as the cactus, are especially well equipped to store excess water as a reserve for use during a period of drought. Most plants, however, allow excess water absorbed by roots to evaporate from surfaces that are exposed to the atmosphere. When too much water escapes from a plant by this process, the plant begins to wilt.

LEARNING OBJECTIVES

After students have completed this demonstration lesson, they should be able to

- account for the periodic accumulation of moisture on the inside of the top of a terrarium.
- identify the role of transpiration in one of nature's systems for water purification.
- predict what would happen if the release of moisture by leaves were to occur at a more rapid rate than the uptake of water by the roots of a plant.
- recognize the elements of the scientific process incorporated in the demonstration.
- describe the events occurring in the demonstration, using *key words:* **transpiration**, **leaf pores**, **evaporation**, and **wilting**.

MATERIALS REQUIRED

potted leafy geranium plant; large plastic garment bag; sheet of plastic or cellophane; string or twistie; tape

PRESENTATION

1. Water a potted geranium plant thoroughly and allow it to stand until the soil is saturated but no water continues to drip through the drainage hole in the bottom of the flower pot.
2. Set the flower pot in the center of a sheet of plastic or cellophane.
3. Draw the plastic up around the stem of the plant so that all surfaces of the pot and the soil are completely covered.

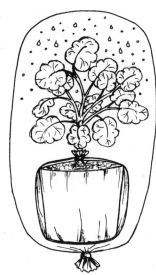

4. After checking to be sure that no part of the flower pot or soil is exposed, tie the plastic around the stem of the plant.

5. Cover the entire plant, including the covered flower pot, with a large plastic garment bag obtained from a dry cleaner's store. Tape shut all openings of the bag.

6. Set the covered plant in a sunny location.

7. Make observations of the activity inside the plastic bag.

RATIONALE

Water is conducted upward through conducting tissues from plant roots to stems and leaves, where moisture in excess of that needed for the plant to perform its life functions is allowed to escape through pores called stomata. Although some energy is expended by the plant to perform this activity, the plant derives some important benefits. Minerals present in small amounts in the soil water are accumulated for plant use when only water evaporates, leaving the minerals behind.

DISCUSSION AND FOLLOW-UP

- Discussion should focus on the demonstration design and on observations made as it progresses. Questions to be asked of students include:
    - What is observed forming on the inside of the plastic bag?
    - Where did the moisture come from?
    - What was the purpose of wrapping the flower pot and covering the surface of the soil with cellophane?
    - How does the water that escapes through the leaves compare with the water taken in through the root system of the well-watered geranium plant?
    - Can you predict what will happen to the leaves of the plant when the entire supply of soil water has been used?
    - What adjustments in the demonstration would be necessary to prevent this from happening?
    - How do plants contribute to the humid conditions that are present in a greenhouse?
- As a follow-up, students should be asked to consider some practical applications of the plant's ability to transpire water by investigating the role that plants play in nature's hydrological cycle.

7-12: A PLANT THAT EATS ANIMALS*
(elementary level)

INTRODUCTION

When plants are eaten by animals, we accept it as a normal event that follows the natural order of things. But when animals are eaten by plants, we consider the chain of events to be unusual. There are a few species of plants whose modified leaf structure enables them to eat insects, thus adding to their diet of carbohydrate food that they manufacture by the process of photosynthesis. Among the commonly known insectivorous plants are the sundew, the Venus' flytrap, and the pitcher plant.

LEARNING OBJECTIVES

At the end of this demonstration lesson, students should be able to

- identify an unusual form of plant life.
- understand the important structure/function relationship illustrated by the insectivorous plants.
- recognize an adaptation that enables a plant species to grow in soil that lacks an essential mineral.
- analyze the effectiveness of digestive enzymes on different parts of food taken in by an organism.
- trace a food chain that does not follow the usual pattern.
- describe the food habits of the pitcher plant, using *key words:* **insectivorous, enzymes, nitrates, protein,** and **digestion**.

MATERIALS REQUIRED

a healthy pitcher plant with mature "pitchers"; razor blade; shallow dish; magnifying lens; forceps

PRESENTATION

1. Obtain a healthy pitcher plant with mature pitcherlike leaves.
2. Examine the shape and structure of the leaves.
3. Hold a shallow dish at the base of an older pitcher and use a razor blade to cut across the base and separate the pitcher from the rest of the plant.

NOTE: Do not allow students to handle sharp razor blades.

*Suitable for teacher-only presentation.

4. Allow the material that is freed from the pitcher to collect in the dish.

5. Make a vertical slit in the tubular leaf to free any of its remaining content.

6. Use a magnifying lens to locate any undigested remains of insects among the collected materials in the dish.

7. Use a fine forceps to sort out insect heads and/or other identifiable insect parts.

RATIONALE

Pitcher plants have leaves that are uniquely adapted for capturing and digesting insects. They are modified in the shape of deep tubular pitchers that collect and store rain water, and have an inner surface covered with hairlike projections that point downward and prevent curious insects from escaping. Consequently, insects that are attracted to the color and odor of the leaf fall into the liquid, where they are digested by enzymes secreted by specialized leaf cells near the base. Heads and shells, which are undigested, collect in the bottom of the pitcher, where they can be sorted out and identified. The insect bodies contribute to the nutrition of the pitcher plant by supplying protein needed for their growth. In this way, insectivorous plants are able to grow successfully in bog areas where mineral-poor soil is especially lacking in nitrogen.

DISCUSSION AND FOLLOW-UP

- Pitcher plants can be maintained in a bog-type terrarium where students can "feed the plants" by introducing fruit flies and other small insects to the environment.

- Discussion based on their observations made concerning the feeding habits of pitcher plants and the examination of the contents of an opened pitcher can help students to develop some important concepts and derive answers to pertinent questions:
    — What kind of food is manufactured by all green plants?
    — What kind of food is needed for the growth and development of all organisms?
    — What is the source of the pitcher plant's protein?
    — Could a pitcher plant live without insects?
    — How would a lack of insects in the diet affect a pitcher plant?
    — How are pitcher plants adapted to live in mineral-poor soil?
    — How might this explain their presence in a bog area where very few plants with traditional leaves are found growing?

- Students should then be asked to research other forms of insectivorous plants and to report their findings to the class for discussion and sharing of information.

CHAPTER 8

Demonstrations Pertaining to Animals

* Suitable for teacher-only presentation.

8-1: PULLING POWER OF A SNAIL
(intermediate level)

INTRODUCTION

Animals exhibit amazing powers of strength and endurance. People have long used animals such as oxen and work horses as beasts of burden, and they have used horses and dogs to pull chariots, wagon trains, and sleds. Examples of great pulling power can also be observed among the lower animals: a snail carries a heavy shell on its back and an ant can carry a large-sized leaf to its burrow. While the pulling power of higher animals is more useful to man, demonstrations involving the lower forms are more practical for use in the classroom.

LEARNING OBJECTIVES

At the end of this demonstration lesson, students should be able to

- associate the pulling power of animals to the strength of their muscles.
- recognize the physical forces to be overcome when moving an object.
- compare the weight of an animal with the weight of the load it can pull.
- describe the pulling power of the organism demonstrated, using *key words:* **strength, muscle activity, friction, inertia,** and **pulling power**.

MATERIALS REQUIRED

a healthy garden snail; piece of glass windowpane; thin wire; stack of books; water; toy truck whose size and weight are several times as great as those of the snail

PRESENTATION

1. Build a stack of two or three books on a table top where it can be viewed clearly by all students.

2. Moisten the surface of a glass windowpane and position it at a 30-degree angle with the table top to make a ramp to the top of the stack of books.

3. Note the difference in size of the snail and the toy truck and ask a student to estimate their comparative weights as well.

4. Place a halter of thin wire around the shell of the snail and attach the other end of the wire loop to the toy truck.

5. Place the snail on the surface of the glass, facing in an up-slope direction and with the load to be pulled trailing behind it.

6. Observe the snail and its progress.

RATIONALE

The smooth, gliding motion of the snail is accomplished by rhythmic waves of muscle contractions in the foot as it moves on a layer of mucus secreted by a gland at the front of the foot. Because of the snail's natural tendency to move away from the earth, it moves up the slope, pulling the toy truck behind it. Although the motion is slow, the inertia, once overcome, keeps the wheels of the truck moving over the almost frictionless surface.

DISCUSSION AND FOLLOW-UP

- As the demonstration is being set up students should be encouraged to predict whether or not the snail will be able to pull the toy truck up the slope.
- As they observe the demonstration they should respond to questions:
  - In what direction does the snail move?
  - How does this compare with snails observed as they move along the side walls of an aquarium?
  - Why was the surface of the glass moistened?
  - Did the truck move more easily when it first started or after it had been set in motion?
  - What structures of the snail provided strength and energy to move and pull the load?
  - How might this ability be useful to a snail?
- Students should be encouraged to comment on observations they have made involving other animals and the size and weight of objects or loads they have pulled.
- As a follow-up, students should be asked to consider some data collected, indicating that some beetles can pull a load more than forty times their body weight. Then, assuming the same rate for humans, they should be asked to calculate their own pulling power, based on individual student weights.

8–2:   DETECTING UPTAKE OF OXYGEN IN RESPIRATION
(intermediate level)

INTRODUCTION

All living organisms engage in the process of respiration. This includes all stages in the life of a plant, an animal, or a human. Although it is difficult to observe directly the intake of oxygen being used by a small animal or a tiny embryo plant as it respires within a germinating seed, evidence of oxygen uptake from the environment by small organisms can be demonstrated with the use of a common substance.

LEARNING OBJECTIVES

After having completed this demonstration lesson, students should be able to

- identify a life process that is common to all living things.
- apply an indirect method of obtaining scientific information.
- analyze a chemical reaction that is reversible.
- understand the use of a chemical indicator.
- describe the demonstration and explain the activity observed, using *key words:* **biochemical reaction**, **reversible reaction**, **respiration**, and **aerobic**.

MATERIALS REQUIRED

living ant lion larvae or doodlebugs; methylene blue aquarium treatment solution; thread or string; water; gauze pad; jar with screw-cap top

PRESENTATION

1. Place two to three drops of methylene blue solution in a jar that is two-thirds full of water.

2. Place ten to twelve doodlebugs in the center of a gauze pad that has been fully opened.

3. Arrange the gauze to form a basketful of doodlebugs in the mouth of the jar: drape the outside edges of the gauze over the rim of the jar and hold the basket in place—suspended above the level of the liquid—with a string tied around the gauze where it overlaps the rim of the jar.

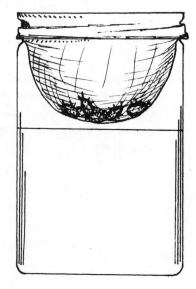

4. Check to be certain that the basket holding the doodlebugs is above the level of the liquid in the jar and carefully place the lid on the jar.

5. Place the jar on a table top where all students can view it clearly as they observe the color of the methylene blue in the jar.

RATIONALE

Release of energy from food by organisms occurs by the process of cellular respiration. It involves primarily the removal of hydrogen, which is normally accepted by oxygen to form water. In the absence of oxygen, organisms will die quickly unless an alternate substance such as methylene blue—a source of free oxygen and a temporary acceptor of hydrogen—is present. The fading of a methylene blue solution when the colorless methylene blue-hydrogen complex is formed makes methylene blue a good indicator that respiration is occurring in organisms whose breathing mechanism would be too difficult to observe directly.

DISCUSSION AND FOLLOW-UP

- The use of methylene blue as an indicator, as well as a remedy for fungal disease in aquaria fish, should be developed, with attention to basic ideas:
  - the chemical reactions that are involved in respiration
  - the use of chemical indicators in scientific study
- Other common indicators such as iodine and cabbage juice should be discussed and their specific use in scientific investigations reviewed.
- After the fading of the methylene blue in the demonstration jar has been observed, the demonstration setup can be dismantled and the doodlebugs returned to their habitat in the classroom.
- Attention should then focus on the jar containing the faded methylene blue solution. Reasons for its loss of color, except at the surface, should be discussed and related to the doodlebug respiration. Then a student can be asked to shake the contents of the jar gently, while others note the change in its appearance and discuss the restoration of its characteristic blue color when oxygen was introduced by shaking. This may be used to develop the concept of reversible chemical reactions and the use of methylene blue as a chemical indicator.
- After the discussion has been completed, students should be asked to write a report about the demonstration in which they explain how chemical indicators can be helpful in revealing information about some biological processes.

8–3: AN INSECT THAT TELLS THE TEMPERATURE
(intermediate level)

INTRODUCTION

Many animals appear to be more active and more numerous in warm weather than in cold. This is particularly noticeable among animals that hibernate in winter and among the great hordes of insects that buzz about in summer and virtually disappear completely with the coming of cold weather. The sensitivity to change in the temperature of the surroundings is most easily demonstrated with tree crickets, whose rate of chirping can be used to calculate the temperature.

LEARNING OBJECTIVES

At the end of this demonstration lesson, students should be able to

- calculate the temperature based on data collected.
- recognize the dependence of some animals on the environment to supply the temperature requirements for their chemical reactions and activities.
- understand the narrow range of temperature that is favorable for life on earth.
- explain why insects are more active in summer than in winter, using *key words:* **temperature**, **enzymes**, **chemical reactions**, and **life activities**.

MATERIALS REQUIRED

live crickets; shoe box; clock or watch with a sweep second hand; Fahrenheit scale thermometer; Celsius scale thermometer (optional)

PRESENTATION

1. Place an active cricket and a Fahrenheit scale thermometer in a shoe box in a quiet room.
2. Listen for the chirping sounds of the cricket to begin.
3. Count the number of chirps in a period of 15 seconds.
4. Calculate the temperature according to the formula:

$$\text{temperature in degrees Fahrenheit} = \text{number of chirps in 15 seconds} + 39$$

5. Take a temperature reading inside the box.

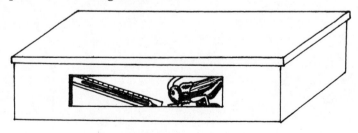

RATIONALE

The life processes of some organisms are strongly affected by the temperature of the surroundings. This is true of all animals that do not maintain a steady body temperature; they must depend upon the temperature of the surroundings to provide a favorable temperature for their enzymes to engage in the chemical reactions that are necessary for their life processes. There is a close relationship between temperature and the physiological activity resulting in the chirping sounds made by crickets. Quite interestingly, the temperature in degrees Fahrenheit can be calculated with reasonable accuracy by adding 39 to the number of chirps counted in a period of 15 seconds.

DISCUSSION AND FOLLOW-UP

- There are opportunities for students to be active participants in this demonstration lesson. Individuals should be asked to bring in crickets they have collected, to time the 15-second time period, and to take a temperature reading. All students, of course, should count the number of chirps and calculate the temperature (in degrees Fahrenheit) from the collected data.

- Discussion should focus on several key points and be guided by direct questions:

  — How did the temperature calculated compare with the actual temperature reading on the thermometer in the shoe box?

  — What do you predict would happen if the temperature in the box were changed?

  — How does this compare with actual experiences of what happens to the occurrence of cricket chirping sounds as the weather gets colder at the end of summer?

  — Why is temperature a critical factor for life processes?

  — How is your body equipped to permit life processes to occur in winter as well as in summer?

- Students should then be allowed to observe the cricket directly as it chirps and relate the energy needed for moving the scraper of one wing against the file of the other to chemical reactions occurring within its body structure.

- As an option, another dimension can be added to the demonstration. By placing a Celsius scale thermometer in the shoe box with the cricket, the temperature calculated—by adding four to the number of chirps counted in a period of eight seconds—can be matched with the temperature reading in degrees on the Celsius scale thermometer. A comparison of two different temperature scales for the same temperature condition in the box can then be made for the development of a better understanding of the relationship between Fahrenheit and Celsius scale thermometers.

- As a follow-up, students should be encouraged to repeat the procedure for calculating the temperature based on the number of chirps counted on some evening during an appropriate season. They should record their findings in their Science Demonstrations notebooks, for reference when reporting to the class on the accuracy of the results.

8-4: CRUSTACEAN RESPONSE TO MOISTURE
(elementary level)

INTRODUCTION

A colony of sow bugs scurrying from beneath a rock or a log that has been disturbed quite suddenly is a familiar sight. These terrestrial crustaceans are related to both aquatic and marine forms such as crayfish, crabs, lobsters, shrimps, and water fleas—all of which are completely adapted for life in a watery environment. Sow bugs and pill bugs may be collected easily and raised in the classroom, where their activities can then be observed.

LEARNING OBJECTIVES

At the end of this demonstration lesson, students should be able to

- identify the breathing organs of crustaceans.
- name two terrestrial crustaceans.
- name two aquatic crustaceans.
- name two marine crustaceans.
- infer that animals survive in many situations because they instinctively make the "right" choice.
- explain how the sow bugs' instinctive preference of a damp location to a dry one helps them to survive, using *key words:* **terrestrial**, **gills**, **moisture**, and **oxygen**.

MATERIALS NEEDED

absorbent paper toweling; 8 to 10 live sow bugs or pill bugs; water; transparent bowl; spray bottle; tray; scissors

PRESENTATION

1. Cut some absorbent paper toweling to form two rectangular pieces of equal size.
2. Place one piece of toweling on one side of a tray.
3. Dampen the second piece of toweling and position it on the tray also, but at a distance of about one-half inch from the first, so that the dry and the damp towel pieces lay side by side with no direct contact between the two.

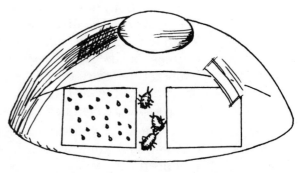

4. Place the live sow bugs in the space between the dry and damp toweling.

5. Cover the entire towel section on the tray with a transparent glass or plastic bowl.

6. Observe the activity of the sow bugs.

RATIONALE

Unlike most terrestrial organisms, sow bugs are equipped with breathing organs that are more suitable for use in a watery environment. Their platelike gills are arranged along the lower surface of the abdomen and must be kept moist to enable their respiratory process to occur. The sow bugs' instinctive response in "choosing" to make contact with the moist towel makes it possible for them to breathe—and survive.

DISCUSSION AND FOLLOW-UP

- Both the sow bugs and their activity should be discussed as the demonstration progresses. Discussion can be developed by encouraging students to comment about their observations and to answer leading questions:

  — Did the sow bugs appear to prefer the moist or the dry toweling?

  — What would probably have happened if the sow bugs had not made the "right" choice?

  — Where are sow bugs usually found in nature?

  — How does this help them to survive on land?

  — Where do most crustaceans live?

  — What kind of respiratory organs do crustaceans have?

  — Does it appear that sow bugs prefer light or darkness?

- After the discussion has been completed, students should be encouraged to set up a terrestrial habitat for the sow bugs. A schedule can be set up for gathering damp rich soil and small rocks and logs under which the bugs can hide, and for a feeding regimen that includes occasional bits of raw potato or carrot.

8–5: AN ANIMAL RESPONSE TO LIGHT
(elementary level)

INTRODUCTION

The name *earthworm* accurately describes a group of land-dwelling organisms; they are the segmented worms that live in soil that is rich in humus. While they do come to the surface mainly at night, to mate and to eat bits of organic debris, they spend most of their daytime hours burrowing tunnels. This activity, plus the fact that they are also known as nightcrawlers, provides an important clue as to how they respond to light.

LEARNING OBJECTIVES

At the end of this demonstration lesson, students should be able to

- relate responses made by animals to their survival.
- describe the earthworm's response to light.
- associate the terms *positive* and *negative responses* with an organism's movements toward or away from a stimulus.
- recognize the presence of alternate mechanisms for light sensitivity in organisms that have no eyes.
- explain how the earthworm's response to light helps it to survive, using *key words:* **light-sensitive nerve endings**, **negative response**, **moist skin surface**, and **harmful light rays**.

MATERIALS NEEDED

living earthworms; damp paper towel; flashlight; tray; black cloth

PRESENTATION

1. In a room with subdued light, arrange a damp paper towel on a tray.
2. Lay a piece of black cloth over one end of the paper towel.
3. Place a live earthworm on the moist paper towel.
4. Using a flashlight, shine a beam of light on the earthworm.
5. Observe the response made by the worm.

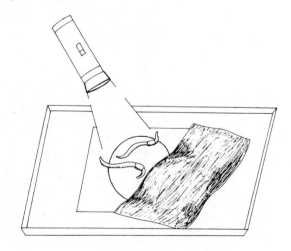

RATIONALE

Although the earthworm has no eyes, it is sensitive to light. When light is shone upon its anterior end, the worm adjusts its body position quickly and crawls away from the light source. This negative response is accompanied by a close nervous-muscular coordination; certain light-sensitive cells in the skin receive the stimulus, and impulses are carried immediately to the muscles, causing the earthworm to make decisive movements that, in its natural habitat, helps it find its way into the soil, where it will be protected from exposure to harmful ultraviolet radiation from the sun.

DISCUSSION AND FOLLOW-UP

- As the demonstration is being set up, students should be encouraged to predict how the earthworm will respond. They should then check their prediction against the actual response made and discuss the demonstration by responding to selected guide questions:
    - What was the response of the earthworm to light?
    - Was it a positive or a negative response?
    - How could this response be helpful to an earthworm?
    - What might happen to the earthworm if it could not move away from light?
    - Why is light harmful to the earthworm?
    - Is the name *nightcrawler* appropriate for an earthworm?
    - Which end of the earthworm appears to be the more sensitive to light?
    - How does this assist the earthworm in making movements that enable it to avoid unfavorable light conditions?
- Students should be encouraged to report experiences in observing earthworms digging tunnels and burrows in an earthworm colony display, and in catching nightcrawlers for fish bait.
- After the discussion has been completed, students should be asked to write a report about the demonstration, in which they explain how a negative response to light helps earthworms to survive.

8–6: RESPIRATION IN A FISH
(intermediate level)

INTRODUCTION

Most complex animals are equipped with specialized structures for obtaining oxygen for use by their many cells and for releasing the carbon dioxide waste that they produce. Although the actual gas exchange occurs internally, there are outward signs that can be detected in the form of alternating inhalations and exhalations as air enters and leaves the lungs of air-breathing animals. Similarly, the pathway of water entering and leaving the body of a fish can be traced. In each case the organism is adapted appropriately for obtaining oxygen from its immediate environment.

LEARNING OBJECTIVES

After this demonstration lesson has been completed, students should be able to

- identify a specialized structure/function relationship.
- recognize a similarity in basic needs of all organisms.
- relate the mouth and operculum activity of a fish to its breathing process.
- show evidence of an understanding of the process by which a fish exchanges gases with the water in its surroundings, using *key words:* **mouth, operculum, gills, oxygen,** and **carbon dioxide**.

MATERIALS REQUIRED

goldfish in an aquarium, fish tank, or large jar

PRESENTATION

1. Observe a goldfish in an aquarium or other suitable container that is visible to all students.
2. Locate the crescent-shaped slit at the rear of the gill cover on the side of the head.
3. Look for activity in the mouth region.
4. Look for activity of the flaplike gill covers.
5. Try to observe what is beneath the gill covers.
6. Note any synchronized activity between the mouth and the operculum.

RATIONALE

The observable opening and closing action of the fish mouth and operculum flaps are outward signs that the fish is breathing. Water enters by way of the open mouth. Then, when the mouth closes, water is forced to the throat region, where it passes over the gill filaments and leaves by way of the gill covers on the side of the head. The actual exchange of respiratory gases takes place in the region of the gill filaments. As water passes over thin moist membranes of gills that are richly provided with capillaries, oxygen dissolved in the water diffuses through the thin membranes into the blood and, in exchange, carbon dioxide, carried to the gills from the body cells, is released.

DISCUSSION AND FOLLOW-UP

- Students should be encouraged to report observations of activity of the goldfish.
- They can be assisted by the use of guide questions:
  - What activity do you notice in the region of the mouth?
  - What activity do you notice in the region of the gill covers?
  - Do both of these structures appear to open at the same time?
  - What is the color of the structures under the gill covers?
  - What causes this color?
  - Can fish separate the O (oxygen) from the H_2O (water) when they breathe?
  - What is the source of the oxygen that is dissolved in water that fish use for breathing?
  - Why do fish sometimes come to the surface to breathe?
  - What is the advantage of the thin moist membranes of the gill filaments and capillaries?
  - How does the forward motion of the fish aid its breathing process?
  - Why is an aerator sometimes used in an aquarium?
- After the discussion has been completed, students should be asked to draw a diagram showing how water enters and leaves a fish body and to indicate on the diagram the region in which the exchange of respiratory gases—both kind and direction—takes place between the fish and the water.

8–7: A SPECIAL FITNESS OF BIRD FEET*
(intermediate level)

INTRODUCTION

Birds have feet that show adaptations for different ways of life: for swimming, climbing, capturing and killing prey, and—perhaps most curious of all—for perching. The sight of a bird in a perfectly balanced position on a swinging telephone wire or on a tree branch or leaf stem becomes even more puzzling when we consider that birds can sleep in this position without falling off their perches. An explanation for this can be found in the demonstration of an articulated chicken foot.

LEARNING OBJECTIVES

At the end of this demonstration lesson, students should be able to

- identify a tendon and its action.
- understand the action of tendons in moving the toes of a chicken foot.
- understand the special fitness of some birds to use tendons found in the leg, foot, and toes for perching.
- relate the action of the tendons observed to finger and toe movements on their own hands and feet.
- describe how bird feet are adapted for perching, using *key words:* **tendon** and **muscle**.

MATERIALS REQUIRED

fresh chicken foot with short portion of the leg attached; sharp knife or razor blade

PRESENTATION

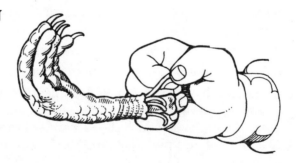

1. Examine the appearance of the individual toes on a chicken foot.
2. Locate the tubelike sheath that lies to one side of the bone on the cut end of the leg attached to the foot.
3. Using a sharp instrument, slit this sheath to expose the group of tendons within it.

---

* Suitable for teacher-only presentation.

CAUTION: Keep sharp instruments out of reach of students.

4. Grasp and pull on each tendon—one at a time—while observing the effect on the toes.

5. Grasp all tendons as a group and observe the effect produced by pulling.

RATIONALE

The foot of a perching bird has very little muscle that is useful for moving the toes. Instead, leg muscles in the thigh and calf are attached to long tough cords that operate the toe action, enabling the bird to flex its toes and grasp a branch tightly. These tendons in the area of the feet are arranged in such a fashion that when a bird lands on a branch, the weight of the bird's body forces the toes to curl around the branch. The tendon that passes over the claw also passes over the leg joint, so that when the bird settles down on a branch to rest, the legs bend more and the claw closes more—resulting in the grasp being tightened around the branch and enabling the bird to sleep while perching.

DISCUSSION AND FOLLOW-UP

- After the tendons have been exposed and demonstrated, individual students may be invited to grasp the tendons to operate the toes and effect a grasping motion. The concept of the tendons continuing to the upper leg can be developed by reminders of the tough cords present in a chicken or turkey "drumstick" and by asking questions relating to structure and function:
  - What effect did pulling a single tendon have on the chicken foot?
  - What effect did pulling all tendons at once have on the chicken foot?
  - Over what joint would the tendons pass to attach to the muscle of the upper leg?
  - How would this affect the toes if the chicken settles down?
  - How does this make it possible for a bird to sleep while perching?

- Individual tendons on the opposite side of the leg can also be pulled and released to observe the effect of stretching the toes. Students can then relate this action to the movement of their own fingers and toes.

- The special fitness of the perching birds for their way of life should then be summarized, with attention to the tendon control over the movement of their toes and feet.

- Then, after the discussion has been completed, student volunteers should be invited to see if they can remove a tendon from the chicken leg by pulling. This too can be related to experiences encountered while eating a drumstick.

8–8:   AN UNUSUAL TONGUE
(elementary level)

INTRODUCTION

Animals have mouth parts that are variously modified to suit their specialized food habits. In different kinds of mammals, teeth may be well developed for biting, grinding, chewing, gnawing, or tearing flesh; bird beaks may be equipped for pecking for worms, crushing seeds, or scooping up fish; and insects may have sucking, chewing, or biting mouth parts. A few animals have mouth parts that are useful for capturing the food they eat. A frog at feeding time illustrates the use of its unusual tongue for this purpose.

LEARNING OBJECTIVES

At the end of this demonstration lesson, students should be able to

- identify an important structure/function relationship.
- recognize the efficiency of an unusual tongue structure for capturing food.
- relate the kind of food eaten by an animal to the mouth parts it possesses for handling food.
- list three adaptations of the frog tongue that enable it to perform its function.
- describe the mechanics of the frog tongue in action, using *key words:* **muscle**, **point of attachment**, **extension**, and **mucus**.

MATERIALS REQUIRED

terrarium; hungry frog; thread; mealworm or insect

PRESENTATION

1. Place a frog that has not been fed recently in a terrarium or other large container.

2. Tie a mealworm, insect, or small piece of fresh meat to one end of a piece of thread.

3. Holding the free end of the thread, dangle the "meal" about three inches in front of the frog.

4. Observe the frog's response.

RATIONALE

The frog acts quickly in response to the sight of food on the wing. It throws out its forked tongue, folds it over the food, and returns it to the mouth, where the food is dropped into the gullet leading to the stomach. The great extension of the tongue is due to its strong musculature and point of attachment at the front of the lower jaw. Even flying insects, once wrapped in the tongue and attached to its sticky surface, cannot escape, and the frog swallows an acceptable meal whole. If food is unacceptable because of a bad taste, the frog will reject the meal and spit it out of the mouth.

DISCUSSION AND FOLLOW-UP

- Students may be allowed to supply insects for frog feeding and dangle the food in front of the frog at varying distances. Attention should focus on the swiftness of the action taken by the frog and on the coordination between its nervous and muscular systems.

- Discussion of the demonstration can be guided by questions:
  - How does the frog respond to food dangled in front of it?
  - How does the structure of the frog's tongue help it capture food?
  - Are there any indications of a relationship between the frog's sense of sight and its tongue activity?
  - How does the frog's tongue extension compare with the length of its body?
  - How does this offer an advantage to the frog?

- When the discussion has been completed, students should be asked to draw a diagram showing how the frog uses its tongue to capture food.

8–9: MOVING AT A SNAIL'S PACE
(elementary level)

INTRODUCTION

Some animals travel at amazingly high speed. For example, the cheetah and antelope can run at the rate of 60 miles per hour, and homing pigeons and dragonflies are even faster, often flying as fast as 90 miles per hour. Other animals, such as tortoises, are known for their more leisurely pace. The proverbial "snail's pace" can be demonstrated in the classroom and compared with the speed at which other animals travel.

LEARNING OBJECTIVES

At the end of this demonstration lesson, students should be able to

- recognize the structure/function relationship involved in an animal's organs of locomotion.
- associate the speed of an animal with its organs of locomotion and its food habits.
- make use of data collected for calculating the speed of an animal.
- show evidence of an understanding of the meaning and proper use of *key words:* **locomotion** and **speed**.

MATERIALS REQUIRED

terrestrial snails; piece of glass windowpane; large sheet of white paper; compass; ruler; wax pencil; watch or clock with a sweep second hand

PRESENTATION

1. With a compass, draw concentric circles at one-half inch intervals on a large sheet of white paper.
2. Place the circle pattern under a glass windowpane where all lines can be viewed clearly.
3. Place a snail on the glass surface at the center of the circle pattern.
4. Prod the snail gently.
5. Observe the snail's motion.
6. At the end of five minutes, make a wax pencil mark on the glass plate to indicate the snail's location.

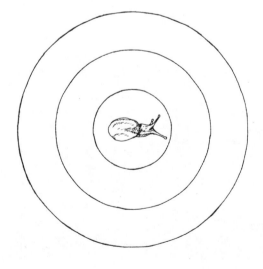

214

7. Measure and record the distance traveled by the snail in five minutes.

8. Measure and record the distance traveled in one or more additional five-minute runs.

RATIONALE

As the land snail moves from one place to another, it carries its shell on its back. This offers protection for the soft body but also causes the snail to be one of the slowest moving of all mollusks. To move, it uses its flat muscular foot to secrete slime, over which it then travels in rhythmic waves, attaining a speed of about ten feet per hour.

DISCUSSION AND FOLLOW-UP

- Individual students should be given opportunities to act as timekeepers for the five-minute snail marathons and as measurers and recorders of the distances traveled.
- Discussion should focus on methods employed in the demonstration as well as on observations of the snail's activity, by posing pertinent questions:
    - Did the snail travel the same distance during each five-minute run?
    - Why was more than one marathon run by the snail?
    - What was the average distance traveled in five minutes?
    - At the same rate, how far could the snail travel in ten minutes?
    - At the same rate, what is its hourly speed?
    - How does this speed compare with that of a jack rabbit or a dragonfly?
    - How does the snail's shell influence its rate of travel?
    - Is a slow speed suitable for a snail?
    - How is the rate of travel of an animal related to its food habits?
- After the discussion has been completed, students should be asked to write a short report in which they describe the snail's method and rate of travel and in which they explain what is meant by the expression, "a snail's pace."

8–10: COLOR CHANGES IN A CHAMELEON
(intermediate level)

INTRODUCTION

Although some animals are brightly colored, most have a more subdued coloring that blends in with their surroundings and enables them to remain undetected as they escape from enemies or lie in wait for food. Some respond to seasonal changes, making themselves inconspicuous against a snowy winter background as well as barren ground or a lush overgrowth in other seasons. A few rare species are able to change their coloring temporarily, often changing to blending colors or camouflage patterns as they find themselves in a new and different situation. Some interesting color changes can be observed in the small lizard known as the chameleon.

LEARNING OBJECTIVES

At the end of this demonstration lesson, students should be able to

- name one animal that changes its color on a seasonal basis.
- name one animal that changes its color temporarily when faced with a new situation or condition.
- name two factors that may stimulate an animal to make a response that results in a color change.
- describe how an animal's ability to change its color is advantageous to the animal, using *key words:* **color pigment cells**, **protective coloration**, and **camouflage**.

MATERIALS REQUIRED

live chameleon; small cage with removable door made of vertical bars; tree branch; flashlight

PRESENTATION

1. Place a small chameleon in a cage with vertical bars that contains a horizontal tree branch positioned parallel to the door.
2. Allow the chameleon to remain undisturbed until it has adjusted to its new surroundings.
3. When the chameleon is quiet and perched on the branch, direct the beam of a flashlight on the animal's side, allowing the cage door to cast

216

vertical shadows on the chameleon's body.

4. After a few minutes, remove the door from the cage and, in condi-

tions of subdued light, observe the color pattern on the chameleon's body.

RATIONALE

The chameleon is the best known among lizards that can change the color of their skin. However, the color changes are not brought about by any conscious effort on the part of the animal. Instead, bright light and increased temperature cause dark pigment cells in the skin to expand, sending a flood of dark pigment cells over the exposed surface, while protected areas—being cooler and less brightly lighted—are seen to be comparatively light. The striped effect produced when the chameleon is placed behind bars in a strong light can be seen to persist for about one minute after the bars are removed.

DISCUSSION AND FOLLOW-UP

- The demonstration should be discussed as it relates to the chameleon directly and to other animals in which a color change is produced also.
- Students should be asked to respond to direct questions:
  - What color is the chameleon's skin?
  - How does this help it to remain unnoticed in its natural surroundings?
  - What happened to the skin areas that were exposed to heat and light from the flashlight?
  - How might this help to explain the color change of a snowshoe rabbit's fur in summer and winter?
  - Why does the rabbit's fur color change last throughout the winter season, while the chameleon's stripes can be seen for only a very short time?
  - Does an animal have any conscious control over when and how to change its skin color?
- For a follow-up activity, students should be asked to make a list of animals that nature has provided with the ability to engage in color changes, and to describe how these color changes are related to changes in the environment to which the animal is capable of making a favorable response.

8-11: THE CASE OF THE JUMPING "BEANS"
(elementary level)

INTRODUCTION

Spontaneous movement of an organism is usually associated with the characteristic activity of a leaping frog, a flying insect, a squirming worm, a swimming fish, or a running dog. It is the spontaneous movement of plant forms that we view as extraordinary. Careful observation of Mexican jumping beans provides an opportunity for students to develop some insight into the actual cause of their unusual jumping action.

LEARNING OBJECTIVES

At the conclusion of this demonstration lesson, students should be able to

- recognize some misleading names given to some objects and organisms.
- identify the jumping beans as the seeds of a plant grown in Mexico.
- associate the jumping action as due to something inside the seed coat of the "beans."
- gain some insight into how larvae gain entrance to seeds.
- explain the action of the Mexican jumping beans, using *key words:* **seed, larva, moth, protection, spontaneous movement,** and **response**.

MATERIALS REQUIRED

8 to 10 Mexican jumping beans; ticking clock or watch; wooden tray

PRESENTATION

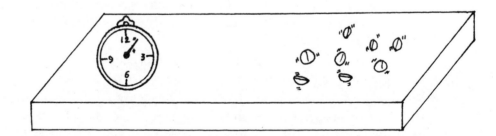

1. Place several Mexican jumping beans on a wooden tray, positioning them close to one end.

2. Allow the seeds to remain undisturbed until activity is noted.

3. Place a ticking clock or watch on the tray, positioning it at the end opposite the seeds.

4. Over a period of time, observe the activity and eventual location of the seeds.

218

RATIONALE

When left undisturbed for a short time, Mexican jumping beans make small spontaneous movements, accompanied by faint clicking sounds. Such movements and sounds result from the convulsive activity of the larval stage of an insect within the shell of the seed. Having been hatched from an egg laid by a species of moth in the flower of a specific plant species, the larva develops within the seed coat, during which time it becomes active and appears to respond positively to sound vibrations such as those made by a ticking clock. After a time, the seeds appear to become inactive as the larvae within progress to their pupal stage of development on the way to becoming adult flying moths.

DISCUSSION AND FOLLOW-UP

- Students should observe closely to detect signs of motion and sounds produced by the seeds. They should be encouraged to report these observations and to answer related questions:
    - What kind of motion was observed?
    - What kind of sound was produced?
    - Did the ticking clock appear to have any effect on the direction of the movement?
    - What caused the movement of the seeds?
    - How did the moth larvae get inside the seeds?
    - How does this habit of the female moth benefit the larvae that develop from the eggs laid in the flower?
- There are opportunities here for developing the concept of names of some organisms that are misleading. Starting with the Mexican jumping beans, students can be encouraged to add others, such as starfish, jellyfish, vinegar eel, and others.
- As a follow-up, students should maintain the demonstrated seeds in a box for about one week, or until they become inactive. Then, interested students can be encouraged to devise ways for locating the seed chambers in which the larvae had lived and caused the seeds to jump.

8–12: INSECT RESPONSE TO TEMPERATURE CHANGE
(intermediate level)

INTRODUCTION

The activities in which animals engage involve certain chemical reactions that are temperature related. Some animals are capable of regulating their internal body temperature so that the chemical reactions necessary for their life activities can occur, despite some temperature variations in the surroundings. Lower animals, however, lack this capability and have approximately the same body temperature as their surroundings; only when the external temperature is suitable for these chemical reactions are these animals able to engage in their normal life activities. This can be demonstrated with insects in the classroom.

LEARNING OBJECTIVES

At the end of this demonstration lesson, students should be able to

- recognize the effect of temperature on insect activity.
- relate the activity of the flies observed to the rate at which chemical reactions occur within their bodies.
- identify insects as organisms with great dependence on the temperature of their surroundings.
- name other animals whose life activities are directly related to the temperature of their surroundings.
- explain the response made by flies to a change of temperature in their surroundings, using *key words:* **environment**, **temperature**, **chemical reactions**, and **activity**.

MATERIALS REQUIRED

several flies or other insects of one kind (grasshoppers, ants, or crickets); glass jar with screw cap; shallow bowl or basin; thermometer; thread; crushed ice; water

PRESENTATION

1. Place several captured flies or other insects in a glass jar fitted with a screw-cap top that has a series of air holes punched in the top.

2. Insert the thermometer so that it hangs freely while being suspended from a thread held in place by the cap when screwed on the top of the jar.

3. Observe the activity of the flies in the jar.

4. Have a student take a temperature reading of the inside of the jar and record it on the chalkboard.

5. Place the jar in a shallow bowl. Then pour a small amount of water into the bowl and pack crushed ice around the base of the jar.

6. Observe the flies. When a change in activity is noted, have a student take another temperature reading.

7. When all activity has stopped and another temperature reading has been taken, remove the jar from the ice-water bath and allow both the approximate room temperature within the jar and the accompanying activity of the flies to be restored.

RATIONALE

As the temperature is lowered, so too is the activity of the flies being observed. Their activity is related to energy needs for the performance of the activity, and the energy released is due to biochemical reactions that depend upon certain temperature ranges for their occurrence within the insects' organization. Unable to regulate their temperature from within, the insects must depend upon the environmental conditions to provide the temperature of their bodies. Only some of these temperatures are suitable for the chemical reactions yielding energy for life processes; there are both upper and lower limits, beyond which all activity stops.

DISCUSSION AND FOLLOW-UP

- Discussion should focus on the effect of temperature on the activity of the flies and on chemical reactions involving energy release. This can be developed as students report their observations, make comments, and respond to questions:

  — What effect did a drop in temperature have on the activity of the flies?

  — Recalling the involvement of water in chemical reactions previously demonstrated, how does the slowing of molecular motion and the formation of ice affect chemical reactions for the release of energy?

  — How does this help to explain why some animals die and others hibernate in cold weather?

- After basic relationships between temperature and activity of insects and other simple animals have been understood and the relationship of temperature to chemical reactions has been established, students should consider the advantages of being able to maintain a suitable internal temperature for chemical reactions, despite the temperature of the surroundings. They should then be asked to prepare lists of so-called coldblooded and warmblooded animals, and to research more scientifically accurate names for these two groups.

CHAPTER 9

Demonstrations Pertaining to Humans

9-1: HEIGHT VARIATIONS AMONG STUDENTS IN SCIENCE CLASS
(intermediate level)

INTRODUCTION

All humans resemble each other in significant ways. Specific structural features of the right kind, number, and placement on the body link all humans together and distinguish us from all other living species. All members, of course, are not exactly the same; there are variations within a range of size, height, weight, and other measurable features that allow for successful interaction with the environment. When studied, these variations are generally found to be distributed in predictable patterns.

LEARNING OBJECTIVES

After having participated in this demonstration lesson, students should be able to

- recognize differences in height of students as variations within the human species.
- identify the distribution pattern in a random sample.
- name three examples of variations in the human species.
- understand the value of measurements in gathering scientific information.
- prepare a graph from the collected data.
- interpret the graph prepared from data collected, using *key words:* **variations**, **normal distribution**, and **bell-shaped curve**.

MATERIALS REQUIRED

tape measure or height chart attached to a wall area; graph paper; markers

PRESENTATION

1. Measure and record the heights of individual students.

2. Determine the range of heights represented and divide into five height groups of equal spread.

3. Assign a name or a number to each group.

4. Have students line up by height, from shortest to tallest.

5. Place a marker at the boundary line between groups.

6. Count and record on the chalkboard the number of students in each group.

7. Use the collected data to prepare a bar graph—groups of measured values placed on the horizontal axis and number of students in each group placed on the vertical axis.

8. Construct a line graph that connects the midpoints of the top of each bar.

9. Then smooth the straight line graph into a gentle curve and analyze the pattern that develops.

RATIONALE

With some exceptions, student height measurements tend to exhibit continuous variations from the shortest to the tallest. When plotted on a graph, the frequency distribution approximates that of a bell-shaped curve, with more individuals represented in the mid-range than at the extremes of the height variations. As with most variations among members of the same species, height differences are relatively small and too insignificant to affect the organism's chances for survival. They may, however, influence an individual's ability to excel in a specific physical activity or sports event.

DISCUSSION AND FOLLOW-UP

- Students should become actively involved in the demonstration. On the basis of the height measurements taken, they should respond to questions:
  - Are all members of the class the same height?
  - What is the height of the tallest class member?
  - What is the height of the shortest class member?
  - Which height group has the greatest number of members?

- They should participate in the processing of data collected and in a discussion of the graph showing the distribution of the variations.

- Attention should focus on the pattern of the distribution curve and on other physical features of students that might show a similar pattern of variation in their expression.

- As a follow-up, students should be asked to use the graph to determine why relatively few individuals qualify to become star basketball players or jockeys, but that most of us have been provided by nature with a mid-range favorability.

9–2:   THE MECHANICS OF BREATHING
(elementary level)

INTRODUCTION

Our bodily needs for oxygen are more critical than our needs for food and water; people have been known to live for more than 60 days without food, and up to one week without water—but after a period of only several minutes without oxygen, the body loses consciousness and may suffer serious brain damage. When we inhale air during the first phase of the breathing process, activities of some body structures and changes in pressure within the chest cavity are involved. As a result, supplies of oxygen enter the lungs, from which they are distributed to body cells for use in cellular respiration.

LEARNING OBJECTIVES

After having completed this demonstration lesson, students should be able to

- recognize that the lungs cannot breathe by themselves.
- identify the work of the diaphragm and the creation of areas of unequal air pressure as critical factors in forcing air into and out of the lungs.
- recognize the advantages and disadvantages of using a working model to study a life function.
- explain how the working model demonstrates the human breathing mechanism, using *key words:* **inhalation, exhalation, diaphragm, air pressure, trachea,** and **bronchial tubes.**

MATERIALS REQUIRED

clear plastic food container; plastic drinking straw; small balloon; O ring cut from rubber or plastic airline tubing; large balloon or rubber sheet; thread; tape; rubber bands; yarn loop

PRESENTATION

1. Construct a breathing model:
   - With thread, attach a small balloon to the lower end of a plastic drinking straw that has been inserted through a small hole in the center of the base of an inverted clear plastic food container.
   - Place an O ring around the straw to hold it securely in place and make a tight seal

with the plastic food container.

- Stretch a cut balloon or piece of rubber sheet over the open end of the food container, and use rubber bands around the outside rim of the container to hold the rubber sheet taut. Then tape a yarn loop to the center of the sheet.

2. Grasping the loop with one hand, gently pull the rubber sheet downward and watch the balloon.
3. Release the pressure on the sheet, allowing it to return to its normal position.
4. Observe the action of the balloon.

RATIONALE

In the model, the balloon fills and empties because of changes in air pressure created within the food container by lowering and raising the rubber sheet. Lowering the sheet reduces the pressure in the container below that of the outside air mass and air is forced into the balloon. When the sheet is raised, air in the container is compressed, increasing its pressure and forcing air out of the balloon. In real life, the lungs cannot move by themselves either. The muscular diaphragm moves up and down and, like the sheet, changes the size of the chest cavity. This causes air pressure within to be either greater or less than that of the surroundings, which either forces air into or out of the lungs.

DISCUSSION AND FOLLOW-UP

- Students should be permitted to manipulate the model and to analyze the activity as it relates to their own breathing process.
- Attention should focus on the values as well as the shortcomings of a model to represent a living structure:
    — What part of your body does the plastic container represent?
    — What part of your body does the balloon represent?
    — What part of your body does the drinking straw represent?
    — What part of your body does the rubber sheet represent?
    — In what way does the model not represent the actual structure properly?
    — How could the model be restructured to include two lungs?
    — What structure does the actual work involved in breathing?
    — What causes air to enter the lungs?
- After students have compared the demonstration model with the breathing mechanism in their own bodies, they should be asked to describe the events that are involved in inhalation and in exhalation during the process of breathing.

9–3:   SEEING A "HOLE IN THE HAND"
(elementary level)

INTRODUCTION

Things are not always what they appear to be. Distant objects appear to be smaller than those of the same size that are close; a series of separate still pictures flashed quickly on a television screen, in a movie, or on a set of flip cards, gives the impression that the objects and people pictured are actually moving; straight lines sometimes appear to be curved; and a circle surrounded by large objects appears to be smaller than a circle of the same size surrounded by small objects. These and other unusual and misleading effects are produced when the brain is fooled by information received by the eye, causing the picture of what we see to be perceived incorrectly.

LEARNING OBJECTIVES

After having participated in this demonstration lesson, students should be able to

- relate optical illusions to occurrences during the process of seeing.
- name three cases that involve optical illusions.
- demonstrate one optical illusion.
- tell why optical illusions are important to the scientist and to the science student.
- name three practical uses of optical illusions.
- explain the appearance of a "hole in the hand" using *key words:* **optical illusion** and **focus**.

MATERIALS REQUIRED

rolled paper tube or cardboard tube from a roll of paper toweling

PRESENTATION

1. Obtain a cardboard tube from a roll of paper toweling or roll a piece of paper to make a tube that measures about two inches in diameter.

2. Holding the tube in your right hand, place the tube close to your right eye and focus on a wall clock or other object across the room.

3. Keeping both eyes open, place the outside edge of your left hand, with palm outstretched and facing you, alongside the length of the tube, just a few inches in front of your left eye.

4. Observe the composite picture.

RATIONALE

Your eyes report to the brain the stimuli they receive, for interpretation in the visual center of the brain. Since the demonstration involves differing stimuli being received by each eye, the brain tries to put them together in the form of a unified "picture." However, it is confused by the fact that each eye is focusing on a different object at different distances. The result is one image superimposed upon the other—or a distant object, such as the wall clock, viewed in a circular field of vision superimposed on the near object, the hand. The unusual and misleading effect produced is that of a clock being seen through a hole in the palm of the hand.

DISCUSSION AND FOLLOW-UP

- Individual students may need assistance in placing the tube properly in relation to their hands and eyes, and may need to be reminded of the importance of keeping both eyes open throughout the demonstration.
- After each has successfully demonstrated the illusion, students should be asked:
  - What did you see?
  - What would you expect to have seen if you kept the left eye closed?
  - What would you expect to have seen if you kept the right eye closed?
  - How does the brain become confused and tricked into producing the effect of a hole in the hand?
  - Why does this effect not occur unless you use the tube and keep both eyes open?
- Discussion should include other forms of optical illusions. Students should be encouraged to report personal experiences and to bring in examples of illusions appearing in magazines and on puzzle pages of newspapers. The idea of flip cards should be developed, and students should be encouraged to make flip cards that show a dog running, a bird flying, or a skier traveling down a slope.
- The impact of illusions on our sense of sight should be considered, and its importance to scientific work should be determined. Students should then be asked to write a summary report about illusions and to explain why a scientist must always check what he sees in order to obtain accurate scientific information.

9–4: KEEPING COOL BY SWEATING
(elementary level)

INTRODUCTION

Profuse sweating experienced during hot weather or while engaging in vigorous exercise or sports events involving running and jumping is accompanied by an uncomfortable feeling of excess body heat. Actually, the sweating cools the body and prevents it from overheating. It is one of the mechanisms that allow the body to maintain its constant internal temperature at 98.6°F.

LEARNING OBJECTIVES

After having participated in this demonstration lesson, students should be able to

- relate the production of excess body heat with body activity requiring energy.
- identify the vaporization of water at the surface of the body as an example of a physical change involving a transfer of heat.
- recognize the use of a simulation to represent an actual event being investigated or demonstrated.
- understand something they have discovered about the operation of their own bodies.
- describe sweating as a cooling process, using *key words:* **sweating, evaporation, vaporization, heat transfer,** and **constant body temperature.**

MATERIALS REQUIRED

water; medicine droppers; paper fans

PRESENTATION

1. With a medicine dropper, place a few drops of water on the backs of the hands of all students participating in the demonstration.

2. Have students use paper fans to fan the air and create air movement to hasten the evaporation of water placed on their hands.

3. Observe the "disappearance" of water as it evaporates into the air.

4. Have students report the sensation associated with the demonstration.

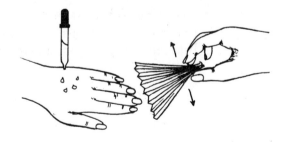

RATIONALE

Body temperature is controlled by several different processes operating within the body and over its surface. Surplus heat that is not needed immediately by the body for warmth and mechanical energy is removed, mostly through the skin. If the blood is not cooled sufficiently by radiation of heat at the surface when blood vessels dilate and bring more heated blood to the surface, internal regulators increase the production of sweat. Evaporation of sweat at the surface then cools the skin as heat necessary for evaporation is taken from the body. Thus, the body is cooled as surplus heat is allowed to escape and the body, using a feedback system much like that of a thermostat, stops the sweating process and maintains the temperature at a fairly constant 98.6°F.

DISCUSSION AND FOLLOW-UP

- Students should be encouraged to relate the demonstration to experiences they have had and to report some of the occurrences. Discussion can be initiated by questions:
  - Why do you feel hot when you have been playing ball?
  - What other activities have caused you to feel hot?
  - How did your body react to being hot?
  - What causes you to sweat on a cool day when you have been skating?
  - Why should you put on a sweater or sweat suit after you stop exercising?
  - Why is more heat produced in your body during your Physical Education class than during your Science class?
  - Why do we refer to sweating as a cooling process?
- Discussion should focus on sweating, shivering, and reddening of the skin as signs of physiological processes engaged in by the body to regulate its internal temperature.
- Then, as a follow-up, students should be asked to explain the importance of sweating to the well-being of a basketball player whose physical activity during a single game sets free enough heat to kill him—*if* his body did not have a way to cool off during the game.

9–5:   LOCATING THE BLIND SPOT
(intermediate level)

INTRODUCTION

The world we see is primarily the world we know. It is through our sense of vision that we gain most of our firsthand knowledge about the world around us from both our immediate surroundings and from millions of miles away when we view the stars. By converting light waves traveling at a speed of 186,000 miles per second into nerve impulses that are then transmitted to the brain for interpretation, we see a reasonably accurate picture of something we are looking at. Nature has even equipped us to see that small point that comes to a focus on each eye's "blind spot."

LEARNING OBJECTIVES

After having participated in this demonstration lesson, students should be able to

- locate the blind spot in one or both eyes.
- understand how light waves are received by light-sensitive receptors in the retina of the eye.
- recognize the absence of receptors at the point of optic nerve connection to the eye.
- appreciate the value of having two eyes.
- explain the occurrence of the blind spot, using *key words:* **retina**, **light sensitive receptors**, **optic nerve**, and **blind spot**.

MATERIALS REQUIRED

white file cards; rulers; pencils; black felt-tip pens; model or diagram of human eye structure

PRESENTATION

1. Instruct each student to prepare one-half inch figures of a pea and a walnut shell spaced three inches apart on a white file card. The figures can then be filled in, using fine-tipped black felt-tip pens.
2. Instruct students to locate the blind spot in the right eye:
   - Place your left hand over your left eye.
   - With your right hand, hold the card at arm's length in front of your face.
   - Focus your right eye on the shell figure and note that the pea figure can be seen also.
   - Slowly move the card closer to your eye until you reach a point at which the pea disappears.

231

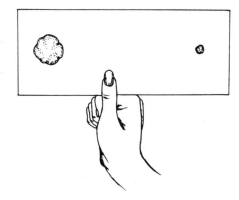

- Move the card closer until the pea reappears.
- Repeat the procedure and hold the card steady at the point where the pea disappeared from view. Then remove your left hand from in front of your left eye and note what happens.

RATIONALE

The human eye is constructed so that light stimuli can enter through the pupil, pass through the lens, and finally reach the light-sensitive cells in the retina. However, there are no light-sensitive nerve endings at the point where the optic nerve joins the retina. The result is that light impulses coming to a focus at this location cannot be sent to the brain for interpretation, and a blind spot is created. It is fortunate that light impulses from the same object are received at a slightly different angle by each eye so that the focus is not reached on the blind spot of both eyes simultaneously. What one eye misses the other eye sees.

DISCUSSION AND FOLLOW-UP

- Students should prepare their cards carefully and repeat the demonstration until the blind spot is located. They may test the left eye as well by focusing on the pea.
- By referring to a model or diagram showing the structure of the human eye, the pathway of light stimuli received should be traced and the changing position of its focus on the retina determined as it approaches, reaches, and passes the point at which the presence of light-sensitive cells is briefly interrupted by the spreading of the optic nerve into the retina. Students should consider:
  - What is a blind spot?
  - What is a main disadvantage of one-eyed vision?
  - Why is it a good practice to look both ways twice before crossing a street?
- After the discussion has been completed, students should be asked to give specific reasons why two eyes are better than one.

9-6: THE SENSE OF TASTE
(elementary level)

INTRODUCTION

Although the taste buds on the tongue can distinguish only sensations of sweet, sour, bitter, and salty, we enjoy foods that come in a great variety of flavors. One popular brand of ice cream even offers 128 different flavors! Actually, as with other forms of information, our bodies perceive taste as a result of information received by more than one of our senses. The clue to involvement of other senses in the determination of taste sensations lies hidden in the fact that the real and enjoyable flavor of even our most favorite food is seldom experienced when we have a heavy cold or suffer from head congestion.

LEARNING OBJECTIVES

At the end of this demonstration lesson, students should be able to

- be aware of the dependence of our senses upon each other.
- recognize that we rarely depend upon one sense alone for information.
- identify taste and smell as chemical senses.
- tell how it is possible for us to taste a wide variety of flavors, using *key words:* **taste buds**, **sensory cells**, **nasal passages**, and **moist membranes**.

MATERIALS REQUIRED

small slices of food (apple, raw potato, onion, cabbage, cheese, chocolate) cut to the same size and stored in separate closed containers; blindfold; toothpicks

PRESENTATION

1. Select student volunteers to take part in the demonstration:
    - one student subject to identify food samples placed on his/her tongue
    - one student recorder to list taste identifications made by the subject
    - one student helper to assist with food samples
2. Blindfold the subject and ask her to sit so as to be seen by other members of the class.

233

3. Using a toothpick, place a slice of raw potato on the subject's tongue and hold a slice of apple near the subject's nose.

4. Remove the food samples and ask the subject to identify the food tasted.

5. Repeat the food taste tests, using other combinations of food samples.

6. Examine the record of responses made and determine correct and incorrect identifications of taste.

RATIONALE

If limited to taste receptors on the tongue alone, we would be able to distinguish only sensations of sweet, sour, bitter, and salty. However, most foods have distinctive odors that greatly influence the sensation of taste that we associate with them. When placed in the mouth, these foods emit vapors that pass into the nasal passages, where they stimulate the receptors for smell. Hence, taste and smell of food are blended together to form its characteristic flavor. With the nostrils closed, these "tastes" cannot be distinguished.

DISCUSSION AND FOLLOW-UP

- As the demonstration progresses, attention should focus on some related conditions:
    - Why is it important that all food samples be the same size?
    - How do moisture on the tongue and mucous membranes in the nasal passages contribute to the functioning of receptors for taste and smell?
    - Why are taste and smell said to be "chemical" senses?
    - Why do we sometimes smell food to find out if we might like it?
- Students should also consider some *what if* situations:
    - *What if* the tongue were dried with tissue before each food sample was placed on the tongue?
    - *What if* the blindfolded subject pinched his nose shut before a piece of onion was placed on his tongue?
- Experiences relating to the demonstration should be reported, such as diminished taste perception when a heavy cold and swollen tissues in the nose prevented air from reaching the smell receptors.
- Then, as a follow-up, students should incorporate some of the elements of the demonstration into a short explanation that accounts for the expression, "We can almost taste the dinner cooking in the oven."

9–7:   A SIMPLE REFLEX ACTION
(intermediate level)

INTRODUCTION

Fortunately, we do not need to think about what action to take when we accidentally touch a hot object such as a hot stove; instead, as the result of a reflex action, we jerk the hand away almost immediately—probably before it has been burned seriously and certainly in less time than it takes to talk about it. In a similar manner we blink our eyes, jump out of the way of an approaching vehicle, and shield our face when something is hurled at it, in what we know to be defensive and protective reflex actions that have definite survival value. Certain vital actions such as breathing, heart action, secretion of digestive enzymes, and swallowing are also controlled automatically, thus freeing our brain to concentrate on reading, talking, and problem-solving kinds of activity that require conscious thought and attention.

LEARNING OBJECTIVES

At the end of this demonstration lesson, students should be able to

- trace the pathway of a simple reflex.
- identify simple reflexes and their survival value.
- name three reflex actions that are automatic.
- name three reflex actions that are not automatic.
- distinguish automatic responses to a stimulus from those responses that are not automatic, using *key words:* **reflex**, **reflex action**, **automatic**, and **inborn response**.

MATERIALS REQUIRED

piece of clear plastic; wad of crumpled paper

PRESENTATION

1. Select two student volunteers to participate in the demonstration.
2. Ask one student to hold a piece of clear plastic at a distance of about eight to ten inches in front of his/her face.
3. Ask a second student to throw, without warning, a wad of crumpled paper at the plastic shield.

4. Observe the response made by the student holding the plastic shield.

5. Throw several more wads of crumpled paper, each time noting the response made to the unexpected attack.

RATIONALE

The demonstration response—blinking of the eyes—is a reflex action in response to a stimulus—a wad of paper thrown toward the face. It involves only a sensory nerve receptor in the eye, a connector nerve to the spinal cord, and a motor nerve to a nerve fiber in the muscle of the eyelid. Because this short pathway bypasses the brain, the response is almost immediate. Shortly after a reflex action has occurred, the sensory nerve message is also relayed via the spinal nerves to the brain, where it is interpreted as a possible danger and threat to the safety of the head, face, and/or eyes.

DISCUSSION AND FOLLOW-UP

- During the demonstration, students should be cautioned about safety measures to be practiced. They should be cautioned about throwing objects toward a person's head and, during the demonstration, to proceed only when the plastic shield is properly in place.

- The focus of the demonstration should be on the responses made by the subject to the stimulus applied. Students should observe closely and report their observations:

  — What response was made by the subject when the paper wad was thrown toward his face, even though protected by the plastic shield?

  — Was this an automatic response?

  — Was it an immediate response?

  — Did the person making the response need to learn what response to make?

  — Why is this type of response called an "inborn" response?

  — How could this kind of response be useful to a person?

- Students should be encouraged to report other reflex actions that they have witnessed or engaged in personally. Examples such as jumping out of the way of an approaching automobile should be considered for their protective and survival value and compared with a *what if* situation requiring time to think about what to do before taking action when a car is bearing down upon you as you stand in the roadway.

- As a follow-up, students should be asked to draw a diagram showing the pathway of a reflex action that accounts for its fast action and built-in survival value in a specific instance selected by the students individually.

9–8: THE UNIQUENESS OF FINGERPRINTS
(intermediate level)

INTRODUCTION

No two individuals are exactly alike. Although we usually recognize a person by his physical features, voice, and facial expression, it is the skin of the individual that marks his greatest distinguishing feature for identification purposes. Beginning with the "footprinting" of newborn babies in hospital nurseries and continuing later with standard fingerprinting practices, the details of skin patterns and ridges—which are unchanging with age, habit, or fashion trends—serve as reliable marks of identification of their one and only owner.

LEARNING OBJECTIVES

After having participated in this demonstration lesson, students should be able to

- recognize that each human individual is unique.
- understand that criteria used for identification of individuals must be lifelong features that are not subject to change.
- name three practical applications of the use of skin prints for the identification of an individual.
- understand the basic classification scheme used in fingerprint identification.
- explain why fingerprints of every individual can be unique, using *key words:* **skin patterns**, **whorl**, **loop**, **arch**, and **friction ridges**.

MATERIALS REQUIRED

white cards; soft lead pencils; transparent tape; paper; copies of basic fingerprint pattern reference guides

PRESENTATION

1. Instruct and assist students working in groups in the making of a thumb-print for each student:

   - Use a soft pencil to make a heavy black smudge on a piece of paper.

   - Rub a thumb over the black smudge.

   - Press your thumb against a white card and, using a rolling motion from left to right, transfer the black smudge material from your thumb to the white card.

   - Cover the thumbprint with a small piece of transparent tape.

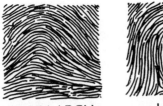  

PLAIN ARCH   LOOP   PLAIN WHORL

2. Examine and compare thumbprints made by all students in the group.

3. Use fingerprint pattern guides to identify the basic print patterns represented in the group.

RATIONALE

Details of the unique skin patterns of individuals are used regularly for identifying people. Small elevations of the skin on the palm surfaces of hands and fingertips and on the sole surfaces of feet and toes are arranged in rows like miniature mountain ranges, forming the basic pattern—loop, whorl, or arch—characteristic of the individual's skin. Further subdivisions, which include pattern variations and number of friction ridges, make it possible to identify a set of prints as belonging to one individual and no other.

DISCUSSION AND FOLLOW-UP

- An examination of the thumbprint made by each member of the group should identify basic patterns, as shown on the reference guide, and focus on key points for their classification:
    - How many of the three basic patterns were represented?
    - How many of each basic pattern have the same detailed variation?
    - How many friction ridges showing the same pattern variation were counted on each print?
- Student groups should be encouraged to make and compare print patterns for a finger, such as the index finger, and, applying the results to an entire set of prints, to explain why it is possible for every set of prints to be completely different. They should also give consideration to
    - the value of fingerprints for establishing evidence in solving a crime.
    - fingerprint files for assisting in the location of lost children and missing persons.
    - the usefulness of friction ridges on the hands and fingers in the performance of certain tasks by human hands.
    - the use of fingerprint records for all but newborn babies.
- As a follow-up activity, students should be asked to relate the demonstration to Mark Twain's observation in *Life on the Mississippi* that " . . . fingerprints are the only indelible signature of man."

9–9: PRODUCING STATIC CHARGES ON OUR BODIES
(intermediate level)

INTRODUCTION

The mild shock we feel when we touch a doorknob or handle after walking across a rug or sliding across a plastic car seat cover results from the buildup of electric charges. In some cases, if the charge is large enough, there are crackling sounds and/or sparks produced as well. How electric charges can be built up and transferred can be demonstrated in the classroom with willing students and an inflated balloon.

LEARNING OBJECTIVES

After participating in this demonstration lesson, students should be able to

- understand how electric charges are produced.
- understand how electric charges are transferred.
- predict the behavior of two electrically charged objects when brought close to a human body.
- give three examples to illustrate how a person's body can become electrically charged.
- explain the demonstration, using diagrams and *key words:* **static charge**, **static electricity**, **positive charge**, and **negative charge**.

MATERIALS REQUIRED

large balloon; string; wool mitten or piece of fur; cup hook or tape

PRESENTATION

1. Inflate a large balloon and twist the neck tightly to prevent the air from escaping.

2. Tie one end of a piece of string around the twisted neck of the balloon.

3. Using a cup hook or piece of tape, fasten the other end of the string to the top of a doorway so that the balloon hangs free at a level that is about the head height of students.

4. Rub the balloon briskly with a wool mitten or piece of fur.

5. Invite a student to approach the doorway.

6. Observe what happens.

RATIONALE

When the rubber balloon is rubbed with wool or fur, the rubber picks up electrons. This gives the balloon a negative charge, which has a strong attraction for a positively charged object. It also has an attraction for neutral objects such as the human body, which has an equal number of positive and negative charges on its surface. Negative charges on the balloon repel electrons on the student's skin and hair—forcing them away and leaving only the positive charges close to the balloon. This creates a force of attraction between the student's head and the balloon, causing the balloon to cling. If the balloon is about the same size as the student's head, it suggests a "friendly" balloon.

DISCUSSION AND FOLLOW-UP

- Several students may wish to be active participants in this demonstration. Discussion can be developed as students respond to leading questions:
    - What happened when the student approached the balloon?
    - What caused this attraction?
    - What kind of charge was on the balloon?
    - What caused the balloon to become charged?
    - How does combing your hair with a hard rubber comb relate to this demonstration?

- Discussion should focus on the nature of static charges and the conditions that promote and/or control their occurrence in human experience. Students should be encouraged to report personal experiences, such as feeling a shock when touching an electric light switch after having walked across a rug or having freshly washed hair tend to be "flyaway" on a cold dry day in winter.

- As a follow-up, students should be asked to suggest reasons why the use of water and hair spray helps to control unruly hair due to static charges.

9–10: CARBON DIOXIDE IN EXHALED BREATH
(elementary level)

INTRODUCTION

A child who threatens to hold his breath is unknowingly making an idle threat. Although he does shut off the supply of oxygen to his body cells, his control over his breathing mechanism lasts only about one minute. After that the carbon dioxide waste from oxidation of food in body cells stimulates the breathing center in his brain and restores the normal breathing pattern.

LEARNING OBJECTIVES

At the end of this demonstration lesson, students should be able to

- identify the presence of carbon dioxide in exhaled air.
- trace the origin of carbon dioxide waste found in exhaled air.
- employ a chemical indicator in a scientific test.
- understand the chemical change involved in the chemical indicator test.
- explain the usefulness of the limewater test, using *key words:* **limewater, calcium hydroxide, calcium carbonate, carbon dioxide, chemical indicator, cellular respiration**, and **chemical change**.

MATERIALS REQUIRED

peanut butter jar; soda straws; limewater

PRESENTATION

1. Pour clear limewater into a jar until it is one-fourth full of limewater.
2. Ask a student to exhale through a soda straw by bubbling his breath into the limewater.
3. Allow several other students, using individual straws, to take turns exhaling breath into the limewater.
4. Observe the activity in the jar during the demonstration and note changes in the limewater.

RATIONALE

Carbon dioxide is produced as a waste product when food is oxidized in body cells. It is then transported by the blood to the lungs, where it is exhaled. The presence of carbon dioxide in exhaled breath is confirmed by the use of the limewater test; in a chemical reaction between gaseous carbon dioxide and limewater, a white precipitate is formed. If the carbon dioxide concentration is high enough or if excess water in the cloudy precipitate is allowed to evaporate, the formation of a solid limestone deposit may be observed.

DISCUSSION AND FOLLOW-UP

- During the demonstration, attention should focus on changes in the appearance of the limewater as students blow their breath into it. Changes should be reported and analyzed. The respiratory pathway should be traced to the cell level, where oxygen and carbon dioxide are exchanged through cell membranes for oxidation of food and removal of waste.

- The use of limewater as a chemical indicator should also be developed, with students relating the change in appearance of limewater from clear to cloudy with a chemical reaction between carbon dioxide and limewater and the formation of a new substance, calcium carbonate.

- Students should respond to questions:
    - What accounted for the cloudiness of the limewater when exhaled air was bubbled into it?
    - Where did the carbon dioxide come from?
    - What scientific use of limewater was demonstrated?

- The relationship between breathing and cellular respiration should be developed. Then, as a follow-up, students should be asked to write an account of how the body produces carbon dioxide and how this waste is removed.

CHAPTER 10

Demonstrations Pertaining to Health and Physical Fitness

* Suitable for teacher-only presentation.

10-1:   INTERNAL BODY TEMPERATURE VERSUS
EXTERNAL TEMPERATURE
(intermediate level)

INTRODUCTION

Many activities of living organisms involve chemical reactions that will take place only within a very narrow range of temperature. Fortunately, humans can regulate their internal environment and maintain a fairly constant internal body temperature at a level that is suitable for these reactions. This gives us a tremendous advantage over many animals; it enables us to remain active year-round, despite the intense heat of summer and extreme cold of winter.

LEARNING OBJECTIVES

At the end of this demonstration lesson, students should be able to

- identify the range of normal human body temperature.
- associate the regulation of body temperature with both internal and external factors.
- demonstrate the proper usage of two kinds of thermometer.
- understand the advantage to humans of being able to maintain a constant body temperature.
- explain the mechanisms involved in regulating body temperature, using *key words:* **sensory receptors, nerve impulses, involuntary, oxidation, heat energy, radiation, evaporation, sweating,** and **shivering.**

MATERIALS REQUIRED

clinical thermometer; submersible room thermometer; water; bucket or large basin; crushed ice; towel

PRESENTATION

1. Partially fill a bucket or large basin with water.
2. Add crushed ice to the water until there is no evidence of ice melting.
3. Use a room thermometer to determine the temperature of the ice water.
4. Using a clinical thermometer and a room thermometer, take the oral temperature and the skin tempera-

ture at the forearm of a student who has volunteered to be the subject in the demonstration.

5. Ask the student to place her forearm in the ice water.
6. After two to three minutes have elapsed, ask the student to remove her hand and forearm from the cold water and dry the forearm by blotting with a towel.

244

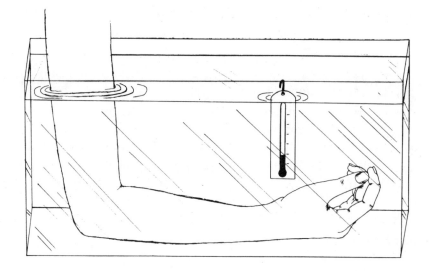

7. Again take readings of the skin temperature and of the oral temperature.

8. Note and record the external and internal body temperatures both before and after exposure to a cold environment.

RATIONALE

Although the outside temperature may be lowered by many degrees, the internal temperature of the body remains about the same. Reacting to signals of cold received at the skin's surface, the body makes certain automatic responses: blood vessels in the skin contract, reducing the amount of blood flow and escape of heat at the surface of the skin, and nerve impulses originating in the temperature-regulating center of the brain step up muscle activity, thereby increasing the rate of oxidation of food and production of heat. Together, these completely involuntary responses act to maintain the body temperature by producing heat and conserving it. Equally effective mechanisms for increasing the rate of escape of excess body heat are activated when cooling the internal environment is necessary to maintain its constant temperature.

DISCUSSION AND FOLLOW-UP

- As the demonstration progresses, students should be asked to take temperature readings and to distinguish between the two thermometers used. They should be asked to report specific temperature readings:
    - the internal body temperature at the beginning of the demonstration
    - the skin temperature at the beginning of the demonstration
    - the temperature of the ice-water mixture in the basin
    - the skin temperature after exposure to cold water
    - the internal body temperature at the end of the demonstration

- Discussion should focus on key questions relating to the demonstration:
    - Was the internal body temperature affected by the outside temperature?
    - How does the body make adjustments to maintain its normal internal temperature?
    - Why is it important for the body to maintain a warm internal environment?
- Students should also be encouraged to report personal experiences in which their bodies have responded to temperature changes by sweating and/or shivering, and in which a change in body temperature resulted in a fever that accompanied an illness.
- Students should then be asked to write a report of the demonstration in their Science Demonstrations notebooks.

10–2: OBSERVING PULSE MOTION
(elementary level)

INTRODUCTION

Each time the heart muscle contracts, blood is sent rushing through the arteries to be distributed to all parts of the body. This results in blood being pushed through the arteries with the same rhythm as the heartbeat. The characteristic arterial blood flow can be observed in the spurting of blood from a cut artery or in the rhythmic pulsing of an artery close to the surface of the body. While the pulse can be detected in the temple or carotid artery in the neck, the pulse at the wrist is the most convenient location for determining pulse activity.

LEARNING OBJECTIVES

After having participated in this demonstration lesson, students should be able to

- associate the pulse rate with the rate at which the heart beats.
- know how to locate the pulse and count its beats.
- know how to calculate the pulse rate per minute.
- understand why blood spurts from a cut artery.
- explain how the demonstration gives visual evidence of the way that blood flows through arteries, using *key words:* **artery**, **pulse**, **arterial walls**, and **heartbeat**.

MATERIALS REQUIRED

flat toothpicks; watch or clock with a sweep second hand

PRESENTATION

1. Select a student volunteer.
2. With the volunteer, demonstrate to others how to locate the wrist pulse.
3. Assist all students as they locate the region of the pulse in their wrists.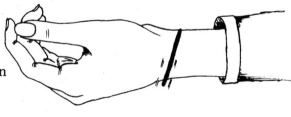
4. Carefully place a flat toothpick on the volunteer's wrist by laying it across the region where the pulse was felt.
5. Observe the toothpick.

RATIONALE

The strong contraction of the heart muscle forces blood into the arteries in two waves: the first expands the muscular walls of the arteries and the second pushes the blood through the arteries to regions of the body away from the heart. This rhythm makes the arteries expand and produces the pulse. In the wrist it is detected by a throbbing sensation near the surface that causes the toothpick to move visibly on the wrist in a motion that is synchronized with the heart's rhythmic beating.

DISCUSSION AND FOLLOW-UP

- Students should observe closely the movement of a toothpick placed across their own or another student's wrist pulse. These observations should prepare them to answer questions:
  - — What happened to the toothpick?
  - — What caused the pulse to throb?
  - — Does the pulse have a regular and rhythmic beat?
  - — Why is the pulse felt only in arteries near the surface?

- Students should be encouraged to keep the motion of the toothpick continuous while they count the number of times it bobs up and down during a timed period of 15 seconds. Then they should calculate the pulse rate per minute.

- Discussion of the demonstration should include other regions of the body where a pulse can be detected, reasons why blood spurts out of a cut artery, and predictions about what might be expected to happen to the pulse rate during periods of exercise or strenuous physical activity.

- As a follow-up, students should be asked to write an account of how the pulse rate can be used as a reliable determiner of the heart rate.

10-3: DETERMINING REACTION TIME
(intermediate level)

INTRODUCTION

Although reaction time is measured in thousandths of a second, we sometimes cannot avoid hitting an object that appears quite suddenly in our path. Usually, we say that we "didn't see it in time." Actually, there is a small lapse between the time our senses receive a stimulus and the time our muscles respond to it. Individuals who are alert and have a short reaction time are able to avert many mishaps.

LEARNING OBJECTIVES

After having completed this demonstration lesson, students should be able to

- relate the demonstration to responses made by the body to outside stimuli.
- associate a short reaction time with the ability to avert a disaster.
- name three situations in which reaction time is important.
- predict the effects of sedatives on reaction time.
- predict the effects of stimulants on reaction time.
- trace the pathway of the nerve impulse involved in the demonstration, using *key words:* **stimulus, nerve receptor, nerve impulse, motor nerve,** and **reaction time**.

MATERIALS REQUIRED

meterstick, yardstick, or long ruler

PRESENTATION

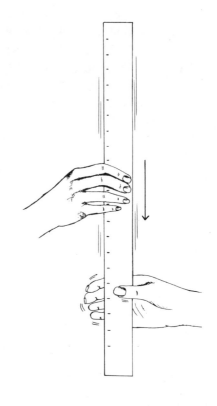

1. Select a student volunteer to hold her hand at a comfortable level in front of herself, with her thumb and index finger slightly separated.
2. Holding a long ruler by one end, lower it so that its opposite end is between but not touching the student's thumb and index finger.
3. Ask the student to keep her eyes focused on the bottom end of the ruler and to catch the ruler between her thumb and index finger if it should begin to fall.
4. Without signal or warning, release the top end of the ruler.
5. Observe what happens.

RATIONALE

The interval between seeing the ruler begin to fall and preventing it from dropping to the floor is called the reaction time. It involves nerve impulses that must travel from the eye to the brain and then to the arm muscles that are used to grasp the ruler between the thumb and index finger. The distance the ruler falls before being caught is related to the student's reaction time—the shorter the distance, the faster the response to the visually received stimulus.

DISCUSSION AND FOLLOW-UP

- The demonstration should be repeated to allow other students to participate and test their skills. While differences in reaction time will be noted, attention should focus on common factors:
  - What sense organ was stimulated?
  - What nerve was used to carry the message?
  - Where was the message carried?
  - What instructions were sent to the muscles?
  - Were the instructions received quickly enough to prevent the ruler from falling to the floor?
- Students should be encouraged to report personal experiences involving similar situations in which the time required to respond to a stimulus determined the success or failure of an attempt to avoid a mishap.
- The effects of stimulants and sedatives on reaction time should also be discussed, with recommendations for their use or disuse when riding a bike, driving a car, or operating some machinery.
- Then students should be asked to draw a diagram in which they show the pathway of the nerve impulse demonstrated, in which a student catches a falling ruler before it drops to the floor.

10–4: THE EFFECTS OF ALCOHOL ON LIFE
(intermediate level)

INTRODUCTION

The effects of alcohol have been well documented. Alcohol slows down the functions of the brain and nervous system, resulting in decreased reasoning powers and judgment, reduced muscular control and reaction time, and blurred and double vision. Its use makes a person who is "under the influence" a menace on the roadway. "Don't Drink and Drive" carries an important message for safety; "Don't Drink" carries a message for health and well-being as well.

LEARNING OBJECTIVES

At the end of this demonstration lesson, students should be able to

- recognize the effect of alcohol as a depressant.
- understand how alcoholism is related to malnutrition.
- explain how studies of animals contribute to our knowledge about effects of alcohol on humans.
- relate specific behavior to levels of alcohol in the blood.
- list six reasons for not drinking alcoholic beverages.
- show evidence of an understanding of the meaning and proper use of *key words:* **alcohol**, **depressant**, and **blood alcohol**.

MATERIALS REQUIRED

small garden toad; 70% rubbing alcohol; shallow bowl; water; toweling; graduated cylinder or measuring cup

PRESENTATION

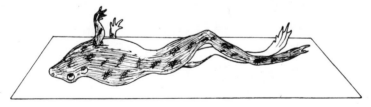

1. Add water to a measure of alcohol to produce an approximate 10 to 1 mixture.
2. Pour the diluted alcohol to a depth of about one inch in a shallow bowl.
3. Place a small garden toad in the alcohol and allow it to remain for several minutes.
4. Remove the toad from the alcohol and lay it on its back on a layer of toweling placed on a table top.

5. Observe the toad.

6. Transfer the toad to a bowl of fresh water and allow it to recover.

RATIONALE

A normally active toad is visibly affected by alcohol. Normally reacting by turning over quickly when placed on its back, its activity is slowed by alcohol to the point where it moves only slightly and—eventually—not at all. The alcohol acts as a depressant, decreasing its breathing and heart rate. It eventually could become unconscious, as is the case when an alcoholic passes out. When the toad is placed in fresh water, it eventually revives and recovers from the alcoholic binge.

DISCUSSION AND FOLLOW-UP

- The behavior of the toad before and after being exposed to alcohol should be compared and discussed. Also, other studies involving the effects of alcohol on animals and humans should be considered:
  - Spiders spin haphazard webs after imbibing alcohol.
  - Human behavior changes when blood alcohol levels are as low as 0.02 percent.
- Students should be encouraged to report other impaired behavior they have witnessed—such as slurred speech, loss of balance, and tremors of the hands.
- Attention should focus on specific aspects of health and fitness:
  - Why is alcohol considered to be a depressant rather than a stimulant?
  - Which system is especially harmed by alcohol?
  - How does the fact that alcohol provides fuel for energy explain why alcoholics suffer from malnutrition?
- As a follow-up, students should be asked to design and prepare a poster that they think might convince young people not to drink alcoholic beverages.

10–5: DETERMINING LUNG CAPACITY
(intermediate level)

INTRODUCTION

Ordinarily, people use only a small portion of their total lung capacity; their normal breathing pattern is shallow, allowing for an exchange of gases with the outside air that is only a fraction of that which can be accomplished during deep breathing. The amount of air that can be exhaled in one forced breath can be measured. This can be demonstrated with student volunteers.

LEARNING OBJECTIVES

After completing this demonstration lesson, students should be able to

- recognize that we normally do not make full use of our lungs' ability to exchange air with the outside air.
- identify three factors that have an effect on an individual's lung capacity.
- name three advantages of "deep" breathing.
- distinguish between air that can be forced out of the lungs and air that must remain in the lungs.
- make a comparison of "demonstrated" and "calculated" lung capacity.
- describe the relationship between exchange of respiratory gases and physical health and fitness, using *key words:* **vital lung capacity**, **carbon dioxide**, **oxygen**, and **cell respiration**.

MATERIALS REQUIRED

gallon jug; large pan or aquarium tank; plastic airline tubing; water; metric measuring cup; grease pencil

PRESENTATION

1. Fill a gallon jug completely with water and place it in an inverted position in an aquarium tank that is partly filled with water. Be sure that the mouth of the jug is below the water level in the tank and that no water escapes from the jug.

2. Place one end of a plastic airline tube inside the mouth of the jug.

3. Ask a student to take a deep breath and then to force as much air from his lungs as he can by blowing one

forced breath into the free end of the plastic airline tube.

NOTE: Care must be taken to clean the mouthpiece end of the plastic tubing before and after use by each student participating in the demonstration.

4. Observe what happens in the jug.

5. Use a grease pencil to mark the level of the water remaining in the jug.

6. Remove the jug from the aquarium tank and set the jug upright on a table.

7. Using a metric measuring cup, measure the amount of water that is needed to fill the jug to the level indicated by the grease mark made on its outside wall. Identify this volume as the student's vital lung capacity.

RATIONALE

To prevent the lungs from collapsing, some air must remain in them at all times. Breathing deeply, however, is necessary to maintain a high level of physical fitness by supplying sufficient quantities of fresh oxygen to the body cells and preventing accumulations of carbon dioxide. The demonstrated vital lung capacity—the amount of air that can be forced out of the lungs after they have been fully inflated—can be compared with an approximation of its potential, calculated for students of different height and sex.

DISCUSSION AND FOLLOW-UP

- Possible reasons for differences noted in the vital capacity of different students should be discussed:
  - Does the height of the individual affect his vital capacity?
  - Does the sex of the individual affect his vital capacity?
  - Does the age of the individual affect his vital capacity?
  - Does the student's participation in sports activities or vocal musical groups have an effect on his vital capacity?
- The use of water displacement as a method for determining the volume of air exhaled should be discussed.
- After the discussion has been completed, students should be asked to calculate their vital lung capacities, using standard formulas:
  - Girls: height in centimeters × 20 = vital capacity in milliliters
  - Boys: height in centimeters × 23 = vital capacity in milliliters
- Students should compare the calculated with the demonstrated lung capacities.

10-6:   A MUSCLE FATIGUE EXPERIENCE
(elementary level)

INTRODUCTION

In addition to food and oxygen needed by all cells for engaging in their activities, our body cells also need periods of rest. Even our heart muscle rests between beats and is thereby able to pump blood during our entire lifetime. If muscle cells are not provided with rest periods, they become more and more tired, until finally they can work no longer. In some cases muscle fatigue can be a life-threatening experience—as when a shipwrecked survivor holding on to the side of a lifeboat releases his grasp and slips into the water.

LEARNING OBJECTIVES

After having participated in this demonstration lesson, students should be able to

- understand the requirements that must be met for muscle cells to do their work.
- describe one personal experience involving muscle fatigue.
- explain how muscles become fatigued and how they recover, using *key words:* **muscle**, **contraction**, **energy**, **fatigue**, and **rest**.

MATERIALS REQUIRED

PRESENTATION

1. Ask individual students to hold one hand, unsupported and in an upright or outstretched position, in front of them.
2. Instruct students to
   - open and close the hand rapidly and forcefully.
   - repeat the fist-forming activity in a rhythmic cycle until they note a change in the speed or completeness of the fist closing and opening.
   - report the results to the class.
3. Discuss the demonstration as experienced by individual students.

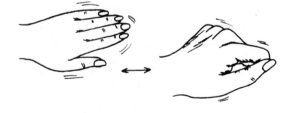

255

RATIONALE

When strenuous or prolonged demands for their contraction are made on muscle cells, they use large amounts of oxygen and give off large quantities of carbon dioxide as a waste. Sometimes, when the oxygen requirements exceed the supply and carbon dioxide is not carried away promptly, the muscle cells become fatigued and can no longer perform their task. After a rest period, during which time the muscle cells replenish their oxygen supplies and get rid of the carbon dioxide buildup, the muscle cells are once again able to contract. The occurrence of muscle fatigue can be averted by frequent rest periods, thus contributing to the body's greater efficiency.

DISCUSSION AND FOLLOW-UP

- Students should be encouraged to report their individual experiences:
    - Did you make a fist faster at the beginning or at the end?
    - Did you make a more complete fist and open hand at the beginning or at the end?
    - What caused your muscles to slow down?
    - How did they get tired?
- Attention should be drawn to the increased demands made on the muscles to form a fist with no provision for an increase in the supply of oxygen to oxidize food for the release of energy needed for the activity.
- Students should then relate the demonstration to personal experiences. They should report incidents while engaging in activities such as swimming, dancing, or running in which they experienced muscle fatigue and needed a rest period to enable them to resume the activity.
- After the discussion has been completed, students should be asked to write a paragraph in which they tell why rest is important in keeping the body fit.

10-7:   EPIDEMIC IN THE CLASSROOM
(elementary level)

INTRODUCTION

It is not uncommon to find a wave of influenza or common colds sweeping through a classroom, a school, or an entire household. The contagious diseases are caused by specific infective agents that travel from an infected person to one who usually develops a case of the same illness. While many of the serious infective diseases that have plagued people in the past have been brought under control by the development of vaccines, antibiotics, and improved methods of sanitation, there is still no cure for the common cold—the most prevalent infectious disease today. A demonstration showing how germs travel suggests several health practices that could help to avert a real epidemic in the classroom.

LEARNING OBJECTIVES

After having participated in this demonstration lesson, students should be able to

- identify one common way that germs can be spread.
- relate the simulated "epidemic" to an actual occurrence.
- list three rules to follow-to avoid the spread of germs.
- list three diseases that are said to be contagious, or "catching."
- tell how an epidemic can occur in the classroom or at home, using *key words:* **germs**, **infectious**, **contact**, **disease**, and **epidemic**.

MATERIALS REQUIRED

candy cane; crushed red or other color chalk; water; camel's hair brush; paper towels; cotton swabs

PRESENTATION

1. Select four or five students to participate in the demonstration.
2. Moisten the surface of a candy cane.
3. Using a camel's hair brush, distribute crushed red chalk over the entire surface of the candy cane.
4. Ask student #1 to roll the candy cane between the palms of his hands.
5. Set up a hand-shaking sequence: student #1 shakes hands with student #2, #2 with #3, #3 with #4, and #4 with #5.
6. Moisten cotton swabs and distribute them to student participants.
7. Ask students to use a cotton swab to rub over the surface of their hands—palm, fingers, and thumb.
8. Examine each of the swabs for evidence of chalk particles.
9. Be sure that student participants wash their hands to remove any traces of colored chalk.

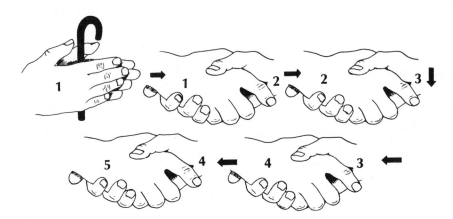

RATIONALE

Chalk dust is spread from one student to another by direct contact during a handshake. Many colds spread from hand to hand also when the infective virus is picked up from the hand of a person who has touched her infected nose. In other methods of the spread of contagious disease, germs may be carried through the air, in food and/or water, or by insects. Knowledge of how germs are spread has led to effective precautionary measures that have reduced the number of deaths formerly attributed to these diseases.

DISCUSSION AND FOLLOW-UP

- The cotton swabs should be passed to all students for close observation. Students should be asked to compare the intensity of the colored particles detected on the swabs and to trace the pathway of the epidemic:
    - If colored chalk particles were germs, could you become infected by shaking hands with an infected classmate?
    - Is it possible for one infected classmate to infect more than one person?
    - Could the spread of infective particles cause an epidemic in the classroom?
    - If all members of the class were involved in the handshaking, is it possible that the spread of infective particles would stop at some point?
    - Why is it not safe to put your hands or objects handled by other people in your mouth?
- Students should report incidents in which several family members suffered an illness shortly after the first one was infected. They should also consider other methods by which germs travel.
- As a follow-up, students should be asked to make a list of precautionary measures—use of paper cups instead of a community ladle for drinking water, disposable thermometers in clinics and hospitals—that can be practiced to control the spread of germs that cause contagious diseases.

10–8: A CIGARETTE SMOKING MACHINE
(elementary level)

INTRODUCTION

Anti-smoking campaigns that call attention to the dangers of smoking take many forms: reference to the Surgeon General's warning about smoking and its effects appear on all cigarette advertising material; products that help smokers break the habit are available on the market; the Great American Smokeouts are well subscribed to by the American public; strong evidence that smoking is linked to respiratory illnesses and that smokers have a shorter life expectancy than nonsmokers is well publicized; smoking is restricted to special areas in some eating places as well as on buses, trains, and planes.

The presence of some of the harmful contaminants in cigarette smoke can be demonstrated dramatically with the use of a simple smoking machine.

LEARNING OBJECTIVES

At the end of this demonstration lesson, students should be able to

- relate the deposits of tar on cotton in a simulated smoking situation to similar deposits on the lung tissue of smokers.
- name three harmful effects arising from smoking cigarettes.
- give reasons that will convince another person that he or she should not smoke.
- exhibit an understanding of the meaning and proper usage of *key words:* **nicotine**, **tar**, **emphysema**, and **lung cancer**.

MATERIALS REQUIRED

clean plastic dishwashing liquid container with screw cap; rigid plastic or glass tube; absorbent cotton; molding clay; cigarettes

PRESENTATION

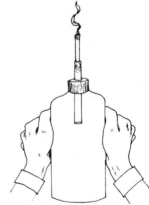

1. Cut a small hole in the center of the plastic bottle cap.

2. Insert a plastic tube into the hole so that it protrudes slightly through the lower end of the cap.

3. Seal the tube into position with molding clay applied near the point where it passes through the cap.

4. Push a loose wad of cotton into the tube.

5. Place the cap on the container.

6. Place a cigarette into the upper end of the tube.

7. Check all connections to be sure that they are tight.

8. Squeeze the plastic container between your palms to force all air out of the container.

9. Light the cigarette.

10. Alternately squeeze and release pressure on the sides of the container.

11. Maintain a slow and rhythmic pumping action until the cigarette has been almost completely "smoked."

12. Remove the cigarette.

13. Remove and examine the cotton plug.

RATIONALE

In addition to nicotine and other chemicals, tobacco contains an abundance of organic particles called tars. These are filtered out by the cotton through which the smoke passed in the smoking machine. In a smoker's body, this tarry brown material accumulates on the lung tissue, forming a barrier that interferes with the normal exchange of respiratory gases. When combined with heat and tissue irritants also associated with smoking, these deposits can damage the lungs so severely that, eventually, they may not be able to function at all.

DISCUSSION AND FOLLOW-UP

- Students should observe closely the smoking machine in action. Then after the cotton plug has been removed, it should be placed on a paper towel and passed to each student for examination at close range, prior to using it as a focal point for discussion:
    - What is the appearance of the cotton?
    - How does it look and smell?
    - Where did the tarry material come from?
    - Where would this material have been deposited if the cigarette had been smoked by a person?
    - What effect would this material have on the smoker's lungs?
    - How is this related to the respiratory problems of smokers?
- Students should report other problems—smokers' cough, husky voice, and shortness of breath—that they have observed among smokers they know.
- Some longer range problems—loss of appetite, nervousness, headache, and sleeplessness—as well as a shortened life expectancy and higher risk of emphysema and lung cancer should also be researched and discussed.
- As a follow-up, students should be asked to prepare a list of recommendations they would make to smokers and to individuals who are thinking about starting the smoking habit.

10–9:   HEALING THE BODY WITH REST AND MEDICATION*
(elementary level)

INTRODUCTION

Both rest and medication contribute to a person's recovery from some common illnesses. Although it is necessary to maintain blood levels of the medication at a proper level until the illness is under control, waking a sleeping patient to take his next round of pills, tablets, and/or capsules may prove to be counterproductive. In some cases it is possible to get the best of both worlds: time-release capsules, taken at bedtime, release medication in the proper dosage at the proper time while allowing the patient to maximize his body's potential for self-healing during a period of uninterrupted sleep.

LEARNING OBJECTIVES

At the end of this demonstration lesson, students should be able to

- recognize that medications are forms of drugs that should never be taken without adult supervision.
- understand how time-release capsules work.
- describe how time-release medication complements the body's natural capacity for self-healing and repair.
- explain the advantage involved in taking one 12-hour time-release capsule at bedtime rather than taking three 4-hour capsules containing the same active ingredients of the medication, using *key words:* **time capsule, dissolve**, **coating**, and **time-release medication**.

MATERIALS REQUIRED

time-release cold capsule; water; small dish or saucer

PRESENTATION

1. Hold a time-release cold capsule over a small dish while you separate the two parts and free the tiny beads that are contained within the capsule.

2. Observe the different colors among the beads collected in the dish.

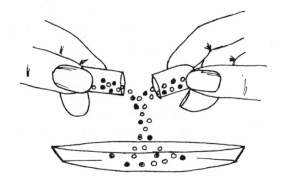

---

* Suitable for teacher-only presentation.

3. Add enough water to cover the tiny beads.

4. Place the dish in a location where

students can view its contents at various time intervals.

5. Note what happens.

RATIONALE

All colored beads do not break open to release their medication at the same time. Those with thin coatings dissolve quickly when in contact with water, leaving only empty shells behind. Those of a different color, with thicker coatings, dissolve and release their medication later. This continues until all bead coatings have been dissolved and all medication has been released, generally about eight hours after having been brought in contact with water. The medication is released according to a time sequence, and remains effective for a few hours after release of the medication by the last group.

DISCUSSION AND FOLLOW-UP

- Students should be alert to the number of different colors among the beads that were freed from the time-release cold capsule.

- They should then observe the demonstration periodically in order to determine the time that is required for the coating material on beads of different colors to dissolve. This should be related to the thickness of the coating and its degree of solubility when in water.

- The advantages of time capsules for the time release of medication should be related to student experiences in taking medication for colds and other illnesses:

  — Why is it sometimes necessary to take medication?

  — Why do the effects of some medications last only about four hours?

  — Why would it not be advisable to double up on the dosage of medication at bedtime?

  — How does the time capsule design combine the advantages of proper medication with provision of plenty of rest?

  NOTE: Special emphasis should be placed on the proper use of medications. Students should be cautioned that all medicines are forms of drugs and that there are potential dangers associated with their improper use. No medication should be taken without adult supervision.

- As a follow-up, students should be asked to prepare an illustration showing how a person's recovery from an illness may be helped by taking a four-hour medication in a time-release capsule that works all night while he sleeps. And, finally, students should be asked to list two important rules they have learned for the proper use of medication.

10–10: ALLERGIC REACTIONS TO FOREIGN SUBSTANCES*
(intermediate level)

INTRODUCTION

Although not all people are sensitive to the same substances, many people suffer the discomfort of itching skin and eyes or fits of sneezing caused by an offending plant or animal. We may be victims of poisons produced by certain snakes, spiders, and mushrooms; and we suffer an assortment of allergies from chemical reactions to pollens, poison ivy, bee stings, insect bites, and certain foods to which we have become sensitized. The fact is that the chemical makeup of a particular organism is not compatible with that of all others. Our allergic reactions are related to our body's immune system, which causes us discomfort while it rebels against the foreign invaders.

LEARNING OBJECTIVES

At the end of this demonstration lesson, students should be able to

- recognize that not all living material is chemically compatible.
- identify some harmful substances produced by plants and animals as protective devices for self-protection against enemies.
- relate allergic reactions to a harmful form of immunity set into motion by the body's defense mechanism against foreign substances.
- show evidence of an understanding of the meaning and proper use of *key words:* **antibody**, **allergen**, and **allergy**.

MATERIALS REQUIRED

block of gelatin; bristle hair from a stinging nettle; needle

PRESENTATION

1. Place a block of gelatin in a shallow dish.
2. Pierce the gelatin with a needle and apply enough pressure to cause the needle to become embedded to one half its length before being withdrawn from the block.
3. Insert the hair from a stinging nettle into the puncture made.

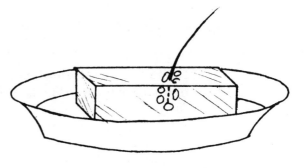

4. Observe what happens.

---

* Suitable for teacher-only presentation.

263

RATIONALE

After a short time the gelatin is affected in a manner similar to that of tender skin that has been stung by a bee. The nettle hair acts like a hypodermic needle, releasing its corrosive liquid into the stab wound that has been made and causing the protein-based gelatin to blister. Human skin may be affected similarly; the histamine and formic acid substances introduced into a skin puncture by many stinging nettles and stinging insects cause skin blisters as well as other allergic reactions.

DISCUSSION AND FOLLOW-UP

- The blistering of the gelatin should be viewed as a simulation of blister formation on human skin caused by the corrosive action of a nettle hair.

    — What was the effect of the nettle hair on the gelatin?

    — What material in the nettle hair caused the blister to form?

    — How does this simulation relate to what happens to the human skin when it is affected by a nettle hair or an insect sting?

    — Of what value are these skin irritants to the plant or animal that produces them?

    — Are all people sensitive to the same allergens?

- The relationship between our body's immune system and the allergies we suffer due to foreign substances should be discussed, as well as some home remedies that have been found to be effective.

- Then, each student should be asked to prepare a list of foreign substances against which the body may use its natural defense system and protect itself by sneezing.

Bibliography

BOOKS ON PHYSICAL SCIENCE TOPICS

Abruscato, Joseph, and Jack Hassard, *The Whole Cosmos Catalog of Science Activities.* Santa Monica, CA: Goodyear Publishing Co., Inc., 1977.

Blackwelder, Sheila Kyser, *Science for All Seasons.* Englewood Cliffs, NJ: Prentice-Hall, Inc., 1980.

Brandes, Louis Grant, *Science Can Be Fun.* Portland, ME: J. Weston Walch, Publisher, 1979.

Cross, Wilbur and Susanna, *Space Shuttle.* Chicago, IL: The Children's Press, 1986.

DeCloux, Tina, and Rosanne Werges, *Tina's Science Notebook.* Mill Valley, CA: Symbiosis Books, 1986.

Downs, Gary, and Jack Gerlovich (eds.), *Science Safety for Elementary Teachers.* Ames, IA: Iowa State University Press, 1983.

Fitzpatrick, Julie, *Magnets.* Morristown, NJ: Silver Burdett Spiral Series, 1985.

_____, *Mirrors.* (Science Spiral Series) Morristown, NJ: Silver Burdett Co., 1985.

_____, *On the Water.* (Science Spiral Series) Morristown, NJ: Silver Burdett Co., 1985.

_____, *In the Air.* (Science Spiral Series) Morristown, NJ: Silver Burdett Co., 1985.

Mebane, Robert, and Thomas Rybolt, *Adventures with Atoms and Molecules.* New York: Enslow Publishers, 1985.

Statten, Mary, *Let's Play Science.* New York: Harper & Row Publishers, 1979.

Stein, Sara, *The Science Book.* New York: Workman Publishing Company, 1979.

Sund, Robert B., Donald K. Adams, Jay Hackett, and Richard Moyer, *Accent on Science.* Columbus, OH: Charles Merrill Publishing Company, 1985.

Wright, Jill D., *Teaching Science Today.* Portland, ME: J. Weston Walch Publisher, 1982.

BOOKS ON ENVIRONMENTAL SCIENCE TOPICS

Asimov, Isaac, *About Earthquakes.* New York: Walker and Company, 1978.

Blaustein, Elliott H., *Anti-Pollution Projects.* New York: Arco Publishing Co., 1977.

Blough, Glenn O., and Julius Schwartz, "The Air and the Weather," *Elementary School Science and How to Teach It.* (6th ed.) New York: Holt, Rinehart and Winston, Inc., 1979.

Challand, Helen J., *Activities in Earth Science.* Chicago, IL: The Children's Press, 1986.

Fraden, Dennis B., *Disaster: Blizzards, Droughts, Earthquakes, Famines, Fires, Floods, Hurricanes, Tornadoes, Volcanoes.* Chicago, IL: The Children's Press, 1986.

Fritsch, Albert J. (ed.), *The Household Pollutants Guide.* Garden City, NY: Anchor Press/ Doubleday, 1978.

Kerbo, Ronal C., *Caves.* Chicago, IL: The Children's Press, 1986.

Lampton, Christopher, *Meteorology: An Introduction.* New York: Franklin Watts, Inc., 1981.

Radlauer, Ruth, *Volcanoes.* Chicago, IL: The Children's Press, 1986.

Radlauer, Ruth, and Lisa Sue Gitkin, *The Power of Ice.* Chicago, IL: The Children's Press, 1986.

Simon, Seymour, *Dangers from Below.* New York: Four Winds Press, 1979.

Zipko, Stephen J., *Toxic Threat: How Hazardous Substances Poison Our Lives.* New York: Julian Messner, 1986.

BOOKS ON LIFE SCIENCE TOPICS

Appel, Gary, Margaret Cadous, and Roberta Jaffe, *The Growing Classroom.* Capitola, CA: 1985.

Busch, Phyllis S., *Cactus in the Desert.* New York: Thomas Y. Crowell Company, 1979.

Claypool, Jane, *Alcohol and You.* New York: Franklin Watts, Inc., 1981.

Cobb, Vicki, *Lots of Rot.* New York: J. B. Lippincott, 1981.

_____, *The Secret Life of Cosmetics: A Science Experiment Book.* New York: J. B. Lippincott, 1985.

Cole, Joanna V., *Cuts, Breaks, Bruises and Burns: How Your Body Heals.* New York: Crowell Publishing Co., 1985.

Fishman, Ross, *Alcohol and Alcoholics.* New York: Chelsea House Publications, 1986.

Glowa, John R., *Inhalants, The Toxic Fumes.* New York: Chelsea House Publications, 1986.

Kuntzleman, Charles, *The Beat Goes On.* Spring Arbor, MI: Arbor Press, 1980.

Mitchell, John, *The Curious Naturalist.* Massachusetts Audubon Society, 1980.

Nelson, Cordner, *Excelling in Sports.* New York: The Rosen Publishing Group, 1985.

Simon, Seymour, *Pets in a Jar.* New York: Penguin Books, 1979.

Sisson, Edith A., *Nature with Children of All Ages.* Englewood Cliffs, NJ: Prentice-Hall, Inc., 1982.

Sonnett, Sherry, *Smoking—A First Book.* New York: Franklin Watts, 1977.

Tully, Marianne and Mary-Alice, *Dread Diseases—A First Book.* New York: Franklin Watts, 1978.

Turner, Edward and Clive, *Frogs and Toads.* Sussex, England: Wayland Publishing Ltd., 1979.

Woods, Geraldine, *Drug Use and Drug Abuse.* New York: Franklin Watts, 1986.

Notes

Notes

Notes

Notes

Notes

Notes

Notes

Notes